On Creation, Science, Disenchantment and the Contours of Being and Knowing

Matthew W. Knotts

BLOOMSBURY ACADEMIC
NEW YORK • LONDON • OXFORD • NEW DELHI • SYDNEY

BLOOMSBURY ACADEMIC
Bloomsbury Publishing Inc
1385 Broadway, New York, NY 10018, USA
50 Bedford Square, London, WC1B 3DP, UK

BLOOMSBURY, BLOOMSBURY ACADEMIC and the Diana logo are trademarks of Bloomsbury Publishing Plc

First published in the United States of America 2020

Copyright © Matthew W. Knotts, 2020

Matthew W. Knotts has asserted his right under the Copyright, Designs and Patents Act, 1988, to be identified as Author of this work.

For legal purposes the Acknowledgements on p. viii constitute an extension of this copyright page.

Cover design by Catherine Wood
Cover image © Godong/robertharding/Getty Images

All rights reserved. No part of this publication may be reproduced or transmitted in any form or by any means, electronic or mechanical, including photocopying, recording, or any information storage or retrieval system, without prior permission in writing from the publishers.

Bloomsbury Publishing Inc does not have any control over, or responsibility for, any third-party websites referred to or in this book. All internet addresses given in this book were correct at the time of going to press. The author and publisher regret any inconvenience caused if addresses have changed or sites have ceased to exist, but can accept no responsibility for any such changes.

A catalogue record for this book is available from the British Library.

A catalog record for this book is available from the Library of Congress.

ISBN: HB: 978-1-5013-4457-2
        PB: 978-1-5013-4458-9
        ePDF: 978-1-5013-4460-2
        eBook: 978-1-5013-4459-6

Typeset by RefineCatch Limited, Bungay, Suffolk
Printed and bound in the United States of America

To find out more about our authors and books visit www.bloomsbury.com and sign up for our newsletters.

On Creation, Science, Disenchantment and the Contours of Being and Knowing

READING AUGUSTINE

Series Editor:
Miles Hollingworth

Reading Augustine offers personal and close readings of St. Augustine of Hippo from leading philosophers and religious scholars. Its aim is to make clear Augustine's importance to contemporary thought and to present Augustine not only or primarily as a pre-eminent Christian thinker but as a philosophical, spiritual, literary, and intellectual icon of the West.

Volumes in the series:
On Ethics, Politics and Psychology in the Twenty-First Century, John Rist
On Love, Confession, Surrender and the Moral Self, Ian Clausen
On Education, Formation, Citizenship and the Lost Purpose of Learning, Joseph Clair
On Creativity, Liberty, Love and the Beauty of the Law, Todd Breyfogle
On Consumer Culture, Identity, the Church and the Rhetorics of Delight, Mark Clavier
On Agamben, Arendt, Christianity, and the Dark Arts of Civilization (forthcoming), Peter Ivar Kaufman

To my parents, Harold and Patricia.

CONTENTS

Acknowledgements viii
Abbreviations of Augustine's works xi
General Introduction xiii

Part One   Creation in Wisdom   1

1 Aspects of (Re-)Creation   3

2 The Problem of Pride   19

Part Two   Divine Incorporeality: Two Dilemmas   29

3 A Re-Descriptive Account of Time as *Distentio*   31

4 Seeing *Sapientia*   47

Part Three   An Interrogative Theory of Knowledge   61

5 Reading the Universe   63

6 Exploring Creation: Acknowledging and Transcending Our Finitude   83

Conclusion 109
Notes 113
References 155
Index of Names 167
Index of Subjects 169
Index Locorum 173
Index of References 175

ACKNOWLEDGEMENTS

According to Augustine, one cannot arrive at truth on one's own. Hence I would like to express my sincere gratitude to many people who have helped me to complete this monograph.

Above all I would like to thank my parents, Harold and Patricia, for their support in a variety of ways, and without whom this would not have been possible, as well as all my family members who have been supportive and encouraging throughout this entire process.

I would like to thank the Editor of this series, Dr Miles Hollingworth, for his direction and encouragement in the completion of the manuscript. In 2013, I read his intellectual biography of Augustine and appreciated it very much, and so I am very pleased by the opportunity to work with him.

I would also like graciously to thank my team of PhD advisors, namely Prof Dr Mathijs Lamberigts, Prof Dr Anthony Dupont and Prof Dr William Desmond. I have greatly profited from their critical remarks and suggestions, as well as their support throughout my time as a PhD student and even earlier. I would especially like to thank Anthony Dupont for going above and beyond the call of duty in helping and advising me along the way, whether by reading various drafts of my work, collaborating on articles and conference panels, or simply providing guidance and direction on a number of questions. For having the opportunity to work with all of my advisors, as well as other members of the University of Leuven, I am extremely fortunate and thankful.

I would also like to thank the Fonds voor Wetenschapelijk Onderzoek Vlaanderen for the financial assistance in completing my PhD, as well as funding research stays abroad at the University of Chicago, the University of Notre Dame and the Institute for Religion and Critical Inquiry at the Australian Catholic University.

In this respect I am grateful to Prof Dr Willemien Otten and many of the professors and students at the University of Chicago, especially Dr Sean Hannan, who welcomed and worked with me in 2015, as well as Dr John Callaghan of the Maritain Institute of Notre Dame for hosting me during that time as well. I am also grateful to Prof Dr James McLaren and other members of the Institute for Religion and Critical Inquiry, who welcomed me in August 2016 and helped me to develop my research further. I also extend my thanks to Prof Dr David Hunter, Prof Dr P. Nehring, Prof Dr Rafal Toczko and Prof Dr Paul van Geest for their hospitality and their guidance to a young scholar.

There are many other friends and associates who have helped me, especially Dr Emmanuel Nathan, formerly of Leuven, now in Sydney, who has encouraged me over the last several years. The same can be said for Prof Dr Robert J. Forman of St John's University (NY), who has been a very strong guiding force in my academic life.

Thanks are also due to the Rev Dr Joel C. Daniels who, in addition to kindly inviting me to give lectures at New York City's renowned St Thomas Church on Fifth Avenue, read drafts of my work, which was far beyond what was required of him. Prof Dr Paul Fry and Dr Sam Pomeroy also read and provided me with helpful comments on my work.

Dr Elisabeth Hernitscheck has helped me immensely, especially with linguistic questions concerning Latin and German. I am also grateful to Dr Els Agten and Dr Eddy Louchez for their help with French. In addition, I would like to thank Ms Rita Corstjens for her help with formatting and my bibliography.

Much gratitude is due to friends of mine in New York, especially Mr Steve Pack, Mr Robert D. Cote and the Rev Dr George W. Rutler, all of whom have hosted me on many occasions and provided excellent conversation partners to help challenge and stimulate my thinking.

For those whom I have forgotten to thank, please accept my apologies. Sometimes the work of a researcher leads to unfortunate lapses in memory.

Note on Text/Translations

Originally I consulted Augustine's texts either in an authoritative translation or using the *Patrologia Latina* text available at augustinus.it. After I composed my manuscript, I consulted the *Corpus Augustinianum Gissense*, and cited Augustine's locations accordingly. Hence all of the texts used for Augustine's works can be located through CAG (Corpus Augustinianum Gissense). Translations are my own, unless otherwise noted.

ABBREVIATIONS OF AUGUSTINE'S WORKS

acad.	Contra Academicos
agon.	De agone christiano
beata u.	De beata uita
c. Adim.	Contra Adimantum
c. ep. Man.	Contra epistolam Manichaei quam uocant Fundamenti
c. Faust.	Contra Faustum
c. Iul.	Contra Iulianum
ciu.	De ciuitate Dei
conf.	Confessiones
cons. eu.	De consensu euangelistarum
diu. qu.	De diuersis quaestionibus
doctr. chr.	De doctrina christiana
en. Ps.	Enarrationes in Psalmos
ep.	Epistula
ep. Io. tr.	Tractatus in epistolam Ioannis
f. inuis.	De fide rerum inuisibilium
Gn. adu. Man.	De Genesi aduersus Manichaeos
Gn. litt.	De Genesi ad litteram
Io. eu. tr.	In Ioannis euangelium tractatus CXXIV
lib. arb.	De libero arbitrio

mag.	De magistro
mus.	De musica
ord.	De ordine
retr.	Retractationes
s./ss.	Sermo(nes)
s. Denis	Sermo Denis
s. Dolbeau	Sermo Dolbeau
s. Dom. m.	De sermone Domini in monte
s. Mai	Sermo Mai
sol.	Soliloquia
spir. et litt.	De spiritu et littera
trin.	De trinitate
uera rel.	De uera religione
util. cred.	De utilitate credendi

GENERAL INTRODUCTION

Background

Hans-Georg Gadamer (1900–2002) held that every statement could be understood as the answer to a question. If that is so, then the following enquiry can in a certain sense be read as a response to a question which Gadamer himself raised in a work published in 1957, 'Was ist Wahrheit?': 'Is science (*Wissenschaft*) really the final authority and the only bearer of truth, as it claims for itself?'[1] Gadamer is suspicious of such a claim and is inclined to answer in the negative. The modern conception of truth and science, which he traces to Descartes, pertains to certainty, domination and scientific method, and represents a break with the prior centuries of western history.[2] After Descartes, the mark of the true became certainty, understood of course according to a particular set of standards.[3] However, Gadamer questions whether science as such possesses the resources to justify its own procedures, and the interpretive element necessary in order to arrive at truth.[4]

Moreover, Gadamer suggests that there are types of truth which exceed the bounds of a univocal form of enquiry.[5] The questions pertinent to religion, philosophy and related disciplines are not answerable by a purely scientific approach,[6] nor do they admit of the possibility of a complete and final answer.[7] As evidence for this assertion, one need only look to the experience of human life. Gadamer concurs with Jaspers when he states that science ceases to be useful and compelling with respect to the questions occasioned by the *Grenzsituationen* of human existence, for instance, the fact of our mortality.[8] In addition to the type of content involved, the modality of communication is different: here it is envisioned as holistic, as persons speak to one another in terms of 'I and Thou'.[9] Gadamer pursued a line of enquiry according to which all understanding involved interpretation, the idea of hermeneutical universality. In this respect, Gadamer turns the tables on the Cartesian dispensation: no longer is it a question of the *Geisteswissenschaften* being dependent on the natural sciences. Rather, all science is seen as dependent upon hermeneutics.[10]

The foregoing ideas are more fully articulated in Gadamer's massively influential *Wahrheit und Methode* (*WM*), published in 1960. In this respect, Gadamer is addressing a question which assumed great importance in the twentieth century, namely the place of interpretation with respect to the empirical sciences, and whether the findings of the latter are completely exhaustive of truth. R. Bernstein situates Gadamer's *WM* with respect to two other monographs that appeared at roughly the same time, namely P. Winch's *The Idea of a Social Science and Its Relation to Philosophy*[11] in 1958 and T. Kuhn's *The Structure of Scientific Revolutions*[12] in 1962. Together the respective monographs by Winch, Gadamer and Kuhn set in motion a series of questions and discussions concerning the human sciences broadly understood.[13] One of the key motivations for these separate enquiries was 'Cartesian Anxiety' and its aftermath.[14] Bernstein characterizes Descartes' epistemological legacy in the following way:

> The idea of a basic dichotomy between the subjective and the objective; the conception of knowledge as being a correct representation of what is objective; the conviction that human reason can completely free itself of bias, prejudice, and tradition; the ideal of a universal method by which we can first secure firm foundations of knowledge and then build the edifice of a universal science; the belief that by the power of self-reflection we can transcend our historical context and horizon and know things as they really are in themselves.[15]

Gadamer thinks that this approach to the world misses something fundamental about what it means to be human, and hence what it means to know. However, he also wants to maintain a robust sense of truth, but not understood according to post-Enlightenment criteria.[16]

The growing awareness in the early twentieth century of the difficulties present in the 'Cartesian persuasion' constituted a motivation to look to sources in earlier times for inspiration. One of these was Augustine of Hippo (354–430), who proved to be a valuable resource for figures such as Jaspers, Arendt, Husserl, Ricoeur, Heidegger and even Gadamer himself.[17] These thinkers were motivated not so much by a nostalgia for a past age, but rather by an interest in Augustine's own thought in the hopes of answering pressing questions of their own time. One of the fundamental ideas of Augustine's understanding of reason is that of a distinction between different types of knowledge. It is here that I believe we can locate resources for critically questioning the prevailing conception of the world as 'disenchanted'.

We inhabit a disenchanted world, one seen as devoid of meaning or purpose. Far from a neutral or impartial perspective, conceiving of the world in this way implies foregrounding certain aspects and minimizing others. In doing this, are we missing something, something crucial about the world, or even more importantly, about ourselves? What would it mean to think of the world as created in the present in such a way that respects and acknowledges our scientific conception of the universe? I believe it would require a different way of looking at the world, viewing it under a different aspect. I shall consider the implications of Augustine's theology of creation, looking at what it says about our identity, constitution and situation within the world, and by extension about what we can know and how we can know it. Before delving into this question, however, I must address what I see as a fundamental theme of Augustine's thought, and one which will serve to frame this book as it proceeds.

Principal and gradual

In my estimation, Augustine's understanding of knowledge and illumination involves two distinct yet inseparable elements.[18] One is the enlightening activity of Christ, present intimately to the soul. The divine light supplies the mind with the resources necessary to grow in knowledge. However, this is not sufficient in order to arrive at the fullness of truth, wisdom (*sapientia*). Created in the image of God, in virtue of which it possesses reason, the human soul is further formed and indeed reformed by continuously turning to its Creator. However, there is a catch. Augustine speaks in various ways of a blindness of the soul or an obstruction of the mind.[19] In other words, though the light is present, we may struggle to see it.[20] This could be for one of two reasons: our finitude or our sinfulness.[21] God is invisible, and so cannot be seen by the bodily eye, but only by the heart, *de iure*.[22] However, de facto, one may not be able to see God, and so must purge the cordial eye. Augustine likens this unto those who wish to see the light of the sun, who must cleanse their eyes.[23] Therefore, our vision needs to be healed and re-oriented. What I wish to emphasize here is the inseparability of these two aspects of illumination in Augustine's thinking, as well as the fact that the latter part, the weakness of the eyes, stems from a twofold source, namely human finitude, which in and of itself is not a moral fault, and sin, by which the intellect is darkened.[24] (This is crucial, as in the final chapter of this enquiry I shall read both of these, namely finitude and sin, as prejudices in the Gadamerian sense of the term.)

A brief passage from Milton's *Paradise Lost* can help to illustrate the principal and the gradual senses of reason as I understand them. In book three, the speaker utters the following prayer for the ability to perceive and communicate truth:

> So much the rather thou, celestial Light,
> Shine inward, and the mind through all her powers
> Irradiate; there plant eyes, all mist from thence
> Purge and disperse, that I may see and tell
> Of things invisible to mortal sight.[25]
>
> MILTON, *Paradise Lost* bk 3, lines 51–5

In these few lines, we see the tradition of the metaphysics of light encapsulated. The ambiguity of the term 'celestial' in the first line bespeaks a qualitatively different type of light from that of the sun. This reading is confirmed in the next line, in which this light is portrayed as renovating the mind ('the mind through all her powers/ Irradiate'). Light implies sight, as light illumines objects so that they can be seen, and without vision, the light shines in vain. In the following line, Milton describes eyes of a certain sort, implying some form of mental vision. However, this capacity itself for intellectual vision is distinct from the perfect realization thereof. Certain blockages must be cleansed and removed. This point is further confirmed by the repetition of 'see'; we already know that one possesses eyes, but apparently this is not a guarantee that one will see. Rather, once the 'mist' has been cleared, one will be able to perceive the objects of intellectual vision, those objects 'invisible to mortal sight'.

In this quotation, we see a number of inter-related themes. For one, we have an implicit schema of light, vision and objects, based in the analogue of our bodily sense of sight. Just as we possess eyes which allow us to see certain objects, and this is facilitated by the light of the sun, so too is this model replicated on the intellectual level. Second, Milton's text implies a distinction between vision and the full realization thereof. This requires help from another, in particular for the purgation of one's rational faculties. Finally, a discussion of illumination is inseparable from a discussion of intellectual vision; in fact, it is the other side of the coin.

This dynamic is neatly encapsulated in *diu. qu.* 46, in which Augustine states that the rational soul possesses a certain capacity for knowing intellectual realities, namely the divine ideas. Light implies a sense of vision, and Augustine states that there is some sort of eye through which one perceives truth: 'However, every soul but the rational is denied the power to contemplate these ideas. This the rational soul can do by that part of itself wherein lies its excellence, i.e. by the mind and reason, as if by a certain inner and intelligible countenance, indeed, an eye, of its own.'[26] In *diu. qu.* 51, Augustine presents a similar reflection, linking *sapientia* and illumination. Here he writes that God's wisdom illumines the mind, and that this light, which is constitutive of the capacity for reason, distinguishes man from beasts.[27] To be a thinking being possessing the capacity for rationality is to imitate God, and this more so than other earthly creatures.[28] When reason rules in the soul, one imitates the image of God within one, just as God's wisdom governs the universe.[29]

Despite the fact that everyone has some access to these ideas in principle – that is, although all rational souls possess some sort of interior capacity for perception *de iure* – the extent to which they exercise this faculty is contingent upon moral and other factors. Hence one may be blind or be absent from the light, such that one cannot see truth. As Augustine writes, 'And indeed, not any and every rational soul is prepared for that vision, but rather, the soul which is holy and pure. It is this soul which is claimed to be fit for that vision, i.e. which has that very eye with which the ideas are seen–an eye sound, pure, serene, and like those things which it endeavors to see.'[30] Here Augustine encapsulates what I call the gradual sense of illumination.

My use of 'principal' and 'gradual' is not a mere word game. Rather, both of these terms reflect Augustine's own language. As for the former, he sees Christ as the *principium*, as the source of all things, not least of all the capacity for reason, which is constituted by his image in the soul. Furthermore, the illumination of the Word provides the 'first principles' of reason, which Augustine describes as the *initia sapientiae*.[31] The latter also reflects Augustine's language, insofar as he speaks of moving *gradatim* towards truth.[32] Indeed, the distinction between the principal and the gradual is reflected most palpably in Augustine's own life, as he recounts how God was (always already) present within him, even if he was unaware of this presence and blinded by his predilection for the non-real creatures of this world. Over the course of time, thanks to God's promptings, Augustine realizes this presence within and then continues to deepen his attunement to that presence.

I argue that Augustine espouses an understanding of rationality which encapsulates the foregoing themes. That is, Augustine holds the principal and the gradual senses of reason and intellectual vision in a productive tension with one another. His ideas seek to balance theoretical commitments and phenomenological insight. The commitment to holding these two elements in such a tension is particularly interesting, as it seems that after Descartes, one has been emphasized to the diminution or even the exclusion of the other.[33] Hence in order to formulate a more adequate understanding of human reason and knowledge, I turn to Augustine's understanding of the world as creation in order to construct an alternative to contemporary theories of knowledge.

The road ahead

This work deals with the implications of thinking of the world as creation for human reason and identity. I engage with the thought of Augustine of Hippo, whose theology is grounded in the creation of the world in the wisdom of God, and indeed, the creation of the human person in the image of God. The context of Augustine's theory of knowledge is his theology of creation. To be created according to God's image means to be given to be and to be enabled to know. This implies that the very conditions of our knowledge lie beyond our complete comprehension and control. Not only is our thinking conditioned by the absolute, but even our very identity is determined by an intimate alterity which nonetheless exceeds our grasp. On the basis of Augustine's thought, I identify and reflect on the key implications of our created nature for human identity and rationality.

In conversing with Augustine, I am not motivated by nostalgia for a past age, nor do I pursue an uncritical apology for traditional Christian theology. Instead I look to Augustine as someone from a radically different time and context whose profound insights into the human condition can challenge us, perhaps to recognize truths concealed by the biases of our own time.

Let us look at the general outline of the book. I ground my understanding of Augustine's theory of knowledge in his understanding of creation *in sapientia*, that is, in the Wisdom of God. We see that creation admits of principal and gradual elements for Augustine. On the one hand, creation is given to be all at once, and always exists in the divine mind. On the other hand, creation in extension fulfils its nature by coming to be in time and space. Moreover, human agents are unique, insofar as they have the choice of turning to God their creator in order to be perfected and fully created.

After an initial treatment of Augustine's theology of creation, I delve into this question of the theological elaboration of *sapientia*. Succinctly put, John's theology as encapsulated in the prologue presents a cosmology of 're-creation', of creation *in principio* through the eternal Wisdom of God, the discarnate Word and redemption through the incarnate Christ. This act of creation has serious implications for the world, as it reflects something of its origin. It also implies something very important about our ways of knowing and thinking, as the rational mind is created *ad imaginem Dei*, in virtue of which it is illumined by the divine light and enabled to know in a normative sense.[34] However, this capacity for reason is inherently limited in virtue of one's creaturely finitude. This limitation is exacerbated by sin, whether original or personal. Adam's folly results in damage not only to human nature, but to all of creation. Hence the principle of creation enters the world of time and space, takes flesh in a miraculous and ineffable way, and by means of his actions heals and redirects the fallen world.[35] This activity is often described in epistemic terms, such as a clearing away of one's moral blindness, or as a reintroduction of light into the darkness. For this reason, Augustine can describe the Son as 'creator and recreator'.[36] Again, Augustine's own words here and elsewhere show us that to think about *sapientia* is at the same time to think about matters of creation and knowledge. Thus the principal–gradual schema applies to creation and to the natures of Christ, or more specifically, the way that creation interfaces with them. Ultimately, Augustine equates beatitude with the possession of wisdom and truth, which are identical with Christ.[37]

Although Augustine does take very seriously the identification of Christ with divine Wisdom, we cannot forget that *sapientia* does not always and unequivocally refer to Christ in Augustine's works. He speaks, for instance, of *sapientia superba*, a pseudo-wisdom of the world. We shall see that to think of knowledge within a context of creation is to commit oneself to the appropriate situation of that knowledge. The acquisition of particular facts, rather than conducting one to truth, can actually prevent one from arriving at it. We see in Augustine an interpretive theory of knowledge, one which requires the parsing and integration of data in order to be made meaningful and coherent. More importantly, Augustine invites us to question the very categories in which we believe we perceive 'empirical' data.

From the treatment of Augustine on *sapientia*, we discover that the theme of incorporeality provides a *locus theologicus* for further study, as Augustine's doctrine of creation generates certain conundrums which summon further attention. For example, Augustine often speaks of the divine Wisdom as the founder of all times, and as incorporeal and invisible. As if this were not mysterious enough, the entry of this divine principle into mutable, finite reality introduces greater difficulties into the way in which *sapientia* can be understood. In Chapters 3 and 4, I deal with two particular implications arising from Augustine's theology of creation: the questions of time and vision. As for the former, we are said to be related to and called to knowledge of *sapientia aeterna* whilst remaining finite and temporal. How can we, in and through time, aspire to that which transcends and conditions it? This is a central question which arises in the *Confessiones* and leads to Augustine's renowned reflection on *memoria*. However, I also seek to demonstrate that this *aporia* concerning time is fundamental to his theology as a whole, and provides insights for his overall theory of knowledge. A close examination of Augustine's texts also reveals, as K. Flasch argues, that time is a logical result of creation in a particular form, such that time and space come to be seen as species of the genus of extension, an insight which will have important ramifications for the final part of this enquiry.

The problem of vision can therefore be seen as a variant on the question of time. God creates the world and can be known through it, but precisely how can we 'see' his vestiges in creation? What are we to make of Christ in the flesh? Can we see him? Indeed, can we see God himself? Questions such as these occasion a series of reflections on vision which recur throughout Augustine's corpus concerning the question of whether God can or cannot be seen, framing the problem as an antinomy generated by the authority of the sacred scriptures. It becomes clear how much of Augustine's thought results from what K. Anatalios has called 'scriptural reasoning', a form of reasoning which takes scriptural claims and authority as a point of departure. My claim is that Augustine acknowledges and attempts to situate himself in the *metaxu* (to borrow a term from W. Desmond) generated by the apparent contradictions of scripture. As scholars such as G. Clark, T. Finan and M. Fishbane note, it is precisely these difficulties in the scriptures which lead us to further knowledge, to thinking more clearly about a particular theological issue.

A theology of creation provides resources for thinking about our knowledge and what must be the case in order for it to function the way it seems to do. For Augustine, knowledge is not so much about moving to some predetermined goal or imposing order on chaos, but allowing ourselves *to see what is already there*, to adjust ourselves in such a way that the images which appear to us cohere into an intelligible whole. His understanding of wisdom also implies that the world admits of 'text-like' properties. Hence knowing reality becomes an interpretive, 'hermeneutical' process. The themes that I distil from Augustine's theology have a certain resonance with the thought of Gadamer.

In the final part, I situate my work with respect to a small but significant body of literature, the common theme of which is to think of knowledge in terms of 'reading' or 'interpreting' the world. The French phenomenologist J.-L. Chrétien, who draws upon various historical figures such as Augustine, describes reason in terms of the dynamic of call and response, and states that the human mind is implicated in a dialogue with the world. The Jewish theologian M. Fishbane presents similar views, drawing upon the Torah and the history of Jewish theology, arguing for an approach to knowledge which challenges our fundamental prejudices concerning ourselves and our situation within reality. Finally, M. Wahlberg has appropriated trends in analytic philosophy to argue for a robust and traditional theology of creation which is consistent with a contemporary scientific understanding of the world. My approach seeks to complement and expand upon the work of these scholars, in particular as I ground the substance of my work in Augustine's theology of creation.

Augustine often discusses his 'speaking' with nature, even claiming that it speaks to him about his soul and about God. Nature speaks in virtue of the beauty it reflects from its source of being, and Augustine is able to see these divine *uestigia* by interrogating creation. We see this especially in *s.* 241, *conf.* 10 and *en. Ps.* 18. In this highly imaginative and scripturally based exchange, Augustine provides us with a 'hermeneutical' template for thinking about one's interpretive interaction with reality. Along the way, we are also invited to call into question assumptions about the nature of the empirical and about 'vision' itself. We also realize that the 'intention' with which one looks at reality is crucial – that is, the aspect under which one views it, and the values one believes to be there or not be there. This is essential to determining whether or not we 'see' what is already there. In the words of William Blake, we must learn to 'cleanse the doors of perception' so that the world can speak to us. Augustine believes it can, and that above all, it tells us that we are finite, or rather, it helps us to recognize this about ourselves.

The conversation which the subject holds with the world foregrounds the prejudice of our ontological finitude. As hermeneutical, rational beings, we have the capacity to distance ourselves at least mentally from our immediate milieu. Augustine's extended reflection on memory in the *Confessiones* takes us a step further, helping us to realize that our way of perceiving the world in terms of time and space is finite and contingent. But Augustine does not stop there; he challenges the very notion of 'dimension' or 'extension' as such, a point which is suggested in his reflection on John's transcendence of all created reality, a feat which results in the utterance of the *in principio*. Without pretending to some neutral position, we are nonetheless made aware that our finitude, experienced in terms of spatio-temporal extension, is a 'meta-prejudice' of our hermeneutical and phenomenological experience of the world.[38] As Gadamer says, the task is not so much to forsake prejudice as to recognize it as such, and hence be better attuned to the ways in which it influences our thought. For example, the (implicit) thought that the physical and the material are the mark of the real comes to be seen not as a self-evident principle of reason, but as a contingent and defeasible assumption about the nature of reality itself. I also identify a further 'prejudice' of sorts, which according to Augustine could be our sinfulness, which causes us to misunderstand the text of the world. Hence I construe *pride as prejudice* and seek to explain how we can re-orient our hermeneutic in order to overcome the obstructions of our fallen human nature.

Let us now proceed to a discussion of Augustine's understanding of creation, which will disclose several points of philosophical and theological significance.

PART ONE

Creation in Wisdom

1

Aspects of (Re-)Creation

Introduction

In this chapter, I shall discuss Augustine's theology of creation as it is expounded in certain select works and how this informs his understanding of knowledge and reason. We shall see how according to Augustine, God is eternal and unchanging, invisible to the bodily eye and beyond all time and space. He exists eternally in himself, and contains the forms of things in his mind. In creation, these things come to be instantiated in matter. In addition to being given to be, they are given to grow and to be formed. Hence it becomes clear that creation admits of two elements which are inseparable if asymmetrically related. This theory of creation is reflected in Augustine's approach to knowledge and illumination. In other words, just as the mind is created in order to know truth, it must continuously seek to be perfected so that it can indeed attain to the truth. The human soul, in virtue of being created in God's image, receives the gift of reason. Moreover, because of this connection to God and the logical link of creation and the divine mind, one can discern something of the order in creation and thereby be led to know God. In what follows, we shall track the elaboration of such themes in Augustine's exegesis of Genesis and John.

Creation in divine Wisdom

In *Gn. litt.*, we read about themes regarding light and wisdom, articulated and elaborated within an explicit framework of creation. God speaks eternally through his Wisdom,[1] his Word.[2] One cannot separate the Father's speech from that of the Son.[3] This speech is part and parcel of God's creative activity. God acts as a unity in creating, even though the three persons of the Trinity each have a contribution to make.[4] Augustine identifies the 'economy' of creation, as the Father creates in his Word insofar as the *rationes aeternae* are contained with him, the treasury of wisdom and knowledge.[5] All of the ideas upon which individual creatures are based are held within the Word together, though not thereby confused, even before each of them is individually named.[6] This creative process is guided and brought to fruition through the love of the Holy Spirit,[7] in virtue of which God sees that creation is good.[8]

The existence and the creation of all things depend on God and his divine Word.[9] Augustine links the psalm in which it is stated, 'You have made all things in your Wisdom',[10] and Paul, who writes, 'since in him were fashioned all things in heaven and on earth, visible and invisible.'[11] The identity of the Word and Wisdom is established, leading to the notion of creation *in sapientia* (*ipsa Sapientia, per quam facta sunt omnia*).[12] Augustine cites the opening verses of John in order to substantiate his claim.[13] One should also note that the discussion of the creation of light in Genesis pertains to the light which is seen by the eyes of the body, the corporeal light, in contrast to God, who is uncreated light.[14]

Drawing upon the text of Genesis, Augustine speaks of two aspects under which to view creation, which I call the 'principal' and the 'gradual' senses, respectively.[15] The former pertains to the way in which all things were made together (*omnia simul*), and the latter to the continuous working of God in the world (*opera eius, in quibus usque nunc operatur*).[16] Thus Augustine can describe all things as having come into being at once, even though they are only subsequently instantiated. In other words, as it pertains to creation, one can speak of creation either 'without any intervals or periods of time between' or 'through periods of time'.[17] As it pertains to the latter, God still works in the world, creating even now in the unfolding of life and movement in its multifarious forms.[18] Scripture speaks of both creation according to a plan of seven days, as well as creation according to one seminal moment.[19] Such difficulties as these pose a challenge to the reader; some may be able to understand, whereas others may require more time and assistance.[20] The temporal character implied by the creation narrative is a result of our existence in time and represents a sort of scriptural condescension which crudely expresses a truth about God's eternity.[21] This narrative form also serves to prevent the proud from arriving at crucial knowledge concerning God and his creation.[22] Augustine suggests that as scripture is wont to do, it can present something in a way which is pellucid to little ones, but nonetheless contains some deeper truth for those who are capable of receiving it.[23]

Augustine further problematizes the foregoing understanding of the senses of creation, deploying a threefold distinction to encapsulate the ways in which creation can be understood and categorized.[24] Creation can be understood as the eternal forms present in the divine Word; the works narrated in Genesis, created together, and from which God rested; and finally as creation unfolding and being realized even now.[25] The last of these three, the works of creation as they are happening now, are available to us through the senses of the body, and are also known by the habit of this life.[26] The former two Augustine describes as unfamiliar to our senses.[27] The eternal ideas are therefore invisible in principle to mortal eyes. In the divine mind, all things are known together, but in creation, when they are made, they are present as individual things, according to their own nature.[28]

Augustine states resolutely that God still acts in the world in a creative way, an argument he substantiates by appeal to Christ's words in the Gospel that he and the Father continue to work.[29] The world and the things in it do not serve as a Demiurge of sorts, nor does God command the world to produce things whilst he himself remains neutral. On the contrary, God is providentially involved with the world (*omnia Dei prouidentia gubernari*).[30] Moreover, Augustine also defends this claim against the objection that Christ's words pertain only to the internal activity of God, and not to any work in the world.[31] Hence Augustine, without employing *ipsissima uerba*, defends a theology of *creatio continua*, as well as the idea that God the creator is still working within the world.[32] From an initial, primordial seed of creation, all other things arose, in particular as this initial thing contained the forms of all subsequent creatures.[33] God can be said to create now in virtue of the potencies he placed in his original creation, as well has continuous providential governance of those things.[34] Augustine describes God as working in and through creation in virtue of the movements of created bodies, or the actions of his human agents.[35]

Augustine's understanding of creation *in sapientia* grounds his theory of knowledge and reason. The rational soul is unique, as it is created from eternal light, and the faculty of reason is placed in it by the Word.[36] Hence to be created in the image of God means to be illumined by the original image of God, the Son, who is also God himself, as we have seen.[37] God's co-eternal Word is identical with his Wisdom (*sapientia*).[38] Hence Augustine can describe the Son in this work as 'begotten wisdom', *genita sapientia*,[39] 'whence the Soule reason receives'.[40] The *principium* Augustine also identifies with the *lumen sapientiae*.[41] This eternal Word-Wisdom illumines the minds of rational creatures.[42] Unlike other creatures, however, we have a free will, which we can use for either good or ill, in the latter case decreasing in goodness.[43] Sin makes the rational creature more like a non-rational beast.[44] Yet despite the pernicious effect of sin, all creation is still essentially good.[45]

As we have already noted, creation involves two elements, to come into being (*creari*) and to be perfected in one's being (*formari*).[46] This is replicated at the level of reason. Created by God, rational creatures fall into darkness by sin, but Christ restores one and renews one in knowledge.[47] This narrative reflects two aspects of the model of illumination, namely the initial illumination of the mind and its subsequent need to be perfected and healed. Augustine claims that illumination consists in turning to the Creator, being perfected by the Word, and so becoming light.[48] In other words, God calls creatures to turn to him and be perfected.[49] What is clearly implied is that there is an element of reason which originates from beyond the self. Augustine states that one must imitate the Word by attaching oneself to the Creator (*inhaerendo Creatori*).[50] The task proper to the intellectual soul is to approach the Creator by imitating his Wisdom.[51]

In this work, we also begin to the see the significance of incorporeality as it pertains to human knowledge and God's wisdom. This theme is even more prominent in the *conf.*, and will constitute a major focus of this study in due course. For the moment, we can mention the following. Augustine writes that the term *in principio* does not refer to a beginning in time.[52] God creates through the utterance of his Word, but this is not a temporal way of speaking.[53] Due to our spatio-temporal situation, we must narrate the eternal activity of God in a similar way, such that we can gradually begin to understand how God exceeds all time and space.[54] The angels do not have any corporeal senses as we do; they see wisdom 'immediately' within themselves.[55] For us, in contrast, the *pulchritudo* of the world is composed in a succession of times.[56]

Augustine and John

The significance of Augustine's theology of creation for a theory of knowledge becomes even more pronounced in the following way: the source of our being and of our knowledge is identified with Christ himself. Augustine identifies *sapientia* with Christ, who is also the *principium*, the *Verbum* and the Son, the source of all creation and knowledge. Hence in order to understand Augustine's account of wisdom, these Christological themes must be addressed. Augustine's language and thematic imagery in this respect are clearly Johannine and elaborated accordingly. Now the task is to examine the theology of John in Augustine more precisely.

Augustine sees John as integrally linked with Genesis. In *sermo* 1, originally preached in the early 390s, Augustine establishes a direct link between the opening verse of Genesis and that of John. He identifies the *principium* of both. In other words, Christ is the Word through whom all things were made, and who took flesh in the Incarnation.[57] As further evidence for this, Augustine cites Jn 8.25, in which Christ speaks of himself as the *principium*. On Augustine's view, this confirms the already strong connection between Genesis and John.[58] In his exceptionally erudite article, G. Van Riel analyses Augustine's exegesis of Genesis 1 in the twelfth book of the *conf*.[59] One of the notable upshots of this essay is Augustine's understanding of *in principio*, not only his linking the term's use in Genesis with that of the Johannine prologue, but also the link of this term with the idea that God created the universe through his Wisdom.[60] This observation motivates an examination of Augustine's treatment of John to be placed alongside his treatment of Genesis. Indeed, Augustine returns to this point less explicitly in *De Genesi ad litteram*, in which he describes *in principio* as referring to the creation of all things in the Son.

Augustine's Johannine theology is pre-eminently present in a set of tractates he composed on the fourth gospel, the *In Ioannis euangelium tractatus CXXIV*. In the first tractate, Augustine collects together several terms which are used to designate God or some 'aspect' of the Godhead, such as *lux/lumen, uita* and *sapientia*, and links them.[61] Terms such as light and truth are only used by Augustine in reference to God.[62] Furthermore, Augustine appears again to link the Gospel of John with the Psalms, and indeed, the OT tradition of the divine *Memra*, the Word of God, through which creation took place.[63] He speaks of God's Wisdom, *sapientia Dei*, and he says, quoting the Psalms, *omnia in sapientia fecisti*.[64] When John refers to the Word, he is discussing Christ in his divine nature.[65] All true wisdom is based in God's Wisdom, which is his (co-)eternal Word, which is to say, the Son. The Word, he maintains, is immutable, truly divine, whereas creation is mutable.[66] In addition, Augustine connects John and Exodus, claiming that the divine Word is the same revelation of God to Moses as *ego sum qui sum*.[67] As we shall presently see, Exod. 3.14 becomes a major proof-text for Augustine's discussion of divine immutability and incorporeality. As Ayres notes, Augustine employs the terms *modus, species, ordo, pondus, numerus* and *mensura* with respect to Wis. 11.21, stating that the order of the universe is produced by God's wisdom.[68]

In the third tractate, Augustine identifies Christ with the second person of the Trinity and the agent of creation, couching this theological principle in Johannine language, and indeed, developing it according to the opening verse of the gospel itself.[69] Augustine proceeds to describe the Son as the uncreated source of creation,[70] around whom from the beginning 'all the Sanctities of Heaven stood thick as Starrs'.[71] As he states also in *Gn. litt.*, the Word did not come to be in the way that the rest of creation came to be; in fact, it did not come to be at all.[72] That which exists now was always present in the mind of God, in particular in the Son:[73]

> Is it perhaps possible that this Word was made by God? No. For 'this was in the beginning with God.' Therefore what? Did God not make other things which are similar to the Word? No. Because 'all things were made through him, and without him nothing was made.' How were all things made through him? For 'what was made in him was life,' and before it came to be, it was life.[74]

This discussion of creation in the Word means that God created all things in his Wisdom, and this *sapientia* is eternal and immutable, in contrast to the things made through it:[75] 'What was made is not life, but before it came to be, it was life in knowledge, this is, in the Wisdom of God. What is made, passes. What is in Wisdom is not able to pass.'[76] One of the major dangers for Augustine is thinking of the divinity of the Word according to some created form, a point which he even mentions in his preaching.[77]

There is an epistemic implication to the foregoing theological principle. Augustine contrasts the 'spirit' (my term) of the OT and the NT, stating that to think in accord with the latter means that one must forsake all carnal images as they apply to God and his relationship with man.[78] In order to begin to conceive of God, Augustine tells one, 'Therefore expel carnal thoughts from your hearts, so that you may truly be under grace, so that you may relate to the New Covenant.'[79] Granted, physical things serve as a means of mediation, but these are simply means, and not ends in themselves. Augustine states (tendentiously) that the people of the OT were held captive by temporal images and conceived of the covenant in purely corporeal terms.[80]

Augustine confirms in the tractates that his theory of knowledge is grounded in his theology of creation. Those who have reason share in the logic of the Word, indeed, are formed in God's divine, rational image; one can be deemed, in Augustine's words, a *particeps Verbi*.[81] The human soul is illumined by God's divine light, for man is made in God's image (*ad imaginem Dei*), which means that man has a rational soul capable of receiving wisdom.[82] The capacity for wisdom thus becomes distinctive and constitutive of rationality and human nature. For Augustine, the image of God is none other than the pattern of the Son, the eternal Logos. The upshot, therefore, is that rationality is a constitutive feature of human nature, and rationality realizes itself fully in the attainment of (divine) wisdom.[83]

Augustine continues the Johannine train of his thought, stating that the divine light is an incorporeal, intelligible light, not to be likened unto that of our sun which is common to man and beast alike:[84]

> but 'life was the light of men.' Is it possible that this light is the light of animals? For that light is of both people and animals. There is a certain light of people, from which we may see that people stand apart from animals, and then we understand what the light of people might be. You are not different from an animal, except by the intellect. Do not boast from anything else.[85]

Our difference from animals and other parts of nature consists in the fact that we possess the image of God within us, in particular in our mind or our intellect.[86] This allows us to think, reason and come to know God in and through his creation, which reflects something of his being and his glory:

> From what are you better? From the image of God. Where is the image of God? In the mind, in the intellect. Therefore, if you are better than an animal, because you possess a mind by which you can understand what a beast cannot understand, then moreover you are a human being, because you are better than an animal. The light of people is the light of minds. The light of minds is above minds, and exceeds all minds. This is that life through which all things were made.[87]

This light of minds is Wisdom, divine and eternal, the source of all form and intelligibility, and ultimately responsible for our rationality as well, which is constituted by the image of God, present in the human mind.[88]

This discussion of illumination leads to a further deepening of Augustine's theory of knowledge. We are mutable, changeable creatures, yet we can also have thoughts about a God who is beyond such categories, indeed, an immutable being. How could such thoughts even arise in mortal minds? For Augustine, the reason for this is clear: it is the intimate presence of God, *qua* Logos, to the human mind (*hoc est uerbum de Deo in corde tuo*),[89] a point in continuity with the discussions of the presence of God to the mind in early works.[90]

On a similar note, Augustine states that this Wisdom is invisible to our bodily senses:[91] 'The Wisdom of God is not able to be seen by the eyes. Brethren, if Christ is the Wisdom of God, and the Power of God, if Christ is the Word of God, and the word of a person is not seen by the eyes, is the Word of God able to be seen in that way?'[92] God is not like anything which we see in this world – that is, those things which we perceive by the bodily eyes.[93] Rather, we see God by means of an interior sense of vision, and indeed, one which is pure and fit to see this.[94] As Augustine puts it, 'all things which are seen corporeally, were not that substance of God. For we see those things by the eyes of the flesh. Whence is the substance of God seen? Ask the Gospel: "Blessed are the pure of heart, for they shall see God."'[95]

The Son is visible to the bodily eyes in the sense that he takes flesh in the incarnation, becoming *lac paruulorum*.[96] Augustine states that the *fides catholica* can accept this.[97] What it cannot accept is that the Son is visible *in se*, in his divine nature, in contrast to the Father, who is ever invisible.[98] In the OT, for example, God took the form of some created being, but in using this as a means of becoming sensible, the substance of God itself (*non utique substantia ipsa*) was not seen.[99] God manifested himself through various corporeal things to Moses, but his substance remained hidden.[100] God is incorporeal, and so whenever scripture speaks of him as if he possesses something bodily, we must interpret this in some analogous terms.[101] This passage anticipates key themes which arise in Augustine's *ep.* 147, dedicated to the vision of God.[102]

Testimony

Because it was created in the Wisdom of God, the world has always borne testimony to him.[103] There is a certain beauty, fittingness and balance to creation, as God has created and ordered it wonderfully.[104] Though God's mysterious plan is invisible, it takes visible form in creation.[105] Augustine speaks of God's *ars*, which is life itself, but not in the individual tokens of their ideal types, which possess life through the divine ideas which sustain their being.[106] Furthermore, God is present to the world as its *artifex*, governing that which he has made, though not as a particular individual thing within the world.[107] Thus the world becomes a means of seeing God, or rather, as Arsenault states, the world becomes an address from God to the soul in virtue of its creation *in sapientia*.[108]

The divine light was always shining in the world, in virtue of which it is also gave testimony to God, but only for those who were prepared to receive it.[109] As Augustine states,

> And where was that [light]? 'It was in this world.' And how was it 'in this world'? Was this light in the world in the same way as that light of the sun, of the moon, of the stars? No. For 'the world was made through him, and the world did not know him.' This is, 'the light shines in the darkness, and the darkness has not comprehended it.'[110]

The problem becomes even more acute in the incarnation, for to see Christ completely is to see him not simply as a man, but as God in the flesh:[111] 'Certainly it is he himself, but not the whole which the Jews saw. This is not the whole Christ. But what is he? "In the beginning was the word." In what beginning? "And the Word was with God." And what kind of Word? "And God was the Word."'[112] Augustine raises the question of why certain people were not able to perceive Christ as God.[113] In a sense, the world's testimonies of God were so obvious that they could not be missed. Hence Augustine appeals to the notion of epistemic darkness as a way to explain why people could not perceive the presence of the divine light: 'if all those things gave testimony, how did the world not know him, unless because the lovers of the world are the world, having the world in their heart?'[114] 'For the world is darkness,' Augustine states, 'because the lovers of the world are the world.'[115] This truth was apparent and present, yet not available to those who were in darkness.[116] He articulates this point again by using the Johannine terminology of the light shining in the darkness, and the darkness not understanding it.[117] This is also the meaning behind the verse according to which the Word came to his own, and they did not receive him.[118] The light is shining and ever present, but we are absent to it in virtue of vice and sin: 'The light is not absent,' says Augustine, 'but you are absent from the light. A blind person in the sunlight has the sun present, but he himself is absent to the sun.'[119] Here we have a clear textual basis for the idea that knowledge for Augustine involves seeing what is already there, and requires removing the blockages or re-envisioning the reality in front of us. In Augustine's own biography, we find an example of this concept. As a free rational subject, one is capable of rejecting the truth and fleeing from the light of God. All the while God remains present to one, even if one is not present to God.[120] One can also see here a clear linkage between epistemic darkness and blindness on the one hand and morally vicious behaviour and activity on the other.[121] Augustine tells his listeners not to be *amatores saeculi*, which amongst other things is constitutive of the aforementioned darkness.[122]

As Berrouard explains, in the first tractate, Augustine draws on Paul (1 Cor. 2.14) in order to substantiate his claim that those who are accustomed to the flesh are unable to understand higher things.[123] He reinforces this point by drawing upon Christ's words about judging according to the flesh.[124] Those who judge accordingly take their own reason and their acquaintance with the created world as the mark of the real, and are thereby prevented from challenging their prejudices and their limitations.[125] They remain blind to the potential enlightenment of the Spirit, which offers them 'une tout autre intelligence'.[126] Those who are imprisoned in the flesh are like the Israelites who saw the manifestation of manna in purely corporeal terms, whereas Moses, for example, saw the deeper spiritual significance of the means of bodily sustenance.[127] Furthermore, Berrouard avers that the source of these different approaches to God's gift of manna comes from the Spirit's illumination.[128]

In his discussion of the flesh of Christ, Augustine intimates that there is a difference between our limitations according to the flesh, that is, simply in virtue of being created, and additionally in virtue of sin, or more specifically, the *tradux peccati* from Adam.[129] The fault of Lucifer, Augustine states, was that even though he was illumined, he did not stand fast in the truth, and looked to himself as the source of his own light and knowledge.[130] It is not sufficient to be capable of receiving illumination, but one must continuously acknowledge, as John the Baptist did, that the source of one's illumination is not oneself.[131] Ultimately, one must be taught inwardly by God himself in order to apprehend something of the humility of God in the flesh.[132]

Augustine writes that if one had not sinned, then one would have remained under the illumination of the Word.[133] Yet foolish hearts are corrupted by sin and thus cannot perceive God's light.[134] The light itself is present to everyone, yet the sinner represents the *tenebrae* which did not comprehend the divine light in the world.[135] In order to perceive wisdom, the eyes of the heart must be cleansed of the obstructions of sin, and for this, one must entreat the assistance of God.[136] Augustine notes that it is fitting that just as we sin and are thus wounded by the flesh, we are also healed in the flesh: 'For all eye drops and medicines are nothing except from the earth. From dust you were blinded, from dust you are cleansed; therefore, as the flesh had blinded you, so now the flesh may praise you.'[137] Christ comes to act on the human soul, cleansing its spiritual eyes.[138] To emphasize this point, Augustine references one of the Beatitudes, according to which those who are pure of heart will see God.[139]

There is a certain fittingness or symmetry to the divine plan for our salvation, insofar as the world becomes the source of our cleansing, just as it was the original source of our wounds (*ut quia terra caecabamur, de terra sanaremur*).[140] Furthermore, just as the eternal, discarnate Word created all things, so too it is fitting that, when creation fell, it would be *re*-created through him: 'Therefore do not believe that it was made, through which all things were made, lest you not be re-made through the Word, through which all things are re-made. For you were made through the Word, but it is fitting that you be re-made through the Word.'[141] Augustine emphasizes the different aspects of Christ's two natures: Christ as the discarnate, eternal Logos, and Christ as the incarnate God-man.[142] However, like T.-J. van Bavel, J. Wolinski warns against reading Augustine as separating the natures of Christ.[143] The theme of the inter-connection of creation and re-creation is reinforced by Augustine's reference to Moses (understood as the author of Genesis, and more specifically, the accounts of creation).[144] Augustine also draws upon the symmetry that Paul discusses with respect to Christ and Adam.[145] Adam, created as the first man, also allows sin into the world, in response to which Christ, the new Adam, comes without sin and rescues fallen man.[146] What is of particular interest here is the way in which salvation is discussed in epistemic terms, incorporating the language of sight and light, and grounding these healing actions in the person of Christ. Appealing to John, in particular the High Priestly Prayer, Augustine identifies eternal life with *knowledge* of God, in particular God the Father and his Son, Jesus Christ.[147]

Critical discussion

At various points throughout this work, an Interlocutor will make an appearance as a devil's advocate of sorts, to present a critical viewpoint:[148]

Your discussion of creation in Wisdom troubles me, insofar as it places an emphasis on things such as eternal ideas and forms, the sorts of things of which, I thought, philosophy had disabused itself. I am especially surprised at your attempt to integrate hermeneutical philosophy and Augustine's theology, as it seems that this synthesis is doomed to flounder on the conflict between Augustine's emphasis on infinity and the necessarily finite emphasis present in hermeneutics.[149] Gadamer was no religious dogmatist and viewed revelation and religion ambivalently at best. Heidegger said that theologians must recognize their own finitude and situated-ness, a task which you have obviously failed to complete.[150] Furthermore, a brief look at the development of hermeneutics in the latter half of the 20th century clearly demonstrates that it has been taken in a direction antithetical to metaphysics. Even those who endorse a more traditional metaphysics, figures such as Grondin, have trouble reconciling hermeneutics with their philosophical positions.[151] Even the work of your own theologians condemns you: Eberhard and Zimmermann, for example, point to Gadamer's hermeneutics as useful for theology, but for completely different reasons than you. For them, hermeneutics has the capacity to correct Christianity's pretensions to absolute truth by introducing an emphasis on the 'incarnational' nature of understanding.[152] Zimmermann also acknowledges the fundamental conflict between the Christian commitment to eternity and transcendence on the one hand, and the hermeneutical emphasis on finitude and particularity on the other.[153] Try as you might, you cannot get away from the fact that hermeneutical philosophy is fundamentally tethered to the here and now.

I accept that there is a tension here, but I do not think it is fatal to the programme I am proposing. As much as Augustine discusses the soul's intimate contact with the divine ideas, he is adamant that human knowledge is inherently limited in this life. If anything, Christian theology provides a firm basis for thinking about our finitude, not only in terms of the emphasis that appears in such writings, which is simply an apparent fact, but also in terms of grounding this finitude in our very nature, indeed, our created nature. Interpreted strictly, the hermeneutical emphasis on human finitude and the limitations of reason becomes an uncontroversial reformulation of the Christian notion of our created nature.[154] But it is just this transience and movement of created being that testifies to God, albeit obliquely: its very finitude suggests an infinite source of its being.[155] Indeed, for Augustine, our finitude is conditioned by and even bespeaks the infinite. A hermeneutic of suspicion can also be useful regarding this issue, as it seems that you take for granted that the eternal, the incorporeal, the timeless cannot be real, and must be excluded from theology or philosophy. If you are to be consistent, you must recognize that this is a fundamental assumption, taken for granted, and it must be critically addressed with suspicion.[156]

All you have said may be convincing; but it is also irrelevant. The arguments above may be sufficient to justify a belief in infinity, eternity, transcendence, or whatever you want to call it. But now you are simply putting it forth as a posit, a sort of Kantian assumption, granted made on a logical basis, but with little relevance for us as human actors. The real crux of the problem, in particular for you, is how we can know something of the infinite in a finite way. Let us grant that there is an infinite; you still have no way of knowing anything non-trivial and substantive about it. And this is a problem for you, insofar as you wish to present a theory of knowledge which includes as an essential part some transcendent, divine source of truth.

Here you touch upon a major issue which has seldom been addressed in the literature, but which I think is of crucial importance for an enquiry of this kind. For reasons I cannot fully discuss here, I hold that in principle, hermeneutical philosophy itself gives us no reason to exclude transcendence from a theory of reality, nor to exclude altogether the human capacity for contact with it. One would want to say perhaps that this contact is always mediated, or somehow incomplete because of our finitude. But nothing in such an emphasis conflicts with Augustine's own admonitions to remember our frailty and weakness when we try to conceive of the infinite and immutable God, not to mention the hindrances caused by sin.[157] It is important to note here that Gadamer distinguishes between comprehension and understanding. The former pertains to the *Sache* in itself. So Christian doctrine is incomprehensible, even if the articulations of it in language are understandable. One cannot completely comprehend the divine, but that is not to say that something is not adequately stated in human language.[158] Furthermore, for Augustine, even in immanent, finite being, transcendence is present. Hermeneutics presents no reason to suppose that the transcendent cannot mingle with the immanent. To appeal to the idea that the transcendent and the immanent are mutually exclusive would be to beg the question, let alone conflict with the general tenor of reacting against the epistemology of the Enlightenment.

Gadamer suggests that philosophy admits of an inherently religious aspect, that it is geared towards searching for that which lies behind our complete comprehension, indeed, the limits of our knowledge, as was the case with Heidegger.[159] As C. Vincie notes, following J. Haught, science and religion are both grounded in the orientation towards questions of deeper truths – that is, explanations and aetiologies.[160] Gadamer also sees a certain convergence of faith and philosophy, insofar as both confront the limitations of human existence.[161] Gadamer suggests that ritual acts as a sort of interruption of one's prejudices pertaining to quotidian life.[162] Ritual and religion witness at a very basic level to the 'overdeterminacy' of the world, and confront one with this inconvenience within the midst of one's typical existence. The questions and the enquiries engendered by ritual are always subject to doubt, especially for the theologian, a fact that one must also learn to accept.[163] Gadamer goes so far as to suggest that the task of the philosopher is to demonstrate that religion responds to a deeper dimension of the human person which can never be totally ignored or eliminated.

What if the message we hear being spoken is a decidedly transcendent, metaphysical one? If we hear a message being spoken to us through the world but with respect to something which exceeds it, Gadamer's thought will be helpful, but only provisionally. The metaxological quality to this message already indicates that we must engage in thought that is not only methodologically and hermeneutically nuanced, but even nuanced in ontological and epistemic terms. I believe that Augustine's ideas can be informative in this respect.

Conclusion

Augustine's understanding of Wisdom includes the identification of *sapientia* with the Son, who is likewise Word, Light and *principium*, as a pre-eminent if not normative element. The eternal, discarnate Word serves as the principle of creation. All things are created in God's Wisdom, in virtue of which they reflect something of their origin and source. Furthermore, the divine image is impressed on the human soul, constituting its rationality, as well as its initial illumination from God. In virtue of this, it can perceive the vestiges of the divine within the world. However, this is inherently limited in virtue of one's created, material being. Human reason is not absolute but is rather conditioned by creation and the inherent deficiencies thereof. These limitations are exacerbated by sin, which is often couched in terms of moral darkness. As a result, the creator enters creation itself and becomes a re-creator. The incarnate Word heals the wounded rational faculties of man, and redirects him to heaven. Hence the darkness and blindness of sin, the damage done to our inner eyes, is cleared away, and we are enabled again to perceive according to our original state. Hence we see that the understanding of two aspects of reason is grounded in Augustine's overall theology of creation and redemption.

The findings thus far from the investigation of Augustine's conception of *sapientia* are compelling and useful, but we can go further still. In the foregoing examination of his works, we have come across a curious theme, namely the incorporeality of God. To be incorporeal means not to be extended in time and space, to be immaterial and eternal in essence. We are temporal and corporeal in virtue of being finite creatures, made by God. We began to be and can cease to be, at least in a particular way. We undergo change, whether good, bad or neutral. We grow and decrease, and we acquire and lose properties. God is not like this in any way. Augustine reiterates with some frequency that the Son is the eternal Word, begotten of the Father without any interval of time. Similarly, he admits of no extension in space, nor of corporeal properties, in virtue of which he is imperceptible to the bodily senses. The commitment to the incorporeality of God results in two closely related epistemic problems which recur throughout Augustine's corpus. One has to do with time and eternity: how is it that we, who are inherently temporal and know in a temporal way, can ever aspire to that which is eternal? Similarly, how can we 'see' God, when he is invisible? What are we to make of the scriptural promises that indicate that we can or will see God, for instance, if we have a pure heart? These two related questions will constitute the focus of the two respective chapters of the second part, being addressed as *loci theologici* for knowledge and cognition. Before that, however, we shall consider further the question of pride.

2

The Problem of Pride

Introduction

One cannot do full justice to Augustine's understanding of knowledge without discussing its dark counterpart, *sapientia superba*. This is the sort of wisdom which leads one to view oneself as wise, even though one is actually in darkness. One way of framing the issue is the following: does the acquisition of more facts necessarily result in greater knowledge? One possible answer is yes, as knowledge is good, and *since good, the more communicated, more abundant growes*,[1] the greater expansion of factual knowledge is clearly to be encouraged. This was the conceit of the Industrial Revolution, in which one envisioned that the acquisition of information would not only mean an increase in knowledge, but would also exert a humanizing effect on society as a whole.[2] Though the affirmative response seems intuitively plausible, Augustine rejects such a position. Then the question becomes what alternative remains, or on what basis does one oppose the indefinite expansion of one's knowledge base? Does Augustine's admonition, for example, to reject the erudition of the *philosophi* in favour of humble adherence to Christ represent an option for obscurantism, anti-intellectualism and fideism? My answer is 'not necessarily', as I think Augustine suggests a third alternative, a 'hermeneutical' view, according to which individual data require an appropriate framework and interpretive key in order to be understood. As Cilleruelo explains, 'la verdad depende de perspectivas más largas de las que ella puede descubrir y de condiciones que limitan el ejercicio de esa misma *ratio*.'[3] For Augustine, this hermeneutical key is Christ, the incarnate wisdom of God.[4]

Sapientia superba

In *s.* 184, Augustine discusses how the impious and the proud are prevented from perceiving truths about God, in particular because he reveals himself in humility and simplicity.[5] The promise to the faithful is that by accepting and embracing the humility of God, they may ultimately arrive at the most esoteric knowledge of his wisdom, a gift denied to the proud of heart.[6] This is in contrast to the *sapientes* (falsely so), who refuse to believe in the humble Christ. As a result, they not only fail to accept the 'simple' revelations of God, but also miss the higher things as well.[7] The theme of Christ's humility is very important to Augustine, a theme motivated by his anti-Manichaean polemic.[8] Augustine particularly has in mind the Incarnation and the teachings associated with it, e.g. the virgin birth, which the prideful view as more fiction than fact.[9] Evoking biblical language, Augustine states that the prideful possess a wisdom of this world, not of its creator.[10] They lack the proper perspective for interpreting reality, and hence do not possess true knowledge or wisdom.[11] Because they lack true wisdom, the proud ones are not capable of accepting the mysteries of the Incarnation, and the fact that God entered the world in order to save it.[12] Christ takes flesh and humbles himself by entering the time which he himself created, standing under the sun which he had made, for our own sake.[13] Augustine locates in the Christ child a humility which can instruct those who are prepared, even (or perhaps especially) because the divine infant cannot even speak in a human voice, and yet his very presence on earth says so much.[14] Christ's humility serves as a healing medicine for our pride. He comes into the world to counteract it, to heal and uplift our nature, a task made more difficult by our pride, a severe prejudice indeed.[15]

Augustine warns us against placing our hope in human knowledge (*scientia*), pridefully putting it before the precepts of God.[16] As Harrison writes, Augustine is concerned about philosophies which do not seem to take seriously the limitations of human rationality, especially those engendered by (original) sin. He criticizes the Manichees in this regard, articulating a less optimistic (but not thereby less than optimistic) view concerning post-lapsarian reason.[17] Augustine learned from his own experience how human reason can be limited, especially if it views itself as self-sufficient.

Svensson also reads Augustine's conception of *scientia* with respect to man's first sin, according to which Adam attempted to detach *scientia* from any higher norm or knowledge, to become a ruler unto himself.[18] As Svensson notes, the fall 'da lugar a una *scientia* autónoma respecto de la *sapientia*–que quiere gobernar sola'.[19] Reason and knowledge are integrally linked with issues of pride, sin, creation and salvation, and these are inherently theological topics. This also implicates other aspects of the Christian life, such as biblical, ecclesial and liturgical dimensions. In addition, it implies that the acquisition of knowledge is ultimately a matter of a personal, holistic encounter.[20]

Similarly, Augustine is also concerned with the vanity associated with intellectual enquiry and is concerned about the vicious potential of *curiositas*.[21] In certain cases, it is better to accept one's ignorance than to place an exceedingly high trust in one's own knowledge.[22] A statement such as this clearly raises the spectre of obscurantism. However, attention to the context of this claim casts it in a more favourable light. Augustine makes his statement in preference for a sort of 'pious ignorance'[23] within the context of thinking of God as not bound to a particular location. Commenting on the difficulty, if not the impossibility of conceiving of such a thing, for it is not *a* thing at all, Augustine says it is better not to think something than to think something which would give one a false sense of God.[24] On the contrary, by fulfilling God's commands, one is led to understanding.[25] However, Augustine reminds us that any vision of God on earth is incomplete and provisional; we are still *in spe*, and not *in re*.[26] Augustine links the opening verses of the Gospel of John with 1 Jn 3.2. The Word in the beginning is what we shall see when we become like God in heaven. This is the vision promised to the faithful children of God.[27] He also invokes Paul, claiming that we do not yet see God face to face, but *per speculum*.[28]

Typology

As Augustine reflects on the Prologue of the Gospel of John, he enumerates a three-fold typology of persons according to how they relate to God.[29] Augustine writes of (i) the great ones; (ii) the little ones; and (iii) the prideful ones (Brachtendorf's terms). The first category consists of those of great faith and great intellect, who believed in the truths of the faith with great fervour and love, who embraced it with their hearts, but who also were intellectually gifted so as to understand and expound upon transcendent truths.[30] Augustine gives the example of John the Divine, the 'disciple whom Jesus loved',[31] whose esoteric reflections on the nature of the *Logos* epitomized the ideal of faith seeking understanding.[32] But what makes John a great one is not simply his intellectual abilities, but his ability to balance these God-given talents with faith and humility.[33] Second, Augustine describes the little ones, those of a simple, humble faith, who, unlike the great ones, have neither the time nor the intellectual capacity to study philosophy and theology or to understand in a cognitive way the teachings of the Church. However, like John and the other great minds, they do possess the humility of faith which enables them to come to Christ.[34] For these little ones, reliance on scripture and authority was sufficient in Augustine's mind. However, that did not exempt one from deepening one's understanding. As Berrouard notes, the reception of the Christian mysteries at baptism implies an 'existential' commitment to growing in and deepening one's understanding.[35] Following Paul, Augustine talks of those who are not yet adults in Christ, but only infants.[36] They remain at a physical level and judge things accordingly.[37] In particular, they look upon the faith as a set of facts or propositions to be memorized, but not thereby internalized in the hopes of arriving at deeper illumination and understanding.[38] Augustine's critique here is not one of mere pedantry. A pedestrian approach to Christianity makes one susceptible to a variety of problems, such as the fomenting of heresy and schism.[39]

Finally, the proud ones were the philosophers, even and especially the Platonists, who were able to reason effectively and lucidly, but who, because of their admiration of their own knowledge, were unable to acknowledge its limitations or errors. Platonic pride consists in failing to acknowledge one's need for divine aid.[40] According to Augustine, the Platonists did not sufficiently address human finitude and its epistemic implications.[41] Nonetheless, they did accomplish great things.[42] Augustine goes one step further, claiming that even though the prideful ones may arrive at similar conclusions, they fail to see the implications of those truths.[43] Hence, in the words of Paul, the hardness of heart of the prideful ones is 'inexcusable'.[44] Rather than serve God, in their pride they attempted to imitate him.[45]

The reader should note that Augustine does not criticize them primarily for an *intellectual fault*.[46] In fact, he grants that at some minimal conceptual level, they did in fact apprehend God. Rather, Augustine's critique is of a moral nature. Whilst he could basically agree that the task of the soul was to integrate itself with the divine and the eternal, Augustine wanted to insist that this being who would aspire to the transcendent was a temporal and historical being.[47] This is why Christ is so necessary, as he manages to reconcile time and eternity within himself.[48] Augustine rejects the Platonic idea that we ascend to God, especially without any aid; the process in his mind is reversed, as God first comes to us, enabling our ascent.[49] Furthermore, these philosophers knew something of God, but did not *love* him, did not give thanks to him and worship him as he ought to be worshipped. Yet this lack of love, rooted in pride, leads to a darkening of one's intellect. Augustine's critique here is drawn from his own experience, in which he saw his pride as the cause of a failure to acquire knowledge and wisdom.[50] The clearest example of this rejection concerns the Incarnation. Augustine sees philosophy as only possessed of provisional character, and emphasizes the necessity of Christ and his revelation for the attainment of salvation.[51] Augustine's understanding of wisdom and knowledge is grounded in Christ, a position motivated especially by what Augustine sees as the error of philosophizing without a mediator.[52] Although the possession of human wisdom requires purification,[53] one's own efforts are not sufficient to cleanse the heart, but rather constantly require divine effort, and are even enabled by it.[54] One does not cleanse oneself so that God can enter there; rather, he is part and parcel of that cleansing so that one can dwell with him more fully.[55] The philosophers knew Christ *qua* Word, but not Christ in the flesh. On Augustine's account, the prideful Platonists refused to recognize Christ, his humility and condescension, his lowliness and his pity for the sinners of the world. It was their obstinate refusal to allow for the possibility of an incarnate God, an *Emmanu-el*, that led Augustine to view their approach as inadequate precisely because of a lack of faith and humility.[56] As it concerns the acquisition of wisdom, the importance of humility cannot be overstated.[57]

Augustine uses the Virgin as an example of how the soul should approach the essence of the Christian mysteries. Rather than attempting to understand or 'univocalize' the message she received from the angel Gabriel, she assented to the divine plan of which she had been chosen to be an integral part. From this she bears fruit, spiritually of course, but also in her body, palpably in her conception of Christ.[58]

With all that has been said about Christ's divinity and transcendence, his supernal wisdom surpassing all human understanding, one might expect him, when he comes in the flesh, to give us at least some intimation of how he made the universe, what this entailed, to give us some glimpse into the divine life. However, our expectations are frustrated, Augustine says, as what Christ comes to tell us first and foremost is perhaps the last thing we would expect, as we think according to our earthly categories.[59] Christ takes on humility for our sake, a movement which we should likewise follow, also for our own sake.[60] God is not affected by our decisions, as he remains whole and complete; rather, our choices are for our betterment.[61] The Lord tells us that we should be humble, just as he is humble, and lives this example throughout his entire life. He does not regale his audience with Miltonian tales of creation and cosmic conflict, but rather encourages us to love one another with a simple, humble, indefatigable love. Indeed, M. Comeau holds that Augustine's preferred term for Christ is *Christus humilis*.[62] In the encounter with the incarnate Word, all human expectations are completely reversed; Christ throws a mean curveball.[63]

Incarnation

The liturgical celebration of Christmas becomes for Augustine not simply the observance of the Incarnation, but the revelation of God's humility. From a theological perspective, it provides the occasion for him to elaborate his Christology, which he does in a specifically Johannine way. This divine humility is expressed especially poignantly in *s.* 185, in which Augustine describes the incarnation of the divine Wisdom, and his first fleeting moments on earth as an infant, infinite yet finite born.[64] Augustine is confronting his listeners with the paradox of the omnipotent God in the form of a powerless new-born.[65] Yet even in the Incarnation, Christ is inseparable from God the Father.[66] The ineffable mystery of God's becoming man is magnified by the humility of taking the form of a child. Christ was *et infans, et Verbum*,[67] remaining silent in the form of a child, and yet allowing the angels to announce his birth.[68]

It is just this recognition of divine humility that furnishes us the opportunity to ascend to wisdom, going to sublime things by way of small things: 'Do you wish to grasp the height of God? Grasp first the humility of God.'[69] Augustine also suggests a gradual growth in understanding once one accepts the humility and other commands that God enjoins on one.[70] Just as a tree grows upward by first establishing its roots firmly in the ground, so too must we be humble, rooted in the fulfilment of God's precepts and the practice of his love. Only then will we be able to ascend to the heights of divine Wisdom.[71] Humility and confession of our weakness is essential to growth in wisdom.[72] Augustine condemns those who believe that they can be the source of their own righteousness or salvation.[73] For this reason Christ comes to us, so that we may have true righteousness, that of heaven, rather than our own (pseudo-)righteousness.[74] Augustine contrasts the true path to salvation offered by Christ with the false ones of the pagan world. The pagans thought themselves to be purged through philosophy, their worship or by their own powers.[75] Augustine contrasts Christ, the true source of *purgatio*, and the pagan tradition, charging that in their attempt to purge their souls, they have become worshippers of demons and partakers in sacrilege.[76]

'Logique chrétien'

It becomes clear that Augustine reads his philosophical sources through a biblical and Christian hermeneutic, and not vice versa. This is not simply a matter of preference, as Augustine sees a theological (and I would say even a biblical) reason for this. As Madec writes, 'Si Augustin trouve de l'aide chez les platoniciens, c'est parce qu'ils ont philosophé selon le Verbe, sous l'illumination du Verbe. Leur malheur est de ne pas avoir reconnu le Christ.'[77]

Indeed, as Bochet writes,[78] Augustine viewed scripture itself as containing true philosophy.[79] Augustine held that anything true and good in philosophy in point of fact belonged to Christianity, for whatever the philosophers understood of God, they did so through the discarnate *Logos*.[80] Although one can locate many good and true things in the works of the philosophers, inter alia, as Bochet explains, all of these truths are already contained, even if implicitly, in scripture.[81] Yet because they failed fully to discern the source of the (partial) truths they possessed, they could not appropriately 'contextualize' their knowledge and direct it to its goal.[82] Therefore, Christians, who have the full revelation and truth of God in Christ, are the only ones properly suited to make use of this knowledge, indeed, in order to bring it to fruition and completion.[83] As in other apologetic fathers, such reflections for Augustine arose, amongst other locations, within the context of his exegesis of Exodus, in which God is depicted as commanding the Israelites to despoil the Egyptians of their silver and gold during their egress from the land of their quondam servitude.[84] This is because the pagans, though they have some share of the truth, do not use it properly, and therefore forfeit any right to it which they had enjoyed. As Augustine writes, 'If those, however, who are called philosophers happen to have said anything that is true, and agreeable to our faith, the Platonists above all, not only should we not be afraid of them, but we should even claim back for our own use what they have said, as from its unjust possessors.'[85] The 'normative' truth, therefore, is in Christ, scripture and the Church; it is distinctively Christian. One's starting point, one's very standard, is Christ, according to which all other ideas are judged; Christ, the God-man, is the measure of all things.

The upshot is that Augustine can be read as grounding his view of reason itself in Christ. Remarkably, Augustine came to the conclusion that no merely human discipline could promise true knowledge, for it was only in Christ that all wisdom and knowledge (both *sapientia* and *scientia*) were contained.[86] According to Harrison, at the heart of Augustine's view of knowledge is 'the centrality . . . of Christ as mediator of wisdom'.[87] In other words, the knowledge of Christ is a *sine qua non* of true knowledge.[88] Madec makes a similar point when he writes that Augustine bases his understanding of reason in Christ, describing this as the 'logique chrétien'.[89] Indeed, Augustine's view of reality and man's place within it is grounded in Christ, not only Christ the discarnate, eternal Logos, but also Christ incarnate. According to Madec, Augustine bases his whole intellectual programme not on a distinction between nature and super-nature, but rather on 'deux économies: 1) de la création et de l'illumination par le Verbe, 2) du salut par le Verbe incarné'.[90] Here we see the twofold aspect of

Augustine's theory of knowledge reflected at the level of Christology: the principal pertains to the activity of Christ in his divine nature, illuminating and creating the soul; the latter pertains to Christ in his human nature, as he heals, restores and re-creates the soul.[91]

In Augustine's mind, philosophy, as well as any other idea or text, is judged in light of Christ and revelation, especially the Bible, as read and interpreted by the Church. Philosophy is valuable to the extent that it helps (or hinders) one in growing in the knowledge, and more importantly the love, of Christ. The crucial point is that Augustine's responses to the philosophers are biblically grounded, based in scripture itself.[92] Moreover, in order to provide some account of the pagans' unbelief, Augustine appeals to a biblical idea which appears throughout his thought, namely that a particular truth is universally available, yet also not seen or understood, not because of any defect or concealment on the part of the truth itself, but rather because of the inability of one to see and perceive it.[93] One can see this dynamic at work in the varying dispositions towards Christ himself, who by many was 'despisèd and rejected', yet conquered sinful pride through gentle, loving humility.[94]

Our Interlocutor reappears:

Your treatment of Augustine here troubles me, insofar as it may provide, despite your protestations to the contrary, the basis for justifying obscurantism or anti-intellectualism, in other words, a flight from rather than to truth. Could it not be the case that your Augustinian theory, as nuanced and sophisticated as it may be, ultimately requires us to cease using our reason and defer to another? Then we are in truly Orwellian territory, where Big Brother can tell us that 2 + 2 = 5, and we accept it on the basis of authority, an authority which requires us to acknowledge a dimension to existence which transcends our limited human reason. Is this approach to knowledge not one which can be easily abused and manipulated, or rather, one which allows others to abuse and manipulate the naïve and the credulous? It seems to lend credence to the critiques of Christianity, from Kant's 'Beantwortung der Frage: Was ist Aufklärung?' to Nietzsche's understanding of Christianity's message as a dysangel. Is this updating of Augustine nothing more than a novel exercise in the will to power?

I appreciate this objection, but I think it is important to note that this is a question of the interpretation of fact versus 'fact' itself, a question which is central to any rational enterprise. Interestingly, the debates between the empiricists and the rationalists in the late nineteenth century reflected something of this dynamic.[95] For the former, 'fact' was deemed ultimately definitive of truth,[96] whereas the latter camp, which included scientists such as Claude Bernard and Nikolay Strakhov, was appalled by what they saw as the 'unscientific nature of raw empiricism'.[97] Rationalists maintained that enquiry must be based on theoretical principles, and that these should provide guidance in disclosing the meaning contained within data.[98] Ultimately, the empiricist model only allows one to collect more and more facts, but offers little by way of truly understanding or making sense of them.[99] That is, an empiricist approach to enquiry tends to diminish if not dismiss the place of theory, resulting in a focus, if not a fixation, on particular facts, to the exclusion of the broader framework in which they should be understood.[100] Moreover, as figures such as Gadamer and Kuhn would later argue, the very discernment of a fact requires the operation of a more basic intellectual faculty.[101]

That being said, I think the objection is really aimed at a different point, as suggested by the reference to *1984*. I am not prepared to provide a full answer here, but I believe we can settle for this: perhaps the crucial point is to raise this question, to invite one to candid self-examination, to foreground the true motivations behind our actions and beliefs.

PART TWO

Divine Incorporeality: Two Dilemmas

3

A Re-Descriptive Account of Time as *Distentio*

Introduction

Augustine speaks of *sapientia* as the source of all creation, and identifies this divine Wisdom with the second person of the Trinity, the Son, the Word in whom all the forms of creation are present. Augustine also speaks of the way in which the world reflects something of its maker, and the way in which the Son is present within the world, sustaining and continually creating it from within. As a result, one can know something of God through his vestiges in creation. God is even within us. However, Augustine encounters a difficulty in this respect: he holds that God is both invisible and eternal, but all the things we see in the world are temporal, mutable and finite. What Augustine is trying to understand – and what we are supposed to come to see as remarkable[1] – is how we know in and through time, and yet seem to know beyond it as well. This problem arises on the basis of his approach to creation, which is grounded in his understanding of *sapientia*, and hence is important for our understanding of how we as human agents come to know that which is timeless in and through time.

Herein I demonstrate how Augustine sees time as a conundrum – that is, how he grapples with the inherently temporal way of our knowing. It will become clear that Augustine understands our corporeality – our extension in both time and space – as an essential ontological feature of our own particular created nature. In other words, I shall suggest that in formulating his understanding of the integral connection of time and space, Augustine anticipates

Einstein, more specifically the metaphysical implications of relativity theory. Such a study will prepare the way for me to talk about a re-descriptive account of time which Augustine proposes and how this can challenge our own categories for thinking about human identity and reason.

Division

Augustine's understanding of time is firmly situated within the context of creation, and in particular the hierarchical order of reality it implies.[2] This framework provides the foundation for Augustine's thinking on time and the implications thereof for human knowing. Simply put, Augustine divides reality into that which is God and that which is not God, the immutable and the mutable.[3] God cannot suffer change in any way, nor does he admit of parts or pieces.[4]

The context of Augustine's early discussion of time and creation is his anti-Manichaean polemic. As he writes in *De Genesi aduersus Manichaeos*, the Manichees refused to accept Genesis as a canonical book, and dismissively asked what God was doing before he made heaven and earth.[5] Augustine responds by arguing that *In the beginning* should not be understood as temporal, but as atemporal, eternal, as the foundation of all things in a conceptual and intelligible sense. In other words, the *principium* is the Son, the source of all the forms of creation.[6] As a result of his exegesis of Gen. 1.1, Augustine states that time is a result of creation, and hence there is no time with God.[7] This position is further articulated in later works of Augustine, which I shall discuss presently, as well as the significance of this point for his understanding of reason and knowledge.

In various locations, Augustine emphasizes that God's eternity implies no passage of time, indeed, no aspect of time altogether. In his eternity, God is above and beyond all time, and time only comes to be as a result of his creative activity.[8] As God is beyond time in a pristine eternity, he does not perceive time in succession; rather all times are present to him as a unity, indeed, like 'one day'.[9]

In addition to human rational agents who occupy a middle ontological position and are embedded in the flow of time,[10] Augustine also posits intellectual creatures who are not subject to the vicissitudes of time's relentless flow. A brief consideration of these will help us to see more clearly the significance of what Augustine has to say regarding the inherent temporality of human knowing.[11]

Augustine's ontological system departs from his Platonic influences insofar as the division consists no longer of the intellectual and the material, but rather between God and creation.[12] On the latter side, there are creatures who are purely intellectual. The heaven and earth of Gen. 1.1, according to Augustine, are collective terms for designating spiritual, intelligible creation on the one hand, and physical, material, sensible creation on the other.[13] The former, the intellectual creatures (i.e. angels), though created, are closest to God, especially insofar as they know in a way which is not subject to the vagaries of spatio-temporal extension.[14] As Tornau explains, for Augustine, intellectual creatures possess 'non-discursive knowledge',[15] the proper object of which is God.[16] These spiritual creatures are said to know 'together without any change of times'.[17] In *Gn. litt.* 4, Augustine attributes to the angels a facility whereby they can see all things together, rather than in succession as we do.[18]

Therefore, on Augustine's view, though both angels and human rational agents share a spiritual aspect to their nature, they nonetheless differ in the respect of the temporal character of their knowing, or lack thereof. Purely intellectual creatures – creatures without any physical component – can know in a purely intellectual, atemporal way. But due to the ineluctably temporal character of the human person, whose body is extended spatially and temporally, and whose soul, which though only extended temporally, still relies on the body for the acquisition of knowledge, one must know and learn in a temporal way.[19] The upshot is that we occupy a middle ontological place, being rational agents whose souls are not extended in space.[20] God's knowledge differs even further from that of the human mind, as well as of any creature. Hence we know in and through time; but it could be otherwise. Augustine finds this remarkable, and seeks to investigate further the implications of this insight for our knowledge.

In the rest of this chapter, I shall consider three such locations in which Augustine struggles with the question of time, beginning with how he recalls his 'intellectual conversion' to a new understanding of matter during his time in Milan in the 380s.

Confessiones 7

Augustine opens the seventh book of his *Confessiones* by reflecting on a major shift in his thinking about the nature of reality and the divine.[21] He recalls with approval how he had begun to think of God in a way which did not conceive of him in human form.[22] In his commentary, O'Donnell notes the retrospective presentation in *conf.* 7; in other words, after his encounter with Platonic thought, Augustine came to understand his prior beliefs in the way that he presents them in this book of *conf.*[23] With respect to Augustine's shift or 'conversion' to thinking of God as incorporeal, Teske distinguishes two particular developments as recounted in book seven. The first, which is presented in the opening passage of this book, pertains to thinking of God no longer in anthropomorphic terms.[24] This describes Augustine in 385 at the age of thirty-one.[25] Though Augustine began to hear the faint murmuring of truth, this was undermined by his 'materialistic' reflex, namely to think of God in other spatio-temporal terms. Augustine is emphasizing that the attempt to think of God in the familiar categories of time and space is bound to fail to capture him, not simply adequately, as that is not possible, but altogether. God is beyond all categorization, and the logic of such worldly thinking can insinuate itself into one's reasoning process, subtly subverting it. Even when Augustine had disabused himself of the error of anthropomorphizing God, and thought that he had risen to a higher level of understanding, his ideas were still vitiated by material categories.[26] In the next paragraph, Augustine recounts how his way of thinking logically resulted in the conclusion that God could be 'more present' in larger parts of the world and could be divided into various parts.[27] But Augustine thought this way for God had not yet shed light upon his intellectual darkness.[28] In his tractates on 1 John, as in the seventh book of his *Confessiones*, Augustine decries the error of thinking of God according to some corporeal form, even some form which is infinitely extended in space.[29] This is not to deny that God can and does take some form of mediation in order to interact with the world. Rather, the mistake for Augustine is reducing God to the forms of his mediations. As Helm explains,[30] in *conf.* 7 Augustine is describing one of the stages in the process whereby he finally came to the realization of God's incorporeal character.[31] Moreover,

Augustine gradually comes to appreciate the truly radical implications of human creatureliness and finitude, and in particular how they are realized epistemically.

This theme is continued throughout the seventh book of the *conf.*, with particular attention to its implications for human knowledge and the spiritual journey. For instance, later Augustine describes himself as having been plunged into a region of shadows and false images when he was still ignorant of God's incorporeality: 'I found that I was far from you in a region of unlikeness.'[32] As Menn writes, Augustine describes this tendency as the *consuetudo carnalis*,[33] which designates that particular weakness in human nature which causes it to think in merely 'four-dimensional' terms, and to allow itself to be confined to such thinking.[34] In addition to *conf.* 7.17.23, Augustine makes a similar point in *trin.* 8.3 on the misleading nature of sensory images.[35] The result is that one tends away from the contemplation of unchanging truth to particular lesser reflections of it.[36] Augustine notes the contingency, finitude and inherent limitations of all the particular entities he observes in the world around him, and how they differ from God in that they derive their being from him.[37] His thought evokes the metaphysics of participation, according to which particular things instantiate to varying degrees some particular 'form', whether beauty, goodness or being itself.[38] As Augustine writes of created things, they seem 'neither completely to be nor completely not to be'.[39] Moreover, Augustine also describes God in terms of an incorporeal light, far different from the light to which we are accustomed at the physical level.[40] Reiterating the point of God's infinite difference from creation in the fourteenth chapter, Augustine goes on to say that the soul is bound to remain in a state of disquietude and unease if it persists in conceiving of God along the lines of some finite, spatially extended substance.[41] In another location, Augustine expresses this point, stating that it is a great thing to arrive at a conception of God as incorporeal, which according to him means 'something which may not be extended through locations, nor change through times'.[42] This incorporeal character is also distinctive of the form of wisdom, *species sapientiae*.[43]

Continuing with *conf.* 7, one can notice a shift in Augustine's consideration of the transcendence of God. Whereas in the opening stages of this book, his language was redolent of physical and spatial imagery (e.g. *corporeum*; *diffusum*; *per spatia locorum*;

minorem partem; etc.), Augustine takes a step further, including time in this consideration as well, thereby laying the logical foundation for a more extended discussion of time in the later books of this work.[44] For Augustine, time is not the measure of motion (as he makes clear later in the *conf.*), but is itself co-extensive with a type of corporeal motion. Here he suggests a position that will become more clearly pronounced later in his career, namely that time arises as a result of creation. This move to link space and time is neither obvious nor self-evident; what Augustine is doing implicitly is positing an essential link between the two, viewing both of these as ineluctable conditions of finite, material creation. According to Helm, Augustine sees time, and our experience of it in terms of past, present and future, as a subtle if indubitable mark of our creaturely finitude, in contrast to God's eternity.[45] Centuries before Einstein's relativity theory revolutionized our conception of space and time by viewing them not as two distinct realities but as two aspects of the same material universe, Augustine's intuition is that extension, both temporal and spatial, intrinsically characterizes created being, in contrast to the eternal and immutable God.[46]

The logical trajectory of Augustine's thought on time and distention comes as a result of his doctrine of *creatio ex nihilo*.[47] The attempt to think of God as eternal, whilst we are situated within time, occasions one of the seminal reflections on the notion of time.[48] In this sense, one can view Augustine's programme in the *conf.* as an expression of the 'scriptural imagination', or what K. Anatolios calls 'biblical reasoning'.[49]

In *conf.* 7, Augustine describes the way in which he gradually came to appreciate the truly radical implications of human creatureliness and finitude, and in particular how it is realized epistemically. In addition to thinking of time and space as the results of *creatio ex nihilo*, Augustine also addresses the epistemic implications of God's eternity and our finitude. One can see these reflections as rooted in the realization that it is remarkable to think that it is precisely in and through time, not only that we know, but that we can come to know, the eternal and immutable God and source of creation, who is fundamentally different from anything we experience.

As we have seen, Augustine in *conf.* 7 establishes the incorporeality of God which, in addition to spatial categories, is also taken as applying to time. Augustine returns to this point later in the *conf.*, noting how God's eternal being differs from ours, as well as certain ways in which it is realized. In what follows, we shall see the way in which Augustine's understanding of incorporeality is deepened in two other works, namely *Gn. litt.* 5 and *ciu.* 11. From this, it will become clear how Augustine continues to link time and space, seeing the former as a logical result of the latter. Moreover, he nuances his view on the nature of material reality with respect to time; in other words, it is *formed* and *formable* space and the movements thereof which are constitutive of time itself. We shall continue to see how God's ultimate transcendence bears implications for our situation as human knowers. After the consideration of these two passages, I shall return to the latter portions of the *conf.*, in which Augustine offers the initial suggestion of a solution to the problem of knowing the eternal God.

De Genesi ad litteram 5

In *Gn. litt.* 5, Augustine describes God as incorporeal,[50] beyond time and space, admitting not even of the possibility of change.[51] Augustine sees this as the meaning of Exod. 3.14, which depicts God speaking to Moses through the burning bush, identifying himself as *ego sum qui sum*.[52] God's nature is unchangeable and eternal, and he is the source of his own being in himself.[53] Even in acting in the world or performing creative actions, God himself does not admit of temporal change or motion.[54] Whilst God's nature may be beyond comprehension, we can speak intelligibly about it to a certain extent, provided we scrupulously avoid discussing time and space, as God is beyond these corporeal categories altogether: 'that substance is inexpressible and can only be presented by one human being to another in words taken over from space and time, though it is before all times and all places.'[55] In addition to identifying the Wisdom of God with the Son, Augustine also states that this Word-Wisdom is co-eternal with the Father.[56] Augustine likewise identifies this Word-Wisdom with divine light, an identification which follows a Johannine logic, and for which he even cites the prologue of this gospel.[57]

God creates heaven and earth by bringing into existence corporeal matter, which is partially formed already and admits of the possibility of being formed further, as its form is not yet totally realized.[58] The created world involves not simply the existence of matter, but matter which is formed at a number of levels, from types of things in general to their individual instances and the constituent parts thereof.[59] Augustine suggests that time itself begins with the creation of the world.[60] He presents an argument for the coincidence or co-creation not only of matter and form, but of time and space.[61] In *Gn. litt.* 5.5.12, he begins by stating his thesis: 'creatures once made began to run with their movements along the tracks of time.'[62] He proceeds to state that without motion, there cannot be time, and there cannot be motion without things which admit of the possibility of movement and change.[63] Although both proceed from and are grounded in God's creativity, time and space, or in Augustine's words, *tempus* and *creatura*, admit of an asymmetrical relationship. That is, time comes to be as a result of creation.[64] As Teske explains, 'for Augustine God creates time in creating the world.'[65] Without creation, there is no time.[66] The existence of time presupposes the change of one formed thing into another type of formed thing.[67]

As K. Flasch argues, time is a logical result of creation on Augustine's view. Time only comes to be as a result of the movements of created bodily things. As Flasch writes, 'Die Zeit ergibt sich, wenn Naturprozesse ablaufen. Folglich gab es keine Zeit, bevor es eine Schöpfung gab.'[68] But there is a further point here which Flasch brings to light. It is not simply the existence of created reality as such which gives rise to time; rather, it is creation according to *form* that allows time to be. Movement implies change, and change implies one particular thing becoming another type of thing. As Flasch explains, 'Dies impliziert auch, dass es Zeit nur gibt, sofern die völlige Formlosigkeit der reinen Stofflichkeit überwunden ist, also sofern spezifisch geprägte Wesen existieren. Die Natur muß *Unterschiede* aufweisen, damit Zeiten möglich sind.'[69] Therefore, Augustine 'auch die erste Materie als zeitlos ansehen und die Zeit als eine Folge der Form beschreiben kann'.[70] Tornau concurs with this assessment, stating that in the *conf.*, Augustine also identifies matter with mutability.[71] Such a theological move is significant for the purposes of a theory of knowledge. Intelligibility is a matter of formal determination; there has to be something to be thought. In this instance, one can see the integral link of a theology of creation and a theory of knowledge. What we have also established is that time is neither an ad hoc dimension of creation nor some reality created distinctly or even separately from matter. Rather, time is a logical result of created and formed matter, or put more provocatively, time and space are inherently, integrally connected.[72] One must recall that elsewhere in this same work, Augustine states that form and matter are created together.[73] He reaffirms this point in book five, saying that the treatment of the creation of heaven and earth and day in Genesis are not two different things, but one and the same. In other words, it is not that heaven and earth are created, and then 'day' is created afterwards, but that these are two aspects under which to view one and the same act of making.[74]

Augustine provides the example of the beauty (*pulchritudinem*) of a tree as a way to understand the way in which God created all things together, and yet still creates even now. In the seed of a tree the entire entity is pre-formed, even if it has not yet been realized in space and time. Hence God can create the world and all things in it at one particular point, and can continue to create as he providentially guides the realization of these things in their own natures.[75] (One can also relate this passage to *s.* 241, not only in terms of the speaking of beauty, but also in the way in which all of the aspects of the tree testify to the perceptive, attentive mind.)

The apparent tension between two opposing understandings of creation is resolved by the distinction between creation in temporal succession and in causal priority.[76] In other words, this concept allows Augustine to say that God created all things at once, even though it had not been realized in time:[77] so matter is created first and is subsequently formed by God's command, though the existence of matter is primary, not in a temporal way, but in a logical one.[78] Augustine suggests a distinction between temporal causation and the bestowing of order according to the 'connection of causes' (*non interuallis temporum, sed connexione causarum*).[79] In other words, these causes are related logically, apart from intervals of time. This helps to explain how matter can be said to be created first, even though it is not prior in time. The primacy pertains to the realm of principle, logic and causality, not to time.[80]

The foregoing cosmological account of creation is important in another way as regards Augustine's theory of knowledge. God knows all things eternally, which is to say in a purely simple way (*illo simplici ac mirabili modo nouit omnia stabiliter et incommutabiliter*).[81] Augustine interprets Jn 1.4, according to which all things are life in the Word, in the following way. One is not the source of one's own life or being, but receives it from God. Moreover, this is received from the source of creation who knows all things eternally apart from their being made.[82] God is ultimately responsible for all knowledge, whether he reveals it to man or angel.[83] The mind receives its light from another source; it is not the source of its own capacity for knowledge.[84]

As in his *conf.*, in *Gn. litt.* Augustine also addresses the epistemic implications of his cosmological account of time. Here he speaks of the different ways in which creation is known to angels and to people, respectively. One could also think of the former category in terms of a mind freed from the flux of space and time, as a result of which, they would be able to know immediately, or as Augustine puts it, 'primordially' (*primordialiter*) and 'originally' (*originaliter*).[85] This type of knowledge corresponds to the aspect of creation that takes place at one distinct point.[86] Our knowledge, which is acquired in time (*per ordines temporum*), corresponds more closely to the continuous act of creation, according to which God works even now.[87] (In any case, God's knowledge is far different from that of any creature, whether angelic or human.[88])

To summarize Augustine's theory of creation and time in *Gn. litt.*, God creates all things in his Wisdom, which means that all things are given to be in a particular form and with particular potencies. These things are created as material, corporeal creation, already formed in some way. In a sense, all things come to be together, and in another sense, God continues to work and create, insofar as due to the logical connection of causes inherent in created things, they unfold and continue to realize their full potential, which is reflected in the eternal ideas in God's mind. This movement of corporeal creation from one form to another is itself constitutive of time.

De Ciuitate Dei 11

The discussion of time as a result of the creation of matter in book eleven of *ciu.* serves as an apt punctuation to Augustine's overall theory of time. Whereas previously this point was addressed to the Manichees, here the context is an anti-pagan polemic. Augustine rejects the idea that the world is eternal, and he harshly criticizes those who accept this idea.[89] God made all things in his Wisdom, knowing all the things he would create.[90] Augustine describes *sapientia* as the treasury of all wisdom and knowledge, as well as the source of the reasons and forms of things.[91] The Father and the Son are of the same co-eternal and immutable substance.[92] God's Word, and indeed, the Word in which he creates, is not a temporal one which sounds through space and time (*Verbo intellegibili et sempiterno, non sonabili et temporali*).[93] Unlike our words, which are bound to time and space, and pass through various temporal intervals, God's Word is always and ever complete.[94] God was not changed in making the world, even if the world admits of change.[95] Rather, Augustine suggests that time and space only come to exist when creation takes place.[96] In other words, time is a result of the creation of formed matter; time does not come to be without the motion of particular objects, changing from one thing into another.[97]

That is, if we begin from the notion that eternity is truly timeless and admits of no change, and that change only comes to be when matter is made, then that 'mutable motion' from X into Y is itself constitutive of time.[98] Augustine punctuates this point when he writes that the world was not made *in* time but *with* time (*procul dubio non est mundus factus in tempore, sed cum tempore*).[99]

As in the previously discussed works, a cosmology of creation provides the basis for a hierarchical and theological theory of knowledge. Augustine speaks of the creation of light as the creation of the angels, who are illumined by the eternal light of wisdom, which he proceeds to identify with the Son, through whom all things were made.[100] Moreover, the angels become participants in Christ as the eternal day by sharing in his light.[101] Christ is the source of all being and light, and all creatures rely on him for this.[102]

In contrast to the angels, 'who *always look upon the face of the Father*',[103] the human soul knows in and through time, but is nonetheless illumined by the divine light. Certain things are perceived by the mind or the soul, and this is enabled by an incorporeal light.[104] Augustine speaks of our senses, both interior and exterior, stating that God is available to neither (*a sensibus nostris, siue interioribus siue etiam exterioribus*).[105] God speaks to man in neither a corporeal nor a spiritual way, insofar as God does not speak to the soul in a way which relies upon corporeal images or the similitudes thereof in the mind.[106] (In the next chapter, we shall see how this reflects Augustine's tripartite understanding of vision as he presents it in *Gn. litt.* 12.) Rather, he speaks 'by the truth itself', though he is only heard by those who are fit to hear this mentally (*si quis sit idoneus ad audiendum mente, non corpore*).[107] (Here we see the dynamic of the principal and the gradual at work.) God speaks to the part of the person which is not only highest in its own nature, but which is surpassed only by God. This capacity of the soul, whether one calls it mind or intellect, is constituted by the image of God within the soul, in virtue of which the human person is superior to the other parts of creation.[108] This part of one's human nature marks one as unique.[109]

The foregoing case studies reveal a consistent view of time and creation spanning several decades of Augustine's career. For Augustine, time is ultimately a result of finite, material creation, and only makes sense in light of eternity. Here we have an illustration of how Augustine's understanding of knowledge is theologically grounded. An interest in knowledge and reason is not far from his mind when he discusses such issues. For example, the hierarchy of creation also reflects different ways in which one knows. What Augustine finds remarkable is how we are situated within the double extension of time and space, and yet our thought is conditioned by that which transcends it. He is driven to understand how these two apparently contradictory commitments can be reconciled with one another. The remarkable point is that on the basis of a theological commitment, Augustine derives significant implications for his theory of knowledge. It is also notable that he first seeks to *describe* the situation in which he finds himself. The significance of this will become clear once we have examined the way in which Augustine proposes to go beyond or counteract the obscuring effects of time.

Re-description

As we have seen, Augustine sees an integral link between creation, matter and time. As bodily creatures, we are inherently spatiotemporal. Indeed, for Augustine, time is a radical part of who we are as created beings; it is deeply ingrained in us, part of the logic of our existence; it is in our 'ontological bones'. Augustine finds himself pulled apart in the relentless flow of time as the 'multiplying villainies of nature do swarm upon him',[110] caught between time and eternity. For Augustine, time requires extended and careful reflection in order properly to transcend it en route to the eternal God. This is easier said than done. Just as Augustine's movement away from thinking of God as in the form of a human body still fell prey to materialistic categories, so too can the attempt to think God's eternity still be subverted by temporal images. As Augustine starts to grapple with the question of time in *conf.* 11, he states that what seems to be distinctive of time is that it tends towards non-being (*tendit non esse*).[111] Thus one can see again, just as in *conf.* 7.1.1, that like spatial extension, Augustine views time as a consequence of created being, which is *nec omnino esse nec omnino non esse*.[112] Because created being is ultimately mutable and constantly subject to deficiency, Augustine can be characterized as 'un Heráclito cristiano'.[113] He proposes the hypothesis that time is like a stretching (*uideo igitur quandam esse distentionem*).[114] Shortly thereafter, in *conf.* 11.26.33, Augustine solidifies this position of time as *distentio* based on an argument concerning the reciting of a poem and its constituent verses.[115] Thus, *memoria* is necessary for the acquisition of *sapientia*.

According to Augustine, time exerts an enervating effect on the soul. In virtue of its temporal extended-ness, the soul is pulled apart and never feels entirely whole. This ontic entropy has effects on the soul and its knowledge; it longs for an escape from such a troubled experience. As Augustine describes it, '[I] lost my desire to dissipate myself amid a profusion of earthly goods, eating up time as I was myself eaten by it; for in your eternal simplicity I now had a different *wheat and wine and oil*.'[116] As he does in other locations, Augustine contrasts the many things of spatio-temporal existence with the unity and simplicity of God's eternity.[117] In order to know truth, the vision of the soul must be simple and unified, and it must aspire to the synthetic unity of God's vision. This implies not so much a sublation of the individual creatures of the world, but rather a simple, which is to say, parsimonious aspect, which enables one to make sense of the various facets of the world. Without the correct framework, one is epistemically upset by the constant stream of images and facts, which do not on the surface bespeak any deeper unity or meaning.[118]

Thoughts of this sort are behind his discussion of time and *memoria* in the latter books of the *conf.* Augustine realizes that the distention of the mind exerts a distressing effect on the soul, which must be suffered, yet also counteracted and ultimately overcome.[119]

In order to overcome this 'entropy', one must constantly and intentionally act to (re-)unify oneself by means of godly things, avoiding the dissolution caused by earthly ones. Hence Augustine in *conf.* calls for a 'renovation of memory as *intentio*'.[120] The memory for Augustine is necessary in order to know God, yet ultimately must be transcended. It provides the starting point, the necessary condition for temporal beings to arrive at the atemporal God.[121] The merely passive collection of data and sense impressions does not suffice for knowledge; that requires mental activity, processing and judgement, for which *intentio* supplies the necessary operation.[122] A somewhat simplistic if not altogether unhelpful formulation would be that *memoria* pertains to the primarily passive collection of sense impressions, whereas *intentio* pertains to a deliberate and active operation of the mind.[123] Augustine uses various terms, such as *intentio*, *extentus* and *meditatio*, to denote a certain mental capacity for unifying various strands of information into a coherent whole.[124] Elsewhere in the *conf.*, as O'Daly notes, the language of extension evokes the mystical ascent of Augustine with his mother.[125] One is enabled to attain wisdom through meditation, which extends beyond mere memory.[126] In *conf.* 11.29.39, Augustine identifies the necessity of *intentio* for arriving at knowledge.[127] As Nightingale writes, it is by means of *intentio* that one is enabled to apply focused attention to memory and expectation, from which the mind derives meaning from the various images and strands of memories present therein.[128]

Relevant here is Augustine's distinction between two forms of memory, as explained by Jeanmart. That is, Augustine distinguishes between the *memoria sui* and the *memoria Dei*.[129] The former pertains to the more common sense of the term memory, which allows one to recall past experiences.[130] The latter, however, is more basic; Jeanmart describes it as the condition of the possibility of the former, and conceives of it in terms of a basic cognizance of cosmic truths, such as an awareness of one's origin.[131] The *memoria Dei* represents a vestige which summons one back to unity with God.[132] This trace is original, however, in that, as Jeanmart suggests, we do not so much discover it as *rediscover* it.[133] We 'remember' God by returning to our original unity, by seeing what was already there within us. Jeanmart emphasizes that the presence of unity within us is *merely* a trace, a vestige, when our lives begin.[134] We begin de facto in the midst of multiplicity and distention, yet we attempt to recover a unity which is imprinted on our memories.[135] Jeanmart specifies a further epistemic implication of the memory. Because we begin to exist in the dispersion of time, we are always in a reflection of reality, always in the realm of representation, of the 'less real'.[136]

This also pertains to the inherently ascetic dimension to knowledge in Augustine. The attainment of knowledge is also an ascetic process.[137] Augustine inherits from Neoplatonism an ascetical dimension to his approach to wisdom.[138] Knowledge and purification belong together, as purification entails dependency on God, not on oneself.[139] In particular, one must purify oneself of the tendency to take the spatial and the temporal as the mark of the real.[140] In a soul in which sin and division reign, the movement within is made dangerous and frightening. One does not wish to confront this and so the problem only festers. According to Chrétien, it takes a certain ascetic violence to impose divine peace on the soul.[141]

Augustine discovers within his memory certain capacities and potencies which enable him to judge, interpret and process information, the reports of the senses. These standards of judgement did not originate in the senses, but rather allow him to interpret those reports, which are contained and stored in the memory.[142] According to Nightingale, *intentio* involves focusing the mind on a particular aspect of memory, enabling certain of the images contained therein to become more unified and coherent, and thereby more meaningful. Whilst one's intention does not promise an escape from the distention of temporal embodiment, it does nonetheless provide a way to mitigate some of its effects, in particular by directing the soul's interior focus towards God, a directedness of looking that will be completed and perfected in heaven.[143]

The upshot of Augustine's enquiry in *conf.* 11 is what I call a 're-descriptive' account of time as *distentio*. By re-descriptive I mean the following: Augustine begins from certain foundational principles and observed phenomena, and attempts to account for these, thinking about the conditions of their possibility.[144] In other words, what do the experiences of our knowing within time and space imply about our condition as finite rational agents, as well as reality more broadly? We see some evidence for this in *conf.* 11.22.28, in which Augustine comments on the intuitive ease with which one speaks about time, especially the measurement thereof and the comparison of that with other stretches of time.[145] Though we never question what we say, there are deeply perplexing aspects to this which are realized upon further reflection.[146] In his article on Augustine and Heidegger on time, S. Hannan too notes how the primarily descriptive account of time in Augustine's thought raises the question of the extent to which the normative does or should enter the discussion.[147] For Hannan, the normative and descriptive are not ultimately separable, and the latter can be propaedeutic for the former.[148]

What Augustine endeavours to do is not so much produce a normative or prescriptive account of what reason should or should not do. Rather, as I see it, Augustine formulates a re-descriptive account of human knowing, working backwards in a sense. That is, he takes into consideration various observations, experiences and other given facts, and tries to determine from them what must be the case about human knowing and identity, based in a Christian framework. Augustine is seeking to describe the way in which we know, and what he produces does so, but in a way that is at the same time novel and different, and goes beyond a mere intuitive reflection on the nature of knowledge. One thought might be that Augustine's account, if it is truly descriptive, is therefore philosophically uninteresting. But sometimes accounting for something is extremely challenging and difficult. Moreover, once this account has been completed, it assumes a normative character, or serves as the foundation for a prescriptive programme that Augustine employs. For the (re-)descriptive account, in its synthetic nature, is not always perfectly reflected at the factual level. Augustine is also keenly aware of human limitations and sinfulness. Therefore, one ought to return to or further realize the faculty with which one has been endowed by God. As Menn helps to explain, the problem in arriving at knowledge of God does not lie with the object of our enquiry, but rather with us the enquirers.[149] Hence the very categories one uses in order to describe or account for a particular phenomenon are very telling. In the final analysis, however, Augustine maintains that our temporality must always be understood with respect to eternity, and any chance we have of true knowledge and peace is based there. As O'Regan inimitably explains this point, 'It is in the Word that the evanescent syllables of our lives cohere into a sentence (3.10–12).'[150]

4

Seeing *Sapientia*

Introduction

The idea of the vision of God is central to Augustine's theory of knowledge. To be human means to be imbued with the capacity to behold God. However, in one's earthly existence, one is not capable of doing so. There is a further point of theological significance which directs us towards an enquiry into the nature of vision in Augustine's thought. As we have seen with respect to incorporeality and eternity, Augustine is confronted with the challenge of how we as finite, embodied agents in time can aspire to some knowledge of the timeless God. The problem is similar when it comes to how we can 'see' the invisible God, or his vestiges present in the created world. Indeed, in *trin.* 12, Augustine states that one is able to perceive sapiential truths in virtue of their being subjoined to material things.[1] In fact, he confronts this question directly in certain parts of his corpus. In grappling with this fundamentally biblical conundrum, Augustine provides us with a profound and nuanced reflection concerning the nature of vision and reason, which discloses further points of contemporary theological interest.

The task of the following chapter is to present an account of Augustine's theory of vision, grounded in his understanding of creation. First, I shall consider several locations in Augustine's corpus in which seeing (God) is a clear focal point. I shall finish with a more focused treatment of the twelfth book of *Gn. litt.*, in which Augustine presents a tripartite understanding of human vision which is integrally connected with reason. We shall see how Augustine's understanding of vision can help us to think about seeing the world as a reflection of divine Wisdom and prepare the way for re-imagining what our sense of sight implies for human identity and knowing.

The senses

Augustine follows the Aristotelian tradition of enumerating five types of bodily sense.[2] Man and beast alike share the five basic senses, which serve the function of discerning corporeal things.[3] As Augustine suggests in *Gn. litt.*, the sense of touch, for example, is closer to our animal nature, whereas hearing and vision are the pre-eminent senses of the body.[4] He concedes that even non-rational animals possess some capacity for memory; in fact, he sees it as an essentially 'natural' faculty.[5] As G. Boersma notes, what distinguishes the rational from the non-rational soul is the capacity to judge and to interrogate reality. Indeed, the capacity for judgement is the mark of true wisdom.[6] The rational soul can judge 'empirical data' in the sense that it can see this content as possessed of a deeper meaning and significance. Intellectual vision is distinctive of rational beings, of the *anima rationalis*.[7] Ayres and O'Daly note that Augustine's thought admits of a basic distinction between the higher soul and the lower soul, the former of which governs and judges the reports of the sense, which are collected in the lower part of the soul.[8]

In locations such as *Confessiones* 10 and *De libero arbitrio* 2, Augustine distinguishes each physical sense based on the object proper to each. For example, the perception of colour pertains to the eye, and the sense of olfaction pertains to the nose or the nostrils.[9] In *en. Ps.* 146, Augustine briefly presents a line of thought that he discusses at greater length in the second book of *lib. arb.* Even though two particular people in very different places think about number or justice, these forms can in principle be equally present to both of them simultaneously.[10] Though this point is discussed only fleetingly in the *enarratio*, a careful look at *lib. arb.* reveals the following. Corporeal objects can only be sensed in an inherently limited way. For example, a particular morsel of a particular piece of cake can only be tasted at one time by one and the same person. Someone else could take another morsel, or taste the piece pre-masticated by someone else, but it is nonetheless not the same.[11] The way in which hearing and vision work is less bound to time and space, but is limited by these conditions. Many people can hear the same thing at the same time, even if each will hear it in slightly different ways and at slightly different times. A better example is vision. If Jones is looking at Michelangelo's *David* from one side, Smith could look from that side, but his perspective will be slightly different, even if they are standing close together.[12] One's vision of immaterial realities, such as number, *iustitia* or even *sapientia*, however, is not limited or conditioned in this way, Augustine notes – an observation which bespeaks the incorporeal character of such objects.[13]

According to Augustine, we possess within ourselves – indeed, within our hearts – the faculties whereby we can perceive and know God. Only within ourselves can we begin to know God, and Augustine states that it is because that is where God's image is impressed.[14] Our interiority and our exploration of our hearts are always already defined and conditioned within a context of the divine presence within.[15]

As Chrétien explains, when it comes to the inner senses, there is a unity and a dynamism which surpass the strictures of those of the body.[16] As Augustine writes in *trin.* concerning interior perception,[17] 'it is not one thing to hear and another to see.' As in *trin.*, Augustine in *ep. Io. tr.* suggests that the 'spiritual' senses are not individual senses corresponding to their corporeal analogues; rather, they are different ways of speaking of one and the same inner capacity.[18] One can see invisible things, such as the virtues of one's soul, by some other type of eye, not by the 'normal' sense of sight.[19] This interior sense of sight is a certain gaze of the heart.[20] Augustine also employs the language of a 'cordial ear', by means of which one understands the content of scripture.[21]

Augustine's understanding of the inner unity of sensation helps to explain why he speaks of 'touching' God, especially when he is so committed to the immateriality of the divine being, as well as the idea that tactile sensation is closer to our animal nature. Furthermore, according to Cilleruelo, Augustine found the language of touching particularly compelling, as it allowed him to capture two aspects of his understanding of intellectual vision which were crucial to him.[22] First, it provided him with a sense of active searching on the part of the rational subject.[23] Second, it provided him with the language fit for expressing the partial touch that one enjoys with respect to an object, that touching does not completely grasp the thing but only a part of it.[24]

Just as there is a different version of 'sense' as it pertains to one's heart or one's mind, so too are there different objects of this vision. The heart, in addition to supervising the function of the senses, also has operations of its own which do not rely on the senses and perceive objects apart from any corporeal determination.[25] The return to oneself, to one's heart, is contrasted with exterior ways, which entail a wandering from God and truth.[26] The inward turn, the movement to one's heart, is at the same time a movement to God. Moreover, Augustine establishes an integral link between knowledge of God and knowledge of oneself, and it is this link which is at the heart of his admonition that one should return within.[27] In this respect, we also get a sense of why the return to the heart also requires a separation from corporeal things.[28]

We can find a similar discussion in *lib. arb.*, in which Augustine discusses how he perceives such properties as 'unity' in things. It seems that he does not have any 'empirical' experience of the oneness of things, since various things are composed of manifold parts. In fact, it seems to be the other way around: some concept of unity seems to be required in order to have intelligible experience at all.[29] Augustine identifies an idea, namely 'oneness', which we do not experience by means of the senses and which we presuppose in making judgements about the material world.

In a work composed several years after *lib. arb.*, Augustine makes a similar point concerning number and our apparently intimate awareness of it, insofar as it conditions our thought and seems inseparable from the 'empirical' realities we observe. As Augustine writes in *conf.* 10, we judge numeral instances in the world according to an innate knowledge of number itself; in fact, the latter provides the very condition which enables one to perceive particular objects in the world. The numbers which we enumerate (*quos numeramus*) when we count are the instances of those numbers by which we count (*quibus numeramus*), and these latter, Augustine suggests, exceed the corporeal senses.[30] By adding that these 'intelligible numbers' exist in a supreme way, Augustine is suggesting a certain link between number and the divine mind, namely that the latter causes the instantiation of the former in reality, and because of our own creation *ad imaginem Dei*, our mental faculties are constructed in such a way that we can perceive such properties instantiated in physical states of affairs.[31] God's being is reflected in nature, in particular in terms of its beauty (*forma, species*) and its unity (*numerus*). The very unity and formal identity of a particular being is itself the divine *uestigium* present in it.[32]

Vision and purification

The principal–gradual logic I discussed previously is also present in Augustine's doctrine of vision. That is, one possesses eyes of the heart or of the mind which are capable of perceiving certain objects, but these eyes often need to be healed or cleansed in order to actualize this superior sense of sight. Augustine's use of *purgatio* figures prominently in contexts connected to intellectual vision, which provides an image for the Christian life as a whole. The mind must be purged in order to discern God's presence in creation, as well as to hold to that light once it has been seen.[33]

Purification is required for the soul to perceive the spiritual things of God,[34] and enables contemplation.[35] This is necessary for intellectual sight, and in a high degree for the 'perception' of God, the Good itself.[36] Intellectual vision requires cleansing since, though in principle one can see spiritual things by this type of sight, this vision requires purgation in order to be perfected. The purged sight of the mind allows one to know the Incarnate Christ as equal to God the Father.[37] Christ as the Son taking flesh can only be seen by the heart, and indeed, one which has been exceedingly purged.[38] In the Incarnation, Christ condescends to our human weakness so that we may be purged and come to know him as the Divine Word.[39] Humility is a necessary precondition of the purgation offered through Christ, the true mediator, as he only purges the humble, indeed, those who reflect his own humility.[40] Augustine also suggests that a purged mind is connected with understanding the divine word in the prophets.[41]

Augustine finds inspiration for his thought on purgation and vision in Matthew 5, the Sermon on the Mount. Suggesting a distinction between corporeal sight and spiritual vision, he describes the *clean of heart* of the Beatitudes as those who perceive by a *purgato oculo*.[42] The light of the sun corresponds to the corporeal eyes which, though in principle they can see this light, need to be purged and clear in order to do so.[43] Likewise, God emits a spiritual light which constitutes the object of another type of vision. Again, though one in principle can perceive this kind of light, one's vision must nonetheless be purged.[44] Purification enables us to come to a certain mental grasp of God by cleansing our intellectual faculties, the mind and the (eye of the) heart.[45] The face of God can be seen only by the eye of the heart, not of the flesh, and indeed, this inner eye must be purged, for God only reveals himself to those who are purged.[46]

The vision of God

Augustine understands God's invisibility as a result of his transcendence, which then calls for some explanation for how he was seen, as it is recorded in the scriptures.[47] As Berrouard suggests, there is an ecclesial dimension to intellectual vision which is presented in Augustine's homilies. Through prayer and the reading of scripture, the faithful will turn from the habit of seeing according to worldly standards and begin to perceive by their cordial sense of sight objects that are invisible to the bodily eye.[48] In *s.* 6, Augustine's exegesis of the Mosaic theophany provides the occasion for a brief if important reflection on the perception of God by the corporeal senses.[49] Augustine holds that God cannot be sensed by human persons in virtue of his transcendent, incorporeal, immutable divine nature. Drawing upon Johannine passages, he describes God as a qualitatively different sort of light, not perceptible by carnal eyes.[50] This type of light, writes Augustine, is that of which John speaks in the prologue, the light of illumination. God dwells in inaccessible light, and his light is that of truth (*ueritas*), wisdom (*sapientia*) and righteousness (*iustitia*).[51] Augustine hints at the qualitatively different character of God, at which one arrives only in the eschaton.[52] This Johannine sentiment resonates in *s.* 4, where Augustine states that the 'joy of the Creator' is perceived not by means of corporeal vision (*non uidetur oculis corporis*) but by a certain sight of the mind (*acie mentis*).[53]

In *s.* 6, Augustine states that because of our incapacity to 'perceive' God directly, he adopts some sensible form, for instance, in the OT theophanies, so that he could be perceived. *Sapientia* deigns to become visible by assuming flesh, a physical thing which is proper to one's corporeal sense of vision.[54] Whilst remaining always divine, Christ assumes a human nature such that one can see him *through* this and ultimately come to know him as he is, as much as is possible in this life, and completely in the next.[55] Whilst remaining God, Christ assumes human nature in order to render assistance to his fallen creation.[56] In *s.* 5, Augustine sees the meaning of *Noli me tangere* as pointing to the constant need to remember that Christ is no 'mere' man.[57] To see Christ this way is truly to see him.[58]

Augustine emphasizes that by taking flesh, Christ never ceased to be God, remaining divine.[59] According to Augustine, Christ came in the flesh so that he might lead us to the knowledge that he is God. Augustine sees this as the very logic behind the Incarnation itself: the eternal Son of God condescends to our human level, making himself visible, assuming a form 'lesser' than that of the Father,[60] yet in virtue of this human nature, using it as a way of conducting the pious to the belief that he is also God. It allows them to see his divinity, precisely in virtue of his humility and presence in the flesh. All of those to be judged will see Christ as the Son of Man – that is, in his human nature, the form of a servant.[61] Augustine writes that since all the living and the dead are to be judged, it is fitting that the judge, who is Christ, will appear in a way that all can perceive him.[62] However, those who have listened to the voice of Christ and have believed in the Incarnation will be shown the fullness of his being, not only as the son of man, but also as the son of God.[63]

In my estimation, in *trin.* 1, Augustine is claiming that two (types of) people can look at the same object and perceive it differently. Although all rational creatures possess this capacity for judgement,[64] some use it to a greater or more excellent extent than others. This point suggests that nature is also saying or speaking something, but one person 'hears' it, whilst another does not. The difference between the two, according to Augustine, is that the one who really 'hears' the testimony of nature compares the reports of the senses with the truth which resides within one.[65]

What is suggested by such passages is a more nuanced notion of sight than that to which we are accustomed. By the same token, it also suggests a more nuanced way of thinking about the relationship between the 'empirical' and the intentional. Augustine's theory of knowledge is one which proceeds *per corporalia ad incorporalia*.[66] It is tempting to separate these two movements in a temporal fashion, but that need not be the case. Rather, these are two aspects or two moments of the same act of looking. The *corporalia*, which are accessible to the 'bodily senses', provide the substrate, the forum for the perception of meaningful, valuable content. They are co-extensive, but the full content of a particular factum is not always perceived due to an inadequacy in one's own intentional way of looking, whether in terms of moral impurity, theoretical commitments or some such.[67]

Augustine maintains the eschatological character of the beatific vision. Even purged intellectual vision is limited in this life.[68] Rationality, and indeed the purification thereof, entails a certain eschatological element. One's growth in rational knowledge ultimately points beyond earthly knowledge and even knowledge of formal realities, to the beatific vision itself.[69] The eschatological element to this vision is clear, as Augustine includes the qualification regarding the degree to which such vision may be permitted in this life.[70]

From the foregoing survey, we have discovered a few key points to keep in mind as we proceed with this study of Augustine's take on vision. He understands the bodily senses as diverse and each oriented towards their own object. In contrast, an inner sense of vision is far different from these, as it is holistic and possesses its own type of objects. Hence we perceive certain formal realities through and not with the bodily eyes. Indeed, these structuring principles provide the basis for sight in the first place. Fact and value are combined inseparably for Augustine, and this is a major theme that not only runs throughout his oeuvre, but also provides a basis for his understanding of vision, with particular respect to the vision of God. However, one must always remember that even if the '*factum* contains the *mysterium*',[71] it does not exhaust it.

Levels of vision in *De Genesi ad litteram* 12

In the twelfth and final book of *Gn. litt.*, Augustine discusses at length the character of human vision, informed by scriptural commitments. For similar treatments of this topic, one could look to his *ep.* 147 and part of the twenty-second book of *ciu.* However, for a case study in this chapter, I shall limit myself to *Gn. litt.*

Augustine frames the twelfth book of *Gn. litt.* based on the theophanic experience narrated in 2 Cor. 12.2-4, in which Paul describes a 'man in Christ' (presumably himself) who was 'caught up' to the 'third heaven'.[72] For Augustine, there is no question that

Paul was taken into the 'third heaven' and that that was what he 'saw'. Augustine bases his interpretation on the text itself.[73] So Paul recounts that he did in fact know that it was the third heaven, but he did not know how exactly he was able to perceive it.[74] Hence Augustine identifies Paul's doubt in this episode as pertaining to the *mode* of his vision, not the object thereof.[75] His exegesis of the Pauline passage provides the occasion for Augustine to propose a problematized understanding of sight. He identifies three types of vision(s),[76] the first of which is the corporeal sort, which is facilitated by the eyes of the body (*per sensus corporis*),[77] and allows one to see objects of sense. Spiritual vision, which seems to be what Augustine has in mind in *conf.* when he discusses *memoria*, involves images being impressed on the mind through one's spirit (*per spiritum*).[78] This spirit is not the soul as such, but a certain faculty of the soul which is able to retain images captured by the senses. Finally, there is the intellectual sense of vision, which is proper to the mind.[79] In a word, this is reason or understanding, vision in a normative sense. This type of vision is incorporeal, as are its objects, which do not admit of any material component. Moreover, when one perceives them with the mind, one is seeing the things themselves (*res ipsae*).[80] So when one truly understands and sees wisdom within one's mind, that is not one's own thought of wisdom, but *sapientia ipsa* (my gloss).[81]

Corporeal

Augustine understands corporeal vision as what we intuitively call to mind when we think about 'seeing' something. Moreover, just as there are different senses of vision, so too are there different objects proper to each. As for corporeal vision, these are corporeal realities immediately available to our sight, hence shown to the bodily senses.[82] Augustine's wording suggests a demarcation between the bodily senses on the one hand[83] and those of the mind on the other. Likewise, there is a distinction between the objects proper to the former, which are accessible to the corresponding bodily senses, and those which are only perceived intellectually, such as *sapientia*.[84] Although God can manifest himself through corporeal objects, and thereby to our human senses, his substance is entirely different from these, and not directly perceptible to them.[85]

Spiritual

As the corporeal sense of vision pertains to *praesentia corpora*, the spiritual vision pertains to the images and similitudes thereof. Augustine writes that the bodily senses convey images to the spirit, where images of those bodies are formed and stored.[86] Corporeal and spiritual vision are not so much two different senses, or two operations separated in time, but rather two aspects of the same act of looking; after the object has disappeared, one realizes the spiritual vision in the form of a memory.[87] Hence spiritual vision is the soul's vision of images which have been impressed on it from the corporeal senses.[88] However, in addition to things one has actually experienced, it is also possible to see images of things that one has never seen, speculating and constructing mental pictures from past experiences.[89] For example, I have been to Budapest, so I can call to mind certain images thereof in my memory. I have not been to Beijing, but based on various memories, I can produce speculative images of what it may look like. Both of these operations are based in the spiritual sense of vision for Augustine which, though not itself corporeal, is concerned with the images of corporeal things.[90]

The use of terms 'spiritual' and 'intellectual' can be a bit confusing. That is true for us just as it was true in Augustine's time. In order to dispel any possible confusion amongst his readers, Augustine qualifies and restricts his use of the term 'spiritual', first acknowledging the various senses which it can take in scripture. These uses of spirit include mind, which pertains to the image of God within the soul, a meaning which really comes closer to Augustine's understanding of *intellectus* in this work. However, though scripture seems to complicate Augustine's schema, it also provides him with the basis for formulating it in the first place. Augustine points to 1 Cor. 14.15 to substantiate his distinction between the spiritual and the intellectual.[91] Thus Augustine makes clear that in this particular work, he is using *spiritus* in his own restricted sense, and hence it should not be confused or conflated with 'intellectual'.[92]

This difference is further clarified as Augustine continues his enquiry into the *tria genera uisionum*. He writes that the spirit delivers its contents to the mind, where the intellect conducts its operation of seeking, parsing and understanding the images contained therein.[93] For this reason, the spiritual sense of vision can rightly be described as a mediator between the mind and the body.[94]

The intellectual sense is superior still, for it has the role of directing the enquiring sensations of the body, as well as making sense of the contents contained within the *spiritus*; the intellect pertains to one's capacity to interpret and understand.[95]

Intellectual

The third and most superior type of vision, the 'intellectual', is unique in that there is a different type of light proper to it, and that its objects do not possess any corporeal properties, such as colour, taste and so on.[96] Rather, they are known by one's intellect; one sees them by understanding and thinking (*intellegendo et cogitando*).[97] Thus there is a strong demarcation drawn between corporeal and spiritual vision on the one hand and intellectual vision on the other. *Intellectus* is proper to the mind, and is responsible for moving from images to knowledge.[98] In the mind, the images delivered by the spiritual sense are judged.[99]

The operation of the mind pertains to one's understanding, one's cognitive grasp of something, in particular non-corporeal realities, which the soul beholds within itself. These are not images but the things themselves.[100] The 'region' of intellectual vision is beyond all corporeality.[101] Here the *claritas Domini* itself is seen, as much as the mind can handle, not a reflection.[102] Augustine writes that 'intelligible things' such as love, virtues and wisdom are perceived by the mind, as these objects are neither corporeal, nor do they possess any corporeal features (*uidetur mente sapientia, sine ullis imaginibus corporum*).[103] Because one perceives such spiritual properties by the mind, one grows closer to God and thereby perfects one's human nature.[104]

Though he speaks of different 'types' (*genera*) of vision, Augustine sees these as inherently connected to one another. Whilst there can be a temporal separation between them, there need not be. This he makes clear by his example of reading a particular scriptural passage, showing how each type of vision can be operative simultaneously:

> Behold, when it is read in this one precept, *You shall love your neighbour as yourself*, three types of visions occur: one through the eyes, by which the letters themselves are read; another the spirit of man by which near and far are thought; the third

through the contuition of the mind, by which the intellectual thing love itself is perceived.[105]

Indeed, we have already seen how corporal and spiritual vision, respectively, are two aspects of the same act of looking.[106] This may well be true for intellectual vision, if one is attuned to perceive and cognize the intelligible forms available before one. For Augustine, intellectual vision implies that one either sees or does not.[107] The intellectual sense of vision in the sense of complete understanding may not happen at the same time. However, one's rational faculties may still be at work in detecting that which one does not (yet) understand and directing the mind to enquire further.[108] In this way, Augustine appears to anticipate what Gadamer and other contemporary figures have to say about the notion of hermeneutical consciousness.[109]

Augustine believes that one can have a sort of 'indirect' intellectual perception, one which is incomplete, yet provides the very basis for its own completion. In this respect, he cites the example of the Babylonian king Belshazzar from the book of Daniel (5.5-28), in which the former has a vision of a hand writing in an unknown language on the wall. Then Daniel is called to interpret the message. Two points are worth noting here. First, Augustine designates Daniel's act of understanding and interpretation as the superior act of vision, though by forming an image of the symbol in his mind, the king was certainly partaking in spiritual vision. Moreover, Augustine identifies Belshazzar's intellectual vision with a certain 'hermeneutical' pre-understanding: though the king's intellect could not understand the writing, he could nevertheless identify it as intelligible and as containing some hidden meaning, which provided him with an intentional object into which to enquire, whether by himself or with another.[110] Even though he lacked complete understanding, his mind was nonetheless able to direct his enquiry and to recognize something of intelligible value in the objects of his perception, the image of which was contained in his spirit. Augustine speaks of this movement in terms of a call or a summons, such that one's mind is called to discover the meaning of particular corporeal images, artefacts and so on, or rather, the meaning contained within those material images.[111] What is suggested here is a variation on the principal–gradual schema: one has some capacity for perceiving non-corporeal objects, which stands in need of being completed or perfected. In other words, one gradually grows in knowledge of a particular object of such vision.

We see a similar line of thought in *f. inuis.*, in which Augustine grapples with the problem of vision, and its highly 'intentional' character. He speaks of intellectual sight in terms of a kind of faith; in other words, before we can begin to interact with someone, we have to have a sense of their identity and their unity,[112] and Augustine locates this in the heart or the soul.[113] There has to be a certain sense in which one perceives an intelligible, coherent reality which, whilst constituted by sensible matter, is ultimately more than the sum of its parts and is thereby not directly 'visible' to the *corporeis oculis*.[114] When we reflect (self-)critically, we realize that our lives seem to make sense in light of these invisible realities; it seems that we are already implicated in them without realizing it, and we proceed accordingly in our quotidian lives.[115] Similarly, Augustine recasts the Meno paradox in *trin.* 8.6, pondering how one can have a desire to know God when one does not yet know him.[116] According to Menn,[117] 'Augustine says that we can pray to God, even before we have knowledge of God, based on *faith* in God.' For this position, Augustine draws upon Heb. 11.6, suggesting that one must have some 'pre-cognition' of God which guides one to seek him and which provides an initial direction for enquiry.[118]

Conclusion

In *Gn. litt.* 12, as in other locations, we see Augustine dealing with vision in highly nuanced terms. Though the question is occasioned by scripture, the application is not so much to the vision of the divine per se but more about the way in which we as human agents perceive sapiential contents (with)in the world. In fact, as I have suggested, there is a somewhat hermeneutical element to Augustine's account of vision. In other words, in virtue of vision in its normative sense, the intellectual type of vision, we can perceive an intelligible content which is nonetheless not completely understood. We are then directed to question and interrogate this object in order to uncover its meaning. This dynamic of being addressed by something, responding to it in the form of a question, and engaging it in a dialogue of sorts, will form the basis for the following chapter, in which we shall follow Augustine as he attempts to converse with the beauty of the universe.

PART THREE

An Interrogative Theory of Knowledge

5

Reading the Universe

Introduction

In her 1995 article on the reception history of the analogy of nature and scripture, W. Otten discusses the foundations, history and eventual decline of this analogy. She looks first and foremost to Augustine's *De doctrina christiana* as a basis for the understanding of nature as analogous to a text. In this work, Augustine takes the radically novel step of identifying both words and things as potentially *significant* – that is, as signs that point to a greater reality, namely the triune God.[1] Augustine's oeuvre yields similar ideas in a variety of other works, such as the latter three books of his *Confessiones*, in which he treats Genesis and the creation of the world, and thus the universe as reflecting not simply the being, but even the goodness and the glory of its Creator.[2]

In her article, Otten continues briefly to trace the reception history of this theme through figures such as Dionysius the Areopagite and Scotus Eriugena.[3] As Otten notes, scripture itself provides a basis for supposing that one can discern vestiges of God in creation.[4] Following this tradition, mediaeval theologians too saw scripture and creation as two complementary ways in which God reveals himself.[5] Creation therefore served as a sort of alternative testament to the pagans, to whom God was speaking in a certain way through the world. However, towards the end of the Middle Ages, according to Otten, the understanding of nature as analogous to a text became gradually attenuated. Small but significant theological shifts of the late Middle Ages laid a foundation for the 'disenchantment' that followed in the early modern period.[6] It was around this time, according to B. Gregory, that the tendency to understand the divine as somehow still located 'within' our universe originated,[7] thinking as though God were spatial,[8] and thus succumbing to a 'univocal metaphysics'.[9] As Gregory writes, the implication is that 'the "spiritual" presence of God is *itself* being conceived in spatial or quasi-spatial terms'.[10] As the theologian V. Austin pithily explains this point, 'God is not a being (amongst beings) but the cause of all beings.'[11] In his divine nature, God is not a 'type' of thing which could be compared with other sorts of things, and thereby exclude the possibility of being present to and within the created order.[12] God cannot be located as a (type of) cause alongside other factors within the universe; rather, it is his divine providence which is the very fundamental condition of the possibility of intelligibility and causality.[13] This theological understanding of God's creative activity helps to explain Augustine's apophatic reflex, an aspect of his theology which, as S. Ticciati rightly notes, is about far more than simply saying no.[14] The result is a subtle but significant reduction of God to exercising a causal role within the universe itself, as opposed to 'beyond' it,[15] such that one loses the notion of creation *ex nihilo*. For example, the philosopher D. Dennett discusses, critiques and rejects the notion of God as a sort of 'craftsman', a notion which in Gregory's view does not correspond to that of Genesis.[16]

The decline of the analogy between nature and scripture represents, in Gregory's words, the overcoming of the 'sacramental view of reality'.[17] A further implication which Gregory identifies as arising within nineteenth-century theological circles is the bifurcation of the sciences, according to which the empirical sciences increasingly come to be seen as the realm of the cognitive – that is, the objective, fact-based and univocal, whereas matters pertaining to religion were considered non-cognitive – that is, merely concerning emotion, feelings and ineffable thoughts.[18]

The upshot of this episode in the history of ideas is that being comes to be seen as disenchanted, as dumb and inert, upon which man imposes a grid in order to elicit understanding. There is no longer an 'overdetermined' charge of value and meaning which is discovered in the world, or which imposes itself upon us. The search for truth becomes one of a monologue, an evaluation of material which of itself does not speak to the human knower.

Systematic and philosophical responses

Despite the disappearance of an analogy between nature and scripture, recent thinkers have revisited this idea from a variety of perspectives. Within the last three decades, three major monographs have appeared on this subject. The common denominator amongst these works is that each of them develops a constructive philosophy or theology according to which one advances in knowledge, in particular knowledge of God, by means of a sort of dialogue with or hermeneutical investigation of the natural world, not simply for its own sake, but as a sign of the transcendent within the immanent realm. The first of these is Jean-Louis Chrétien's *L'appel et la réponse*,[19] in which this phenomenologist, drawing upon various historical sources, not least of all Augustine, construes one's philosophical encounter with reality in terms of a dialogue of the mind with beauty itself as it is instantiated in the world, yet always pointing to something which exceeds it. Michael Fishbane's *Sacred Attunement*[20] represents an attempt to bring Jewish theology into the present day. Though his method is hermeneutical, it is one which does not primarily depart from Gadamer or other contemporary figures, but rather takes its cue from the Jewish tradition itself, especially the multifaceted Torah, which forms the substantive basis of his thought. Mats Wahlberg draws upon contemporary analytic philosophy in order to develop a constructive theological approach to nature as creation.[21] Wahlberg wishes to recover an account of the world expressed by and grounded in sources such as Rom. 1.20, according to which the fact of creation by God is obvious (his term) on the basis of the highly complex properties endemic to the world.[22]

Following the aforementioned thinkers, my task is to complement and confront a contemporary picture of reality and to challenge our fundamental 'ontological' prejudices with respect to the world. The following enquiry will serve to provide meaningful articulation to what it could mean to 'read' the universe.

Chrétien on the call and the response of beauty

Chrétien's work possesses a certain Augustinian quality, and this philosopher is deeply informed by the bishop of Hippo. Like

Augustine, Chrétien believes that the inner senses do not respond to the same logic as those of the body.[23] Hence there is a holistic character to the call of beauty, which is addressed to the entire person.[24] He also wonders whether there is a voice interior to our own voice, which sounds in our mind apart from any of our own input, something like a conscience.[25] Furthermore, Chrétien cites Augustine when he writes that the forms which provide the basis of the world's intelligible structure speak to one, making themselves known.[26] Chrétien is intrigued in particular by Augustine's discussion in the tenth book of *conf.*, in which the latter recalls how he found himself in dialogue with the created world. One of the ways in which nature speaks for Augustine is in its 'apophatic' or negative response, namely that it is not God.[27] That is, creatures speak their finitude and their dependence on the Creator.

A crucial point here is that we are always already engaged in the world whenever we speak.[28] We do not respond unless first addressed.[29] In articulating this notion of the interplay of call and response, Chrétien dedicates a significant amount of his monograph to beauty, noting that the Platonic tradition understands beauty as a call to the soul.[30] We are able to identify something as beautiful, Chrétien writes, when we are engaged in a dialogue with it, a dialogue initiated by the call of the beautiful itself.[31] For Chrétien, beauty calls to us and addresses us; it is the truly 'visible voice'.[32] This initial summons from beauty begins a dialogue between the world's beauty and the human mind. Indeed, this is a truly reciprocal engagement, and not merely a monologue.[33] The significance of this notion of a summons is that it calls us to some form of activity. Even if we first encounter the beautiful as an experience or an event, we cannot remain passive.[34] In this way we truly participate in the dialogue with the world. As Chrétien writes, 'Les choses mêmes nous appellent et nous invitent à les interroger. Leur beauté appelle en répondant et répond en appelant.'[35] One of the key messages communicated to us is the overabundant beauty of the origin of natural things, displayed in their apparent excess.[36]

Pulchritudo

As Giraud explains, aesthetic categories are central to Augustine's theory of knowledge. Contrary to our post-Kantian biases with respect to 'aesthetics', for Augustine this does not represent something non-cognitive, but is a different and perhaps even pre-eminent aspect under which to view truth.[37] The Augustinian understanding of beauty as a call leads one to self-reflection, for it is there that the standards for judging beauty are discovered, and without which no divine vestige may be perceived. The world's reflection of God invokes the images impressed upon the soul which, although obscured by sin, are still present.[38] The divine *uestigia* thus initially address the soul, initiating a hermeneutical process.[39] Aesthetic beauty is a mark of the divine and thereby a mark of truth. Augustine understands beauty primarily in terms of proportion, form, order, unity and so on. Timeless and eternal forms of beauty are instantiated in material objects and states of affairs. God's beauty, his order and number, etc., are constitutive of creation as a whole and each individual created thing, in virtue of which they can be considered *uestigia*.[40]

The way in which God communicates through the various forms and structures of the created world must be understood with respect to their ultimate inadequacy and lack of being with respect to their source. Harrison points to Plotinus as a major source for Augustine's thought in this respect. In *Ennead* 1.6.6, Plotinus describes the ascent of the soul to the One, one of the requirements of which is to eschew one's excessive attachment to worldly realities.[41] In *Ennead* 5.8.9, Plotinus writes that being is integrally linked with beauty, and that one loves something which *is* because of the beauty one discerns to be present therein. That is, one may 'see' the form of the beautiful instantiated in a particular thing, which, through one's gradual participation in it, inculcates in one the desire for its source.[42] In *trin.*, Augustine writes that the movement of rational enquiry takes one from the vestiges of the Creator to the Creator himself.[43] This movement entails a gradual relinquishing of worldly things. However, due to its ontological limitations, the soul suffers from a myopic moral vision, which leads one to flee from the superior for the inferior and become attached to corporeal things.[44] (I shall have more to say about this in the following chapter.) Indeed, the origin of sin is found in the soul's inordinate attachment to temporal, provisional goods, such that the hierarchy of creation is neglected.[45] However, Harrison argues that it does not do justice to Augustine if one sees his thought as implying a devaluation or a diminishment of the goodness of the material order.[46] These things are not evil, they are good. But they are not absolute goods, and they are subordinate to other goods. Hence one must guard against the dangers of pride and curiosity that lead one into these snares.[47]

Augustine's cataphatic theology of *signa* with respect to the created world is checked by an apophatic reflex, though both of these streams have a common font, namely in the doctrine of *creatio ex nihilo*.[48] For instance, in book six of *De musica*, Augustine writes of the way in which the soul may discover and love the beauty of forms in creation, yet after thoughtful reflection will come to the conclusion that these are mere shadows of the source of all form and order.[49] Augustine condemns the error whereby the vestiges of God are prized over their source.[50] When God is abandoned for his signs, the entire 'hermeneutical key' is lost and perverted. The order of the world acts as a sign, leading one back to God, but only if one is properly attuned to perceive the order and to act accordingly.[51] God is always speaking to the soul through his created order, but the soul must be able to recognize these messages, aided by the situating of them in the proper framework – that is, being understood as reflections of God's being and majesty.[52] (I shall develop this point in the following chapter.) Nonetheless, as created beings, God bids one to come and seek him through the things he has made. Thus Giraud describes the created order as a call in the sense of an invitation to seek its source.[53] In a word, as Giraud writes, 'La beauté est un appel.'[54]

Augustine on the speaking of nature

Augustine's understanding of creation in *sapientia* leads him to conclude that it is only logical to expect that the things made by the maker will reflect him and testify to him.[55] The divine Wisdom is infused into the created order, and as the source of order and intelligibility is always communicating through particular creatures.[56] The beauty instantiated in individual creatures reflects God's 'art' (*ars diuina*) through which he speaks to us.[57] According to Giraud, Augustine's theology of creation could also be viewed as the doctrine of the vestiges of the divine Wisdom expressed in material form.[58] The *forma impressa* is communicative, causing an intentional and cognitive operation in the mind, calling it to think of its origin. This is the sense in which Augustine is said to speak of the created world as that which addresses the rational agent. An intentional, rational disposition is a prerequisite of being held or seized by the intelligible order in which one finds oneself. Thus Giraud: 'la création que considère Augustin est l'œuvre de Dieu et, comme telle, transparence à nous adressée de son Verbe.'[59] As Bochet puts it, 'le monde crée est signe du Createur.'[60]

But precisely what does the world signify? What does it say to us, and how? For Augustine, one of the specific things the world speaks is praise, *confessio*. Creation in virtue of its disposition and inherent goodness praises God. It is good and beautiful in its order.[61] Augustine states in *en. Ps.* 148 that the beauty (*pulchritudo*) of nature constitutes its confession to God: 'In a certain way, beauty is the voice of all of those things, of those confessing God.'[62] Here Augustine condemns the idea that God only concerns himself with 'higher' things and is not concerned with or does not govern 'lower' things.[63] If we are attentive to nature, it tells us that it is not the source of its own being. It tells us that God made it. This is its voice speaking to our hearts: 'Heaven cries out to God: "You have made me, not I." The earth cries out, "You have formed me, not I."'[64] Even changeable, created reality can lead us to the praise of God. In a sense, these things exhort us to consider them, whereby we can praise God.[65] The admiration of created things always serves a referential function, insofar as when we consider them we are led to a knowledge of their creator, which must then develop into praise. When we express this, inanimate creation praises God in our voice.[66] 'How do those things cry out? When they are considered, and this is discovered, they cry out from your consideration, they cry out from your voice.'[67]

Augustine conceives of nature as a locus of contact between the human and the divine, as it is created in God's wisdom. Hence it is intelligible, and Augustine describes its manifestation of itself to the soul as speech of a sort. We can see a brief treatment of this in Augustine's two *enarrationes* on Ps. 18, the first composed in 392, and the second delivered as a *sermo* ca. 412-15. Augustine states that Ps. 18, in which it is stated that the heavens declare God's glory, is about Christ.[68] Augustine links Ps. 18 with the Johannine prologue, stating that the glory which the heavens declare is that same glory which was seen in the incarnate Christ, namely the glory *tamquam Unigeniti a Patre*.[69] Employing the language of the Johannine prologue, Augustine states that all things were made through this Word, which is identical to God's wisdom.[70] Within this context of creation *in sapientia*, Augustine immediately proceeds to discuss the speaking of nature.[71] The heavens should and indeed do announce the glory of the Lord and his deeds. The language which Augustine uses is that which is often associated with speaking, especially in terms of explaining or expounding something (e.g. *annuntiat, exponunt*).[72] When the heavens declare God's glory, Augustine claims, it is especially a declaration of one's nothingness and one's utter dependency on God.[73] As Augustine punctuates this point, '"Not to us, O Lord, but to your name give glory." Those heavens had known this, which declared the glory of God.'[74] The heavens serve to remind us that God is the Creator, and not we (*ipse fecit nos, et non ipsi nos*).[75] In other words, the heavens are saying that we are finite, and God infinite. The revelation of the Word during the day, Augustine states, symbolizes the announcement of the eternal Word. It is about this that the earth can be said to speak.[76] Night symbolizes the mortality of the flesh, which for Augustine can point towards *futuram scientiam*.[77] The key point which I draw from this is that Augustine sees the earth not simply as testifying, but as testifying to something which transcends it.

Now let us consider in more detail two particular locations in which Augustine describes the world as speaking to him, from which he is able to learn something about God from his creation.

Confessiones 10

In *conf.* 10, Augustine writes that his 'method' for searching for God involves an active, directed searching, an interrogation. He says that he began with the creatures of the exterior world, and that he asked, or interrogated (*interrogaui*) them,[78] specifically to discover whether any one of them was God. Augustine depicts apparently inanimate natural objects as speaking, responding and, indeed, confessing. This metaphorical and highly imaginative image of nature speaking is portrayed as a dialogue between Augustine's soul and the world, to which he gives some interpretation when he writes, 'my interrogation is my intention, and their beauty is their response.'[79] In the third chapter we encountered Augustine's understanding of *intentio*, and a further significant aspect of it reveals itself here. In other words, Augustine's act of interrogation is an expression for his directed, focused enquiry into particular realities, guided by a pre-sentiment of their intelligibility, whilst the 'response' he 'hears' from various natural bodies is their *species*, their form or their beauty, a property which he is able to perceive by means of his intellect. Augustine writes that natural creatures speak to him, specifically for the purpose that he may be brought to love of God: 'But both heaven and earth, as well as all things which are in them, behold, everywhere they speak to me, so that I may love you.'[80] Moreover, Augustine claims that this speaking is constant, without cessation, and that it is directed to all people, which for him implies that those who do not acknowledge this are *inexcusabiles*.[81]

We also see the language of *intentio* at work in Augustine's dialogue with the natural world as he searches for God. In contrast to animals,[82] man possesses the capacity of reason, which for Augustine is distinctive specifically in its capacity to interrogate and to serve as a judge of the reports of the exterior world (*homines autem possunt interrogare*).[83] Augustine notes that animals have some capacity for memory in the way that people do. What differentiates them is not so much the extent of the memory but the operation it supports in the human knower, that of reasoning, which Augustine likens to judging or interpreting the reports of the senses. Though he perceives and 'hears' the responses of corporeal creation in one way, namely through his bodily senses, Augustine notes that there is an interior and, indeed, qualitatively superior sense at work, judging the reports of the senses and interpreting them in a certain way.[84]

Thus it becomes clear that the brief account of Augustine's *interrogatio* of created reality is something which takes place within himself. Augustine is not talking to himself or daydreaming; rather, he is calling to mind the various images and memories, unifying them as a certain substrate, and then enquiring further into them. In addition, as Nightingale writes, 'This implies not just the reproduction of past images or ideas but creative imagination: one comes up with new thoughts by recourse to past ideas and experiences.'[85] The intellect's faculty of intention aspires to unity, parsimony, synthesis and simplicity, which reflects God's own eternity and immutability. It serves as a faculty by means of which one can begin to overcome the disorienting multiplicity of corporeal reality, enabling one to possess a pure and *simplex cor*.[86]

This beauty of the world's responses inherently includes a double aspect, as whilst they contain some positive, assertive content, that is, in terms of their beauty, the initial responses which Augustine records are negative and apophatic, or at least responses which direct Augustine beyond the very realities he is interrogating and investigating. As for the latter, we read, 'I interrogated the sea and the depths and the creeping things of living souls, and they responded: "we are not your God, seek above us."'[87] There is the apophatic response ('we are not God'), coupled with the referential element ('seek above us'). So as the particular natural realities 'confess', they simultaneously confess their beauty and their lack thereof, or rather their utter dependence upon God for all that they possess and are. We see this especially when Augustine brings his natural investigation to a conclusion by asking creation to say something to him about the God he is seeking: 'and I said to all things, which stand around the doors of my flesh, "Tell me something about my God, which you are not, tell me something about him." And they exclaimed in a loud voice, "He made us."'[88] The failure of Augustine's external search conducts him to self-enquiry, to asking himself who he is, and through such an investigation, seeking what is above him.

Giraud locates in *conf.* 10 the inherently 'hermeneutical' character of human reason on Augustine's view ('Le soi qui constitue l'image est ainsi hermeneutique en son essence'). Engaged in enquiry, the soul is led from the outside world to a knowledge of oneself, which in turn entails a knowledge of the soul's origin from elsewhere.[89] In virtue of discovering the truth about oneself, one is also led to knowledge of the world. Giraud explains this link when he writes,

> L'interrogation du monde sensible et l'accès au soi intellectuel ne suivent pas des voies divergentes. La relation de l'extérieur et de l'intérieur n'est pas d'opposition mais d'implication et d'approfondissement. Foris et intus, loin de s'entraver ou de se nier, se relancent mutuellement, des lors que la trace de Dieu dans le monde ne peut être suivie que par la trace qu'il a laissée en moi, qui me constitue et que je suis.[90]

This image is realized within one, and is thus concrete. From the inner movement Augustine realizes that there is an interior and, indeed, qualitatively superior sense at work, judging the reports of the body's senses and interpreting them in a certain way.[91]

In addition to God himself speaking through the works of the world, Augustine also suggests that creatures themselves speak, but when they do, it is nonetheless on God's behalf, and always directed back to him.[92] In the famous *sero te amaui* passage of the *Confessiones*,[93] Augustine describes God as beauty, and the source of all beauty, in particular the limited instantiations of beauty in creation. Augustine threw himself into these, even though their beauty was inherently limited and less than that of God himself.[94] The prior context of the *conf.* makes clear that the motivation for Augustine's inward move was the fact that he had discovered that God was present within and to him, in particular through the memory.

In discussing Augustine's understanding of creation and formation, he seems to suggest what I have elsewhere called a theology of re-creation.[95] Christ restores the intellectual vision with which we were created and which has been wounded by sin. The fulfilment of this is eschatological.[96] Through free will, the human person has sinned and become a defective symbol of God. Thus the Incarnate Christ restores fallen man, making him once again a fitting symbol through which the Creator can communicate, and which will complement the other divine signs present in the world.[97]

The specific weakness of the inner sense was that it was not able to perceive God, as it was looking at the wrong things and looking at them in the wrong way, a fault which God himself corrects by acting on the soul.[98] Moreover, the language of interiority also serves to make clear Augustine's argument that the perception of God and truth is often a matter of clearing the blockages and the prejudices of our own minds, or re-orienting our intellectual vision so as to be able to see what was already present and available to perception.[99] However, as we have previously noted, though all rational agents possess the same capacity for judgement, not all make use of it, at least to the same extent: 'Indeed, better still, [the world's *species*] speaks to all, but they understand, who compare its voice received from the outside with the truth on the inside.'[100] We have encountered this point already as regards the principal sense of illumination, and now one of its specific aspects can be seen. That is, the truth within tells one that no particular physical thing is God. The upshot of Augustine's external search is that God is not any particular type of 'body', that is, a corporeal, sensible object, nor is he reducible to one: 'for the truth says to me, "Your God is not heaven and earth, nor is he any body."'[101] Of course we have seen this point already, but now we are prepared to ask a further question: if God is *not* like any of the aforementioned things, then what is he like? This challenges our ontological prejudice of thinking of the real in terms of time and space;[102] now we are asked to think of things which are not only outside of our familiar dimensions, but apart from dimensionality altogether.[103]

Sermo 241

We see a similar line of thought in *sermo* 241, delivered in Hippo ca. 405–10. For his understanding of nature's intelligibility, Augustine appeals to Paul's letter to the Romans (1.19-21). In this homily, Augustine credits the *philosophi* with a valid and genuine knowledge of God derived from nature (*de operibus artificem cognouisse*), a knowledge which did not come as a result of the revelation vouchsafed to the chosen people.[104] Augustine affirms that God was addressing these philosophers through creation (*eis Deus quodam modo silens ipsius mundi operibus loquebatur, et eos ad quaerendum artificem rerum, mundi species inuitabat*).[105] This divine call, which echoes through the natural world, is ever present to the soul, ever calling and beckoning: *this way, mortal, bend thy eyes*.[106] Augustine's understanding of *creatio ex nihilo* places nature on a par with scripture, a point which is demonstrated by his assertion that the philosophers are *inexcusabiles* because they did not worship God as they ought.[107]

One can see how Augustine understands the potency and the power of the created world to communicate the divine, even if one can be deaf to its address. Having condemned the pagan philosophers for their rejection of the revelation vouchsafed to them by God through his works, Augustine proceeds to suggest how God can be known through creation, instructing his audience to 'interrogate' the beauty of nature, and to enquire into it as one pursues knowledge of the divine. Thus Augustine:

> Interrogate the beauty of the earth, interrogate the beauty of the sea, the beauty of the wind which spreads and blows, the beauty

of the sky, the order of the stars, the sun which illumines the day by its light, the moon which by its splendour tempers the darkness of the following night, the animals which move in the seas, which roam about land, which fly in the air; interrogate hidden souls, and visible bodies; visible things needing to be ruled, invisible things governing.[108]

Augustine identifies these as particular objects against the backdrop of creation and in defining them can hear what they are saying to him. As Chrétien puts it, 'Augustin définit ici la beauté comme réponse',[109] a point with which Giraud concurs.[110] One should behold beauty and be held by beauty – that is, allow oneself to be grasped by something beyond one's control.[111]

As created beings, God bids one to come and seek him through the things he has made. Thus Giraud describes the created order as a call in the sense of an invitation to seek their source.[112] Contrary to a Kantian aesthetic of enjoyment, the Augustinian understanding of beauty as a call leads one to self-reflection, for it is there that the standards of judging beauty at all are discovered, and without which no divine vestige may be perceived.[113] Even in his much later *ciu.*, Augustine writes that the basic principles constitutive of the world speak to and address one.[114] This calling of the world's *pulchritudo* initiates a dialogue with the soul, which entails a certain reciprocity and dialectic which can be continuously extended and deepened.[115] This speaks to the excess of worldly things, showing forth the beauty of their origin, what Desmond calls the 'over-determinacy' of being,[116] the sapiential saturation of material reality in virtue of its origin in God's creativity. Augustine sees nature as replete with 'question-able' content, which stands in need of being disclosed by directed enquiry.

Augustine's protreptic to interrogation in *s.* 241 is consummated in the following crescendo: 'interrogate those things, all of them respond to you: "Behold, look, we are beautiful." Their beauty is their confession.'[117] Augustine establishes a clear link between beauty and truth: *pulchritudo eorum, confessio eorum*.[118] He even says that creation 'speaks' to one, saying, 'We are beautiful.'[119] In Augustine's view, the world is engaged in a dialogue with the human heart, and the language it speaks is that of beauty.[120] Augustine's understanding of 'interrogating' the beauty of the universe and natural phenomena provides resources for re-conceptualizing epistemology. Moreover, his understanding of *pulchritudo* is interesting here, as he understands it in profoundly cognitive and intelligible terms. But more importantly, in order for one to be able to see this beauty requires an initial vision or intuition which is not ultimately reducible to 'empirical' observation; rather, the latter presupposes the former. So just as is the case with sapiential knowledge, the understanding of beauty requires a concerted effort on the part of the seeker of truth, which is both intellectual and ascetical. However, this intellectual perception presupposes an even more basic faculty, namely that of the mind's gaze, the capacity for discerning objects of intellectual vision and of seeing what admits of the possibility of being interrogated. In other words, *pulchritudo* at a very basic level represents something which admits of intelligible content which can be further disclosed by means of focused and concentrated enquiry; in a word, instantiations of beauty in the created world, or indeed, the created world itself, represents, in Taylor's words, a 'text-analogue',[121] or an object of enquiry which is, as Gadamer puts it, 'question-able'.[122] The very ability to interrogate reality presupposes the capacity to see what can be questioned, and indeed, what is inviting one to question, that which draws one's attention. Such an epistemic model, as we have seen, is grounded in a cosmology informed by Genesis and the concept of *creatio ex nihilo*. The locus of Augustine's *interrogatio* is none other than within himself. Hence the act of interrogating creation is an act which is grounded in a sapiential account of human reason as divine illumination.

The use of the term *interrogare* in *s*. 241 is striking, and bespeaks a certain theological, and indeed, hermeneutical approach to the content in question. According to Burton, this term admits of two senses, one of which involves a directed question, one which seeks to elicit a binary response: a yes or a no. Augustine was aware of this sense of *interrogare*, and a discussion of this term is also located in Cicero's *De fato* 28.[123] The use of the term *interroga* as applied to the beauty of nature is particularly interesting here for another reason, as Augustine uses this very term when he exhorts his audience to 'interrogate' a particular person or biblical book (e.g. Isaiah, John or Paul, 'the apostle') in order to elicit an answer to a difficult question.[124] Chrétien emphasizes that we must interrogate the beauty of nature – that is, we must look with direction and purpose. We cannot look with a simple passivity.[125] In other words, an interrogation is a dynamic, reciprocal process. In my estimation, one only interrogates someone who can respond intelligently. For instance, one cannot interrogate a cash point, but one can interrogate a person, a text or some other sort of thing which is invested with intelligible content.[126] Hence it is interesting that Augustine, who so often speaks of interrogating people and texts, would use the same term to impel his listeners to enquire into nature, even stating that it can 'respond' to one. What I want to say is that the term *interroga* implies a committed sense of searching, even in response to a summons, and hence more than mere curiosity. In an interrogation, one does not ask open-ended questions, or at least has a particular sense of direction in which one is moving and a certain (type of) answer for which one is looking. In fact, in the directed-ness of question, a certain hermeneutical process is at work, for one has a presentiment of an answer which one wishes to complete and to refine in light of further information, a point we have noted with respect to Augustine's exegesis of Daniel 5 in *Gn. litt.* 12.

The place of the act of questioning is crucial to philosophers such as Gadamer, Collingwood and Chrétien. Augustine's approach is consistent with this. We can glean further theological insight from a recent work which approaches the topic of questioning a biblical context. In his brief treatise *What Do You Seek?*, M. Buckley draws upon the questions Christ poses, in particular in the Gospel of John, as a *locus theologicus*.[127] Buckley's work can be seen as arising from the insight that 'We are closer to God when we are asking questions than when we think we have the answers'.[128] One of the main functions of a question, especially one posed by Jesus, is to confront one with oneself, to compel one to engage in self-reflection.[129] Hence for Buckley, every question is a variation on the question, 'Who are you?'[130] The divine source of such a question causes one to be drawn by something greater than oneself.[131] The questioning which confronts us originates in the divine, and we are drawn by the divine and by the promise of our future.[132] Questions give direction and meaning to human life, and the answers they elicit are often a lifetime in the making.[133]

Buckley presents a theory of questioning similar to that of Gadamer as, for him, a properly formulated question leaves plenty of room for answers.[134] Indeed, it opens one to the possibility of acknowledging the truth.[135] As Buckley writes, 'This summons to truth issues from the very heart of the question. To be brought to acknowledge the primordial imperative and supremacy of truth is to come to recognize the presence and claim of God.'[136] Buckley touches upon one of the virtues of an 'interrogative' theory of reasoning, as it forestalls any form of dogmatism and disingenuous argumentation. Moreover, a question is so simple, and yet so profound, as it provides the opportunity for us to see what is 'already there'.[137] In analysing a question and formulating responses to it, one may draw upon previous stores of data and yield new insights from them, or find a new shade of significance or a novel application or interpretation.[138] The ability to ask a question or to entertain it seriously is to acknowledge one's own ignorance and finitude.[139] Questions can disrupt the prior patterns of life.[140] In another idiom, they provide the opportunity for challenging one's prejudices.

The interrogative theory of knowledge elaborated here stands in stark contrast to the way that the modern dispensation understands questioning. Chrétien contrasts a truly open form of interrogation, one which presupposes an 'overdetermined' source to all of reality, with a 'modern' approach, according to which the world is viewed as an empty, neutral space. Such an approach also influences the genre of one's enquiry, and hence the types of questions one asks. The result is that within the latter dispensation, any meaningful sense of dialogue is precluded, and the sense of questioning assumes the form of a forced response. In contrast, the former approach is realized in a certain 'existential' way. Questioning is highly dynamic, as one opens oneself, puts oneself at risk, *en jeu*, as it were, and thereby becomes receptive to what may exceed one, may surprise one or challenge one's prejudices. By questioning, one's interlocutor is valorized, and allowed to speak with some freedom, in a way which is neither compelled nor forced. Chrétien contrasts this model of questioning suggested by Augustine with another way of questioning, which takes the form of forcing a particular (type of) response, rather than asking an open, though directed, question. Thus Chrétien:

> Kant écrit, à propos de la physique, que la raison 'doit obliger la nature à répondre à ses questions,' et qu'elle est 'comme un juge en fonction qui force les témoins à répondre aux questions qu'il leur pose,' cette interrogation ne suppose pas une voix visible, ni que l'œil écoute en étant appelé, surpris et saisi, mais que 'la

raison ne voit que ce qu'elle produit elle-même d'après ses propres plans,' ce qui est le contraire d'écouter. La démarche expérimental est soliloque plus que dialogue. L'idée centrale n'est pas ici celle de question, mais celle de réponse forcée. La réponse ne saurait aucune façon excède notre question.[141]

Chrétien's take on the Kantian approach to interrogation suggests a certain imposition of 'our' categories onto nature, an 'epistemic violence'. In contrast, what I have aimed to show is that there is a dynamism and reciprocity to the Augustinian sense of interrogation, in which the world can also come to one. This movement involves an aspect of hermeneutical intuition: one is summoned, called, invited by the 'question-able' reality in front of one. One simultaneously knows it and does not. One is invited to investigate it further and from that enquiry derive important cognitive knowledge. This whole process, though it certainly relies on 'empirical' sense data, is enabled, as Augustine suggests in *Gn. litt.*, by the direction of one's intellect, of one's perceiving of *cognoscenda* and one's undertaking efforts to examine them further.[142]

One can find some support for this view from a surprising source. In his work on the history of scientific revolutions, Kuhn writes of the directed-ness to scientific enquiry, even at the most rudimentary level. One's experiments are dictated by the theoretical commitments, and therefore the hypotheses, which one formulates.[143] These insights, according to Bernstein, were occasioned by the growing awareness in the twentieth century of the importance of interpretation and how it figures in every form of enquiry.[144] One has a certain expectation, a fore-understanding of what one will discover, and accordingly one seeks to confirm or challenge it. Even the design and deployment of apparatus and instruments involve this intentional element. In addition, the appearance of anomaly, itself a driver of scientific advancement, only appears as such against the backdrop of some rational expectation.[145] In other words, guided by a certain hermeneutical sensibility, one is able to see what is 'questionable'. Indeed, this suggests a certain dialectical relation between the empirical and the intentional, insofar as 'empirical' perception is already linked with the intentional and presupposes it, and further perception encourages theoretical revision and precision, which leads in turn to novel and different sense perceptions. The questioning aspect of scientific investigation is not completely open, but is rather directed and guided by particular standards and expectations.[146] Moreover, certain implied restrictions are placed on the type or the scope of potential solutions to a given quandary, as well as on the methods appropriate to ascertaining an answer.[147]

Conclusion

A major result of the foregoing chapter is a reversal of the way in which reason is understood. In other words, rational enquiry, even if guided by presuppositions and faith commitments, need not result in dogmatism, fideism or question-begging. We can note two key points. First, one's articulation of a question is a response to a summons from outwith. The beginning of one's enquiry is framed by the reality present to one. Furthermore, this framing is always incomplete, in virtue of both the inherent limitations of one's personal knowledge and the finitude of the outside world. As a result – and this is the second key point – true novelty and interruption remain possibilities, whether discoveries in terms of content or the disclosure of previously unrecognized prejudices. Interrogation, as we have noted, involves a certain presentiment of the type of answer one expects to receive, but a true question allows room for surprise or difference. Lawrence encapsulates this point in the following way: 'Conscious intentionality *as questioning* safeguards meaning from becoming a *closed* totality, while not completely forsaking all definition.'[148] Here we also see a felicitous *uia media* between modern and postmodern versions of rationality. We come to see rationality in terms of being addressed first from without, and subsequently responding. Furthermore, as we shall see in the next chapter, this process is deepened and continued especially as one realizes one's prejudices *as* prejudices, and foregrounds them so that one can understand what is already there.

So, grounded in our initial capacity to see in a way which exceeds the bonds of the 'merely' empirical, we are led to a further dialogue with creation around us. In fact, we are led to recognize its beauty and grandeur, in virtue of its intelligibility. From this, our soul conducts a dialogue with the world. What does it say to us? Creation speaks of its beauty, to be sure, but this declaration is always indexed to its source; Augustine reports the inherently apophatic, referential nature of the world's speech. Above all, it declares the glory and the infinite source of its beauty, namely God. An attentive listener to the cosmos realizes in this dialogue the nature of one's limitations. We are directed towards the source not just of natural bodies, but of our own being and our rational faculties. This realization may surprise us. In the hermeneutical process itself, such prejudices must be distinguished one from the other.[149] In this case of listening to nature, our prejudice of finitude is disclosed, which is to say our extension in space and time.

Once the prejudice of our four-dimensional situation is foregrounded, remarkable leaps in knowledge and insight become possible. However, Augustine goes further in what he has to say about our prejudices. He wishes to challenge not simply our prejudices of time and space, but even the notion of dimensionality itself, a result of created corporeality.

6

Exploring Creation: Acknowledging and Transcending Our Finitude

Introduction

The foregoing part of this enquiry has led us to the following point: we are finite. What may seem like a trivial observation is replete with epistemic meaning and significance according to Augustine. We learn this from our dialogue with reality, the result of a more fundamental capacity to see its intelligibility and to listen to it speaking to us. Once we have realized this, we are now ready to deepen our attunement and engage in dialogue. What we have been told by being, however, is even more cryptic, concealing more than it reveals. In order to understand the importance of our finitude, one can apply Gadamer's concept of prejudice to our spatio-temporal situation.

Earlier I characterized Augustine's account of time as *distentio* as 're-descriptive'. By that, I meant the following. Augustine at first blush is not putting forward a normative claim about what time should be, or what it should mean for human rationality. Rather, he is attempting to determine the way in which we interact with(in) time, and from there to determine what if any consequences there are for us as human beings, particularly for our knowledge and reason. From that descriptive basis, as Hannan also writes, one can be led to formulating prescriptive claims. As I see it, at this stage Augustine's re-description of time can be cast in a new light. The very act of identifying time as *distentio* represents a foregrounding of one's spatio-temporal prejudice. By identifying a prejudice *as* a prejudice, one is then enabled to transcend it. This will be the focus of what follows, in particular how the foregrounding of our ontological prejudice is possible and the extent to which that allows us to transcend our finite spatio-temporal situation.

As we saw in the previous chapter, Augustine goes in search of God in the world around him. Finding that the external world is not itself divine, Augustine is re-directed inward, searching for the divine within the recesses of his own heart. However, although his mind is superior to the things it judges, it shows that he himself is finite. In the search for the infinite, unconditioned God, Augustine finds that he must even go beyond himself.

Following Augustine in his search for God, we come to the point at which we must transcend our very selves, for we are also created, and God is unlike anything which has been made. But what does it mean, what could it mean, to go beyond oneself? As curious as the task may seem, Augustine believes not only that this is possible, but also that it has already been accomplished, in particular by John the Evangelist.

Some of the paradox of self-transcendence dissolves when we remember the basic fact of historical distance. As Chrétien explains,

> A la différence de la philosophie contemporaine, 'autrui' n'est pas pour la pensée antique le titre d'une question majeure, précisément parce qu'il va de soi, et que nous sommes toujours avec lui. La 'subjectivité' leur étant inconnue, les penseurs de l'Antiquité ne se demandent pas comment je peux sortir de la mienne pour aller vers celle d'autrui, et saint Augustin à cet égard est en continuité avec eux.[1]

Antiquity knew not the concept of 'subjectivity', nor the sharp contrast between 'self' and 'other'.[2] Furthermore, as Cilleruelo explains, Augustine 'divides' our interiority between the *citerior* and the *ulterior*, the 'nearer' and the 'farther'.[3] God resides in the 'ulterior interior', and hence for Augustine the move to the inside is never a merely subjective move which draws one away from some communal, shared being.[4] The result is that God is 'interioridad trascendente'.[5] In a sense, therefore, Augustine sees one as already beyond oneself by being with(in) oneself.

Furthermore, commentators on Augustine rightly emphasize that the turn inward is a means to an end and not an end in itself: 'Le retour en soi,' writes Chrétien, 'est une étape nécessaire, moment inaugural qui a la force d'une aurore, en vue de la rencontre de Dieu, mais ce n'est qu'une étape, et non le but lui-même.'[6] Were this to become an end in itself, then such a movement would be circular and vain.[7] The goal rather is to surpass even oneself, such that one can be opened to a divine encounter: 'Le but est de se dépasser, de se transcender pour s'accomplir. Qui se franchit seul se trouve, car il se laisse exposer à la rencontre sans laquelle il ne ferait que se consumer circulairement, et vainement.'[8] God resides within, and when we forget him, it is as if we are leaving ourselves and closing the door behind us, even to the point of forgetting that this inner locus of encounter exists.[9]

Finitude

Previously in this enquiry, I discussed Augustine's conception of time and space, and how these are ineluctable characteristics of corporeal, material creation. In fact, Augustine's understanding of time finds its basis in the two creation narratives of Genesis. In one, creation is given to be, whereas in another it gradually comes to be over the course of a 'week'. In virtue of being created, material entities are expressed in material form. As they move, grow and suffer change and decay, time itself arises, indeed, is constituted by this corporeal motion. We of course are material beings, and so we experience space and time in such a way that it impinges upon our very being, our cognition and our capacity for knowledge. In virtue of being situated spatially, our perspective is conditioned and limited. This is true not only of our 'physical' sense of sight, but also of our knowledge in general, insofar as our knowledge is mediated through the material world. Furthermore, in virtue of being spatial, we are also temporal. Especially in Augustine's *conf.* the temporal nature of our being comes to the fore, insofar as we are in tension, torn apart as a result of our call to the eternal whilst situated within time. His description of corporeality and the epistemic implications it entails resonates with Gadamer's understanding of prejudice and horizon, insofar as in virtue of being constituted as material beings we are afforded access to the world, indeed, biases of openness towards the world, and yet in virtue of these same biases we stand in danger of being blinded to truth.

We are led to the conclusion that our four-dimensional world of time and space, and time and space themselves, are not the defining characteristics of the real. Our creaturely status constitutes an inherent limitation on us.[10] Augustine himself suggests such a position when he quotes Paul (2 Cor. 5.6), stating, 'As long as we are in the body we wander away from the Lord.'[11] According to G. Ripanti, the term *peregrinatio* in Augustine refers to the human situation in the grand scope of salvation history, in particular in existential and moral terms.[12] The reason for this distance from God is that in this world, we must combat the constant assaults of the flesh. Even if we resist them successfully, they nonetheless enervate us: 'If however we may be victorious by not consenting, we nevertheless suffer trouble by resisting delights.'[13] Augustine also suggests that the mere bodily necessities of our quotidian existence exert some limiting effect on us, which could be realized in an epistemic way.[14] Moreover, as I see it, in addition to the vexations of our corporeal existence, our spatio-temporal situation inherently conditions our epistemic perspective, a limitation that an incorporeal being would not suffer. Hence man and his measures are not the measures of all things.[15] This is a weighty proposition in itself, but must also be taken into consideration in the revision of one's hermeneutical framework. A major challenge to our prejudices is the concept of the incorporeal, the timeless, the eternal, the implications of which are discussed by Augustine, especially as pertains to human knowing and finite *being-in-the-world*. For Augustine, the active initiation of God is required for transcendence to be realized.[16] But this is mediated through the material world.[17] One's prejudices are not only challenged by new objects; a series of different objects is insufficient without divine aid, re-orienting one's perspective.[18]

In this respect, Augustine lauds the virtue of continence, in particular because of its unifying and ordering effect on the soul, which rescues one from the snares of division and separation in the distention of spatio-temporal existence. As he writes, 'through continence we are collected and returned into one, from which we have flowed out into many things.'[19] Augustine employs the term for collecting (*colligimur*) and describes the effect of virtue as a return to inner unity.[20] Drawing a contrast between the many things of temporal existence as opposed to the enduring unity of the eternal (*inter [Deum] et nos multos*),[21] he claims that the soul's task is to recollect itself, to be collected and made a unity, indeed, the unity which reflects God's eternity and which allows one to contain a serene sight within oneself.[22] As Nightingale explains, the power of *continentia* is to pacify bodily desires – desires for material things – for the sake of unification.[23] Though this virtue is often viewed in terms of avoiding some sort of act, usually sexual, Augustine's approach to this character trait is far deeper and more comprehensive.[24] Rather, continence is that virtue which enables us to be reunited, as we have been scattered and torn apart in the multiplicity of material reality.[25] The need for this virtue stems from the fact that *memoria* alone is not sufficient for the task of attaining *sapientia*; continence therefore is needed to counteract the debilitating and distracting effects of various thoughts.[26] One can then hope for the complete integration of the self in eternity, improving and working gradually here on earth towards that goal.[27]

Though he does not use *ipsissima uerba*, Augustine here invokes a notion found in other writings of his, namely the *simplex cor*, by which he means to designate the unity of the mind's faculty of willing and knowing the good. The heart is pulled hither, thither and yon by multifarious (corporal) desires, preventing one from focusing on the timeless, eternal goal of union with God in heaven, challenging and competing with the divine voice in one: 'But how will [the heart] be simple, if it serves two masters, if it does not purify its vision by the one focus on eternal things, but clouds it by the love of mortal and fleeting things?'[28] When Augustine famously discusses time in the latter books of his *conf.*, one of the points he is considering is the way in which corporal things distract the soul from its ultimate destiny in the immutable and eternal God. The *distentio* of the soul, its condition of being stretched, is caused by the unrelenting flow of time in which one is implicated. This entire process of re-collecting oneself tends towards the acquisition of truth, and hence one's participation in God's beautiful *ordo*, which begets peace in the soul.[29] Thus the task of the soul was to 'synchronize' the clock of one's own incarnate life with that of the celestial cycles, to discern how heaven is reflected on earth.[30]

Augustine's psalm example from the *conf.* serves to illustrate his theory of 'four-dimensional' cognition. Before he begins to recite, the entirety of the psalm is held in his memory (*in totum expectatio mea tenditur*) in a sort of timeless way, all together, yet losing none of its inherent variations.[31] As he begins to recite it, the synthetic concept of the song must be stretched, as that is simply the way in which a song is sung or a poem recited in time.[32] As he proceeds, the psalm gradually extends into the past and the future, the former, as this is the memory of what Augustine has just recited (*cum autem coepero, quantum ex illa in praeteritum decerpsero, tenditur et memoria mea*),[33] and the latter, in preparation for what must follow (*in expectationem propter quod dicturus sum*).[34] This linear process ultimately concludes when the entirety of the recitation has gone from the future to the past via the present, so to speak, and is thus contained in the memory as a past event entirely.[35]

Furthermore, he writes that this description can apply at the macro- as well as the micro-level. In addition to the overall song itself, Augustine sees this process at work with respect to the smaller constituent parts, even to the individual syllables (*quod in toto cantico, hoc in singulis particulis eius, hoc in actione longiore, cuius forte particula est illud canticum*).[36] Moreover, his understanding of time as a stretching or distention is intended to encompass all human activity, whether the recitation of a song or any other aspect of one's life. Augustine's song illustration is very deliberate. He believes that the description of the mind's activity in reciting this psalm reflects its overall activity in a temporal world: 'This in the whole life of a person, the parts of which are all the actions of a person, this in the entire age of the children of men, the parts of which are all the lives of men.'[37] Augustine's identification of the example of the song as illustrative of a broader human reality implies a re-description of time as *distentio*, which is *ipso facto* a foregrounding of the ontological prejudice of temporal extension.

In a sense, what Augustine is outlining in *conf.* 10 and 11 is a programme for challenging and ultimately transcending those spatio-temporal prejudices which constitute our directedness with respect to the world around us. He enables us to see that space and time are not some absolute realities, in the sense that though they condition us and provide us with our initial openness to the world, they can nonetheless obscure and obfuscate the truth as well. Our epistemic faculties are blocked due to a variety of factors, whether deriving from sin or human finitude. Furthermore, and as a result of this, we are 'prejudiced' in favour of physical and material conceptions of God, trying to fit him into our finite categories.[38] Those enslaved to the *carnalis consuetudo* are only capable of conceiving of God according to a spatio-temporal logic.[39] In order to think of God truly, one cannot think of him as spatial (*nullus cogitetur per locorum spatia*).[40] Augustine realizes this, and thus also delineates a path whereby one can counteract, challenge and potentially overcome the inherently limiting effects of the four-dimensional characteristics of human existence, yet passing through them at the same time. This 'horizontal' description of time prepares us for a vertical treatment of the same theme. In other words, we have only begun to bracket our spatio-temporal conditions, as Augustine thinks that this activity of coming to recognize our finitude and our corporeality is propaedeutic to, if not constitutive of, (self-)transcendence.

An early work contains a brief discussion of self-transcendence which can provide some initial guidance on the question at hand. In *uera rel.*, Augustine seeks to plot a course whereby the soul may turn back to its creator, whence it has absconded.[41] Augustine is attempting to understand the meaning of true worship, and he construes this in both philosophical and biblical terms.[42] He envisions the unity of salvation and knowledge in God.[43] As Lössl writes, *uera religio* 'is at the same time philosophy and religion, which is true wisdom, wisdom incarnate'.[44]

In *uera rel.* we find a set of familiar themes which ground Augustine's argument. As in *Gn. litt.*, he asserts that God made all things through his wisdom, or his Son, and in the love of the Spirit.[45] God is the supreme fullness of being, whilst all other creatures are limited in their being and are hence mutable.[46] The One is also described as 'truth itself'.[47] However, Augustine never separates *sapientia* from the practical and the incarnate, even if this is ultimately more than that.[48] He holds that the One becomes incarnate in order to direct the fallen world back to its source.[49] The opposition of being and nothingness forms the basis for a discussion of epistemic matters.[50] As Lössl explains, it is a return from the abyss and the unintelligibility of sin to God, the fullness of light, life and being.[51]

In a phrase which has now become famously associated with Augustine, he writes, *Noli foras ire* – do not go outside, but return into yourself (*redi in teipsum*), for 'truth dwells in the inner man'.[52] Immediately after the call to turn inward, Augustine writes that even this is insufficient, suggesting that one should also transcend oneself. If one discovers that one's nature is mutable (which of course, it is), one must transcend that as well. Augustine is careful to note that in doing this, one even transcends the reasoning soul (*ratiocinantem animam*).[53] One must realize that one is not the truth, even if the truth dwells within one. Rather, one must seek the truth, which is itself superior and absolute, and need not move or go anywhere in search of truth, for it is itself truth. One arrives at this truth not in a spatial way (*non locorum spatio*) but by a mental disposition (*mentis affectu*).[54] Hence the completion of the search for truth is the interior person's dwelling with its neighbour, the truth, who is Christ.[55] As we shall see, this trajectory is replicated in the *Tractatus*, in which John is cited as one who *actually* accomplished this; the admonition to self-transcendence is therefore not 'merely' theoretical.

One lesson that we can derive from the foregoing is that transcendence, aside from being a mental and a non-physical process, is not so much about leaving something behind, namely the soul. Indeed, truth dwells within the soul; therefore, to transcend the soul or one's interiority does not mean to go beyond it or leave it behind. Rather, it seems that transcendence can be understood more in terms of an acknowledgement, an appreciation, a recognition, a disposition, i.e. allowing oneself to be open to the truth within. Hence transcendence acquires a character which is simultaneously active and passive, or even beyond this division. The interior dwelling of God is at the basis of the admonition to return within oneself. But Augustine continues, urging one to transcend the self if one finds that it is mutable. Ultimately one arrives at the realization that the inner self has a permanent guest, as it were.[56] Moreover, Wetzel suggests that the realization of the conversion experience in Augustine consists in recognizing what is already there, namely God and his providential presence to the soul ('his recognition that the divine presence had been there all along').[57] As Chrétien writes, 'pour Augustin, la "vérité" est un nom divin, comme le montrent ses preuves de l'existence de Dieu, et le chemin vers l'intérieur, vers le centre de soi, loin de conduire à se reconnaitre comme source, invite à dépasser ce que j'ai de plus haut ou de plus profond, à me découvrir, au sens fort, habité ou habitable par une autre présence que la mienne.'[58]

John as transcender

To this point the discussion of this chapter may read as abstract, so much so as to be disconnected from the lived experience of the lay Christian. But Augustine does not see it this way. Rather, he views transcendence and contemplation as the essence of the truly religious life. What's more, he sees this as a possibility for everyone. Looking to scripture for theological inspiration, Augustine uses the figure of John as an example for his congregation.

In the twentieth tractate, Augustine elaborates upon the transcendence of John broached in the first tractate. Here he outlines a path of ascent to God, which proceeds from the exterior to the interior to the superior.[59] One can examine corporeal creation, and realize that it is inherently mutable, finite, transitory and unstable.[60] From this, one proceeds to think about 'celestial bodies' which, though of far greater beauty and radiance than the former, are still nonetheless finite.[61] One must transcend even these things (*transi et ipsa*).[62] This is the point at which one moves from the exterior to the interior. Augustine raises the question of how one considered the foregoing corporeal realities.[63] The agent of the consideration of these things was none other than the mind which, although spiritual and not bodily, is nonetheless finite still (*animus ergo iste spiritus est, non corpus: transi et ipsum*).[64] Despite the fact that the mind is superior to the foregoing corporeal objects (*quamuis melior sit omni corpore*) and a great thing itself,[65] it is nonetheless mutable.[66] As we have seen, the mark of the real is not so much that which is seen or not seen with the corporeal eyes, but that which does not admit of (the possibility of) change.[67] Even a spirit or a spiritual being admits of change and flux, even in living eternally, whereas God alone is truly unchanging and unchangeable.[68] Hence Augustine encourages one to 'Therefore go beyond all mutability, not only everything which is seen, but also everything which changes'.[69] Having moved through all corporeal creation, we arrive at our soul, the interior. Yet even here, having discovered mutability, which does not pertain to God in any way, we must also transcend it.[70] As Augustine explains, 'For now that these things have been accomplished, you had come to your mind, but you also discovered there the mutability of your mind. Is God mutable? Surely not. Therefore surpass your mind as well. Pour your soul over yourself, so that you may touch God.'[71] In other words, here Augustine describes the second moment of the process of transcendence, the movement from the interior to the superior.

Augustine states that the mind or the soul is superior to the corporeal creation it considers.[72] Not only is it able to manage and contain these things within itself, but its operations of discursive thought are not bound by the activities of the bodies themselves.[73] In other words, one can call to mind immediately the sun and the moon, or their heavenly gyres, without having to wait for them to perform these in time and space.[74] The first step on the path of transcendence is to move ourselves away from the carnal world.[75] Yet this is still not sufficient, as we are occupied with mental images rather than God himself.[76] Hence Augustine emphasizes the importance of exceeding even the mind itself in order to know God: 'Transcend the body, and taste the mind; transcend the mind as well, and taste God. You do not touch God, unless you will have also transcended the mind.'[77] Hence Augustine encourages one with the following words: 'Take yourself from the body, transcend even yourself.'[78] This process of 'self-transcendence' is described in Ps. 41.4-5, in which the soul pours itself out over itself.[79] Augustine treats this passage, writing that 'I have not poured my soul over my flesh, but over me: I have transcended myself, so that I might touch him. For he who made me is above me; no one attains to him, except who will have transcended themselves.'[80] This demarcation of the soul with respect to created reality shows that for Augustine, self-transcendence is tantamount to transcendence of all creation. For by means of the mind or the soul, one can transcend all of the corporeal world outside of oneself. It remains to transcend spiritual created reality – that is, one's own mind.

What may seem like a hopeless or quixotic task is nothing of the sort for Augustine, for in the following paragraph, he proceeds to counter such a thought with an example of someone who has successfully transcended all of created, mutable reality, and arrived at God himself.[81] As he states in the first tractate, Augustine claims that John transcended himself and all creation.[82] John's transcendence is described in terms of the foregoing ascent from and through corporeal reality, ultimately arriving at his own mind, the inner part of himself: 'he transcended all spirits which are not seen, he transcended his own mind by the very reason of his mind.'[83] Paradoxically, John's mind supplies and sustains the means by which he can exceed it, namely *ratio*.[84] The operation of the rational mind opens it to that which exceeds and conditions it, a movement enabled by the presence of the divine within the soul already.[85]

John had ceased to be 'merely' human and had begun to be angelic in the way he perceived reality.[86] Of course, elsewhere in Augustine's voluminous corpus we read that the angels see God without any passage of time, that they perceive in an eternal way which is not subject to the spatio-temporal extension that we experience on earth.[87] Augustine seems to recognize the surprising nature of this claim, but does not back down. Rather, he substantiates this by appeal to Ps. 81.6, in which we are called 'gods, and sons of the most high'.[88] God calls us above and beyond ourselves, lest we remain ('merely') human.[89] In order to transcend our human nature, we must first acknowledge it.[90] We rise to God by humility.[91] We must recognize our creaturely finitude and our dependence upon God.[92] Paradoxically, when we transcend ourselves we are most human and yet cease to be human; we acknowledge our finitude, from which we can begin to recognize the need for assistance in the quest for transcendence and attaining to God.[93] Paradoxically, one becomes worthy by confessing one's unworthiness.

One must keep in mind that for Augustine, transcendence is a mental activity, and not a spatial or physical one (*non carne transis, sed mente*).[94] This point is crucial for his thought: in its essence, the mind is immaterial and hence offers us a step to transcendence.[95] If one is able, one perceives the incorporeality of God by the mind itself.[96] Elsewhere in the *Tractatus*, Augustine similarly suggests that it is by means of one's thought that one does this (*ut excedas cogitatione tua omne quod factum est*).[97] Hence it becomes clear that he sees self-transcendence as a mental process whereby one comes to acknowledge the finitude and mutability of all reality, in contrast to God.[98] Going beyond the self therefore comes to mean not so much an 'out-of-body experience' or having anything to do with movement or motion, so much as one comes to realize the fact, so obvious that it is hidden, of our created-ness: being created by and grounded in God.[99] We come to see what is already there.[100] This is what one might call the 'Augustinian reversal';[101] it is not truth which is difficult, obscure or opaque, but we.[102] In the previous chapter, we witnessed how a theory of knowledge informed by Augustine leads us to reverse the dynamic of reason as it is commonly understood. We do not begin an investigation on our own; rather, we are first addressed and subsequently respond. In this chapter, we have added a further sense to this Augustinian reversal. Put another way, it is not as if one must go somewhere so much as remove the obstructions in oneself, to cleanse *the doors of perception*[103] and thus re-orient one's vision so as to see what was already present to one.[104] A crucial point follows from this, as such an acknowledgement would require one to exceed the 'merely' intellectual and lead to a confession of one's dependence. As Drever writes, the doctrine of *creatio ex nihilo* essentially means that one is not the source of one's being, but rather that this is rooted in God.[105] This doctrine carries certain implications for how one understands the human person.[106] When one transcends all created things, by recognizing their source in the infinite God, one is said to pour oneself out over oneself as John did (*transcendens ista omnia, super se effundens animam suam*),[107] for it is in this act of recognition that one surrenders oneself to God.[108]

According to Augustine, John's theophanic experience serves as an aid for those of us who are not gifted in the way the Evangelist is.[109] Even so, one needs help in order to interpret or understand his words, for which we require divine assistance.[110] John himself did not accomplish this great intellectual feat by his own efforts. Rather, he was illumined by God, and received special revelations when he rested his head on the Lord's chest at the Last Supper.[111] The transcendence of the self is a gift, indeed, a grace from God.[112] Later in this same work, Augustine confirms that John's perception of the *principium* was a divine gift, and that it was a direct revelation of the Holy Spirit.[113] God's incorporeality is one of those truths which the disciples 'could not bear' when Christ was with them, but which he taught them through the Spirit.[114]

Descent

We transcend ourselves, and yet, due to the frailty of our finitude, we descend.[115] But the descent allows us to see the world anew. Once we have returned to the world, we can begin to see it in its true form, as a reflection of the divine. G. Boersma's treatment of *uera rel.* is helpful in this respect. He suggests that the ascent of the soul consists in perceiving *imago* in a different way; it is not a movement or a discovering of something new.[116] It is a matter of seeing the *imago* according to a different aspect, coming to see what is already there. Boersma also notes the important difference between knowledge or understanding on the one hand and judgement on the other. The former pertains to the descriptive recognition of a fact, whereas the latter pertains to the normative evaluation of this fact with respect to a (superior) standard.[117] For Augustine, this standard is none other than *sapientia*, the source of all being, present to the human mind.[118] Furthermore, the emphasis on understanding an image as derived from its source underscores the importance of Augustine's overarching view of participation, that individual existents must be understood within the broader framework in which they obtain and participate. This framework is that of creation *in sapientia*.[119] Judging the flux and multiplicity of material reality according to the eternal standard of oneness and unity engenders in the soul that state required for perceiving the world in its proper order.[120] As Boersma pithily explains this point, 'The task of true philosophy' for Augustine 'is to judge all material images in light of this unity'.[121] The act of properly judging material reality in light of its source is itself contemplation.[122] The things of the world, when recognized for what they are, act as so many steps (*gradus*) to eternal and immutable things.[123]

We see a similar description in *conf.* 9 within the context of Augustine's ephemeral if direct contact with the divine. In the famous depiction of the mystical ascent with his mother, Augustine discusses rising to the heights of heavenly Wisdom, which admits of no temporal succession. As he writes, '[Wisdom] does not become, but it *is*, just as it was and ever shall be. Indeed, it is not in it to have been and to be about to be, but only to be, for wisdom is eternal: for it is not eternal to have been and to be about to be.'[124] Augustine states that the strength of the divine light was too much for him to bear, and so his ascent was limited in its success.[125] There is certainly clear textual evidence to support this reading (*repulsus; repercussa infirmitate*).[126] The more one enters the divine light, the more one sees one's frailty.[127] However, King complements this emphasis with a broader awareness of the ontological vision of Augustine. Even though Augustine's ascent is far from perfect, it is not thereby insignificant. One always descends with new insights and, indeed, as a new person. As he approaches nearer the light, Augustine is able to discover certain critical truths which will help him to continue this journey, in particular an awareness of his own finitude with respect to the ultimate immutability of God, and the epistemic implications it entails. What is ultimately responsible for Augustine's inability to gaze on the divine light is his finitude and temporal situation. Greater moral or spiritual fortitude, though helpful, would not be sufficient to overcome the ontological gap which obtains between Creator and creature.[128]

The theme of unity and multiplicity is fundamental to Augustine's view of ascent. By becoming more unified, we grow closer to God, imitating his unity.[129] In contrast, the multiplicity of individual created things overwhelms one and pulls one apart in a continuous stream of flux, a process accelerated and exacerbated by the fall: 'For the multiformity of temporal forms has split fallen man through the carnal senses and multiplied his affect in a changeable variety.'[130] In *uera rel.*, Augustine anticipates his later explanation of the morally debilitating effects of time as *distentio*, suggesting that the vicissitudes of time cause a certain attachment to temporal things within the soul.[131] One must purify oneself of the tendency to take the spatial and the temporal as the mark of the real.[132]

In addition to the sense of *imago* which is positive and pertains to the intrinsic being of an image, Augustine also speaks of the darker aspect of *imago* as that which is not real or derivative.[133] He uses *simulacrum* as a synonym for this sense, and relates it to the soul's attachment to the created world.[134] 'The problem with this second, negative sense of image,' according to Boersma, 'is that it absolutizes material, temporal existence.'[135] The result is that the very purpose and function of an image is frustrated, as it comes to block rather than facilitate access to its source.[136] To invoke a familiar Augustinian theme, it is not that the material world is itself evil, but rather the mind itself which judges it incorrectly (=*falsitas*), forgetting its ontological relation and dependence on something other than itself.[137] *Cupiditas* and *falsitas* are two different ways of viewing the same problem for Augustine, or they are two different manifestations of one and the same (false) judgement, namely mistaking a temporal, finite, material good for one which is eternal, infinite and immutable.[138] Put another way, Augustine envisions the same remedy for both vices, namely the correct judgement of material reality.[139] For Augustine, Boersma argues, the soul is led astray when it takes a temporal, transient, finite, created good, and clings to it as if it were infinite; one attempts to enjoy it rather than to use it.[140]

This Augustinian tenet is also reflected in hermeneutical thought. As S. Hannan writes, Heidegger views temporality as an essential aspect of *Dasein*'s situation within the world. In one's confrontation with reality, one must always recall one's finitude and temporal situation. Hence it is a mistake to attempt to 'univocalize' some particular object, treating it as if it were somehow permanent or eternal. Rather, one should let things come and go in their own order. In this way, one becomes a 'shepherd' of being(s) and becomes attentive to the natural order and harmony of being.[141] In Hannan's words, 'As shepherds of *Being*, not of beings, it is not our role to preserve beings in their particularity (thus risking *adikia*), but to instead remember the rhythm in which they arise and pass away.'[142]

It seems to me that the recognition of our finitude and the interrogation of all that it implies is what is necessary in order to advance in true knowledge and wisdom. We must acknowledge and subsequently challenge our ontological prejudices, and these insofar as they impede our epistemic and spiritual progress. In particular, Augustine asks us to leave behind our familiar world of time and space, of three spatial dimensions and one temporal one. According to Menn,

> we wrongly think that the concept of truth is unclear and that we would understand it better if we could picture it, and this attempt to fill out our knowledge of God by means of sensory images is just what conceals God from us. And this dissatisfaction with a purely intellectual grasp of God is in turn rooted in an affective turning away from God and toward the 'accustomed earthly things'.[143]

One turns from God by immersing oneself in the transience and the multiplicity of the world.[144] Knowing God implies going beyond the mutable order of things and recognizing their dependence upon the immutable God.[145] Augustine invites us to think in a way which is at odds with the capacities of our physical (and indeed, fallen) human nature. Nonetheless, as we straddle reality, we can make use of our mind to assemble a variety of elements and view them simultaneously by the mind's eye in a way that we never could with corporeal sight. Such a perception would not be synthetic in the sense that it would eliminate internal differentiation, but would rather be analytic, providing distinctions within the unity of the content.[146] Here we can also find the answer to why Augustine sees memory as so important: it is that capacity, animal though it may be, which allows us as rational beings to aspire to something of that atemporal way of knowing, by viewing the whole – not corporally, for that would not be possible, but according to the vision of our hearts, assembling the various threads of memories which will enable us to reproduce the whole they constitute, a whole which transcends the sum of its parts.

Just as the soul is stretched within space and time, in such a way that it is susceptible to valuing images of God over God himself, there is a sort of counter-stretching which occurs when the soul is 'set on fire' by divine love. As Ayres explains, a fervent 'desire for God stretches the soul away from the *spes saeculi*, the hope for worldly possessions and place'.[147] Such a desire breaks one's prejudice for the things of created reality.[148] The denouement of the foregrounding of this prejudice is to realize that the goal of the investigation of nature with respect to its divine origin is ultimately eschatological in character.[149] Augustine suggests the possibility that when we are perfected, we shall not see and know within a framework of temporal extension, but see all things together, in a way similar to how God sees them: 'Perhaps our thoughts will not be going and returning from certain things into others, but we shall see all our knowledge *together in one aspect*.'[150] Yet even if this is the case, he writes, such unity of vision should not be equated with that of God (*coaequanda [creatura] non erit illi simplicitati*), who is neither changed nor in principle capable of being changed, in stark contrast to his creation.[151]

We arrive once again at the Augustinian notion that everything besides God *tendit non esse*, which Heidegger understood as human non-being. To possess oneself for Heidegger is to recognize oneself in one's nihility.[152] Likewise for Augustine, as it is only when the soul draws near to God that it is, paradoxically, intrinsically complete.[153] This model is appreciated by theorists of hermeneutics and expressed in musical terms.[154] When a cello is played, it realizes its nature in virtue of emitting mellifluous sounds,[155] and thereby transcends itself. This image captures something of the dynamism of the self, as something which is continuously in flux, and in a sense constituted by this very indeterminacy and dynamism.[156] For Augustine, the proximity of the soul to God generates the spiritual resonance which allows the soul to become what it is intended to be. R. Williams captures this point when he writes, 'The image of God, in short, is realized when we come to be in conscious relation to the divine act that establishes the possibility of relation [...].'[157] In a post-Cartesian world, the reified self (what Taylor famously calls the 'buffered self' in *A Secular Age*),[158] against which Heidegger so strenuously reacted, is taken for granted. But for Augustine *the self is not a particular, defined or reified thing*.[159] This point can be seen in his understanding of *conscientia* as well. For Augustine, the conscience is a locus of contact between God and the soul, a place in which God is intimately and innately present to one's mind, always speaking to and communicating with one. Hence the tensile relationship between God and man just is constitutive of the conscience, or rather, *conscientia* is not so much *a* thing but the echoes of the divine voice in the heart.[160] One cultivates this interior space by means of prayer, a response to the silent call of God already present within one.[161] Creatures perfect their natures by turning to God, their light and source of being. In a sense their creation is continuously unfolding,[162] a movement encapsulated in Augustine's pithy prayer, that 'he who founded the earth may draw near to our minds'.[163]

Critical discussion

Our Interlocutor demurs:
Here I would like to renew my prior objection. This is the very point which a contemporary mind finds so objectionable in theology. It seems that you have attempted through a sneaky way to re-introduce the concept of infinity and transcendence into theology. You have ignored the hermeneutical admonition to recall human finitude and incorporate this into your theory of knowledge as a fundamental principle. You have simply re-presented premodern naïveté in a more sophisticated form, but thereby no less misguided. Taking post-modern philosophy seriously means rejecting any notion of the infinite, at least as it pertains to human reason. We are finite; we cannot think the infinite, or claim some knowledge of that type for ourselves. To do so is simply to relapse into the arrogance of past ages, in which we fail to appreciate the importance of our inherent human limitations. Ironically, your epistemic sin is none other than that original fault of pride, as you seek to Ascend to

Heav'n, by merit thine,[164] *thereby mimicking Satan,* Affecting all equality with God.[165]

I appreciate your objections. However, you fail to perceive a fundamental difference between a simple appeal to eternal ideas, and the position I present, namely that the knowledge of God's infinitude, transcendence and incorporeality, is the result of a divine gift and represents something adventitious to reason. As I have intended to demonstrate, Augustine wishes to reframe reason and knowledge by what I have called a reversal: rather than thinking in post-Cartesian terms about the human mind plundering nature for its secrets, secrets disclosed from a purely active investigation, my view holds that reason is first addressed, and only in virtue of being addressed comes to question and discover. Now if reason is understood as initially responsive and from there initiating a conversation, then this passivity of listening must be taken seriously. By passivity I mean that the message has priority over one. One receives it first and must be truly receptive to it. According to Chrétien, theology itself constitutes a response to a summons. It is given a content of which it must make some sense. Most importantly, however, it does not have the prerogative to choose its (types of) gods.[166] Now, on the basis of hermeneutics alone, there is no reason to suppose that a message regarding God's infinitude or his transcendence, for example, should be excluded. According to Romele, Gadamer was informed by the (Protestant) notion that a word from without can truly surprise us.[167] Zimmermann echoes this point, claiming that Gadamer's exclusion of revelation as a basis for philosophy does not necessarily follow from his hermeneutics.[168] In fact, the a priori exclusion of such a message would not only be against the principles a hermeneutical consciousness espouses, but would also subtly fall prey to the very modern view it wishes to critique, namely one according to which transcendence and immanence are mutually exclusive *de iure*. True, the message is always received according to the mode of the recipient. But even the reception of this message challenges those very categories of reception. One is caught between knowing and not knowing. Indeed, this is why a distinction between comprehension and vision is so crucial.[169] Without this, you would likely be correct. One who would want to maintain the place of transcendence within a contemporary hermeneutical theology would need to motivate and maintain a distinction of this type.

Following Fishbane, we can note a further epistemic implication which arises from the foregoing discussion of finitude, which is demonstrated by the plurality of cultures and hermeneutical frameworks in our world.[170] The realization of diversity impels us to conversation and dialogue, to learn from others and to collaborate in the search for truth.[171] The Jewish tradition allows for the maintaining of several truths simultaneously.[172] The call to co-operation, rooted in an authentic appreciation of our finitude, leads us to see God's presence even in the most mundane realities.[173] Gadamer too suggests the possibility of a complementarity of a number of perspectives and approaches to one and the same subject matter.[174] The commitment to a hermeneutical understanding of human finitude results in a methodological approach which is conversational and complementary. 'Such a method,' Wachterhauser writes, 'could never be discovered by one person, however brilliant, but rather it must represent the accumulated wisdom of a community of inquirers.'[175] For example, for Fishbane, death would not represent the dualistic, 'Manichaean' antithesis to life. Life and death together reveal something of the full reality of God. Together they speak of infinity, as both are essential components in the mystery of creation.[176]

Augustine also suggests a similar approach to complementarity in terms of his (biblical) hermeneutics. In the twelfth book of *conf.*,[177] Augustine concerns himself with the various possibilities for interpreting and understanding the term *in principio*.[178] Here Augustine endorses the idea that a variety of interpretations of a particular passage may be apt.[179] This position is grounded in the nature of the biblical text itself. In virtue of being composed by God, scripture can be said to be filled with an inexhaustible depth of meaning.[180] In fact, Augustine claims that this was God's intention in the first place.[181] The basic reason for his position is the idea that God is the author not only of scripture but also of history, and so in his providence the Bible comes to admit of the susceptibility of indefinite true interpretations.[182] Augustine adopts a fundamentally hermeneutical approach to scripture; like literature, it admits of the possibility of an indefinite number of valid interpretations, though that is not to say that just any interpretation is valid.[183] Augustine claims that God ordained it such that many interpretations would be possible, though not all thereby equal.[184] Again, the positing of multiple meanings present in scripture is rooted in the idea that its source is ultimately divine.[185] Augustine's hermeneutic for scripture is a broad one, welcoming a spectrum of readings *de iure*.[186] In my estimation, this leads to an interesting result: In addition to being the author of scripture, God is the principle behind the universe, sustaining within it the plethora of potential truth which can arise out of it.[187] Our finitude implies that we must seek complementarity, but not thereby a misplaced egalitarianism, according to which one point of view is *ipso facto* seen as just as good as another. Hermeneutics also requires hierarchy, order and parsing.

Pride as prejudice

We have seen how every movement of ecstasy also involves a descent, a return. Yet this return is always with new eyes, which allow us to re-orient our perspective on the world. One way in which this occurs is through realizing how our spatio-temporal situation constitutes a prejudice, which in turn leads us to such actions as engaging in a dialogical search for truth. A further implication is identifying another hindrance to our acceptance of truth, what Augustine would call pride or sin.

In my treatment of Augustinian illumination, I identified two aspects to the gradual sense of reason, that is, two ways in which our ability to know is limited, conditioned or hindered. I have construed both of these, namely sin and finitude, as prejudices in Gadamer's sense of the term. I have already dealt with finitude. Now I wish to deal with sin, or more specifically its source in Augustine's view, namely pride. Unlike finitude, which is basically good or neutral, sin is an inherently obstructive prejudice, the sort that Gadamer identifies as a constant impediment to knowledge if it is not foregrounded, critiqued and ultimately jettisoned. In the following section, I elaborate upon my glossing of 'pride as prejudice'.

Our minds fail to comprehend God's grandeur, not least of all when we are led to think in ways that exceed our spatio-temporal categories.[188] In order to do this, we need God's help, and Augustine states that this help comes in the form of illumination, an enlightenment which allows us to have some understanding of God.[189] When it comes to understanding things that are truly, radically transcendent, Augustine states that the proper attitude for approaching them is not one of understanding.[190] From the outset, one is in error if one presumes that all objects of cognition are somehow comprehensible to a human mind, in particular a human mind bound to finite categories.[191] Rather, one must approach them in a spirit of silence, reservation, contemplation and participation; one must enter into them in order to engage with these truths or these ideas.[192] Some things are *de iure* beyond human capacity to comprehend, and so rational minds 'ought not reach out to incomprehensible things as if they are about to understand, but rather about to participate'.[193] At this point, we hardly need to be reminded of Augustine's position that God is beyond all change and mutability, in contrast to creation.[194] Whilst we cannot comprehend this, we can and are even summoned to participate in it.[195] In particular, we are made partakers in God's immortality and eternity in virtue of Christ's Incarnation and all which it entails.[196] Augustine sees a fitting symmetry here, insofar as Christ takes on our nature so that ultimately, we may take on something of his.[197] (In fact, what is suggested here is a variation on the theme of re-creation.) A necessary condition for such participation is not so much philosophical speculation per se, as this is in principle ineffable.[198] Augustine rather encourages confession and penance performed for sins, which will allow God further and further to direct and heal the soul and restore it to health.[199] The key is that with God's help, things which were once considered impossible for the human soul will no longer be so.[200]

If objects of this sort exist, then one's engagement with them cannot be one of univocal, 'mathematical' reasoning. Faith works especially against the pride of philosophical thinking – that is, thinking detached from the grounding principle of the Word.[201] Faith also enables the humility necessary to grow in truth.[202] Faith for Augustine is an existential act, and not merely an external confession. One does not really have faith until one realizes one's utter nothingness or 'nihility' before God and one's dependence on him. Only such a realization can lead one to the intellectual 'hermeneutic' of humility which is so necessary to reason.[203] In this way, one recognizes the order established in creation by God.[204] Pride comes to be seen as an intellectual fault as well, insofar as one fails to appreciate one's epistemic situation. This is the fault that Heidegger ascribes to the modern reification of the self, a forgetfulness of one's 'nihility'.

Humility is like a weight of sorts, keeping one's feet on the path of faith and sustaining one in one's journey, leading to wisdom and truth.[205] Similarly, Augustine describes the opposition between *caritas* and *superbia* as the difference between sustaining one on the path and making one fall.[206] Pride causes one to think that one is in a different place than one actually is. Clearly this can assume multiple senses. Just as one trips and falls on steps when one thinks one's foot is in a place that it is not, so too does pride cause one to falter epistemically, as one thinks that one is in a different conceptual location than one actually is.[207] Hence Augustine encourages one to be humble, which is to think in accordance with the truth of one's own situation.[208] In this way, one's foot will not be moved.[209] Humility provides a sure support against temptation, and sustains one in the ascent to God.[210]

One must acknowledge and appreciate one's limits, and the fact that one is not the source of one's own happiness or satisfaction.[211] Augustine intimates that when we acknowledge the superiority of God, we are able to situate the constituents of reality in their proper normative setting.[212] This lesson is as much epistemic as it is spiritual.[213] This becomes clear when considerations of light are introduced into this same paragraph of this *enarratio*. Even those of great faith and intellect are not the source of their own light but are illumined from beyond. However, when one prefers oneself as a source of light, it only results in one's becoming darkness.[214] Those who are truly humble and happy are those who realize that they are not the source of their own good.[215] The acknowledgement of our dependence on God can amount to a confession which solidifies the heart: 'That confession forms the heart and makes it a foundation of love.'[216]

Augustine recognizes in creation a hierarchy of goods; not all things are created equal.[217] The enquiry into creation moves through images, yes, but there is an inherent hierarchy of images, according to Augustine's schema. The movement from creatures to the Creator passes through the creature who, though not God, is nonetheless given the gift of knowing itself, a gift it possesses in virtue of being created according to that divine image to which it is summoned to return.[218] In order to find truth, it is essential that we know how to perceive this hierarchy of beings and then interpret and relate them appropriately to one another.[219] In my estimation, Augustine is claiming that our sense of values influences the judgements we make, as well as the way in which we interpret the relationships between particular things. In turn, these judgements then influence our hermeneutical frameworks. This relies upon an 'intentional' way of looking, and one which is able to recognize, as Heidegger would say, that there is more present than meets the eye.[220] This tends toward questions which are ultimately metaphysical, normative and theological.

A major error according to Augustine can be explained by appeal to the gospel passage in which Christ tells his followers not to let the left hand know what the right is doing. Augustine interprets this to mean that we should not confuse a temporal good with an eternal one: 'Whatever we possess temporally is called our left hand; whatever eternal and unchangeable which the Lord promises to us is called our right.'[221] Indeed, it is a great error to reverse the understanding of these goods, a belief which influences the rest of one's commitments, such that one requires only temporal goods in order to attain beatitude.[222] As Augustine puts it, 'That man is foolish and perverse, who makes his left hand his right.'[223] He posits a key dividing line between the world of creation, of time and space, change and flux, being and becoming, and the eternal, immutable reality of God in his divine nature. Within the former there is still a hierarchy, of course, but without this basic starting point, Augustine suggests, one will not even be able properly to assess and parse the differences within the created realm.[224] Here we see another facet of the importance of Augustine's theory of creation as the grounding of his theory of knowledge. What I want to suggest is that Augustine is discussing here a misuse of prejudice, according to which we take the temporal as the mark of the real, the true, the valuable, and in doing so, we fail to interpret correctly or foreground our ontological prejudice in favour of the spatio-temporal world.[225] In fact, the failure to do this could even result in the refusal to understand or countenance the possibility of something eternal or incorporeal.[226]

Augustine locates in his own life some form of 'hermeneutical' error. According to Ayres, in *conf.* 4 Augustine is discussing this theme with respect to the social implications it entails. That is, in certain socio-cultural settings, certain types of things are valued over others, and Augustine laments how in his own culture, certain standards of value were presented to him, despite the fact that they only led to vanity and pride.[227] Augustine also laments his excessive grief over the death of a friend, claiming that he did not know how to love people in a proper way.[228] At this point Augustine recalls that he was seriously lacking in the proper perspective of viewing creatures in relation to their creator.[229]

As we have seen throughout the foregoing enquiry, a key factor to seeing truth is the purification of one's mental vision through proper simplicity of heart, which is to say that one sets one's focus firmly on eternal things, the very act of which is both purgative and leads to cordial simplicity.[230] Augustine describes his thoughts as being torn apart in multifarious things, a process counteracted by the purgative effects of God's love, at which point purged can remain firm in God's truth.[231] Augustine suggests that one becomes 'heaven' by ridding oneself of earth and its desires: 'Do you wish to be heaven? Purge the earth from your heart.'[232] The expulsion of temporal desires from the soul enables one to bear the simplicity of the divine light by the sight of one's heart: 'There is a purgation of the inner eye in the turning itself, when those things which were being desired temporally are excluded, so that the sight of a simple heart may be able to bear divinely the simple light.'[233] The reverse of this is the clouding of the eye by its immersion in corporeal things.[234]

In contrast to those who confuse temporal goods with eternal ones, Augustine provides the counter-example of Job.[235] What I want to suggest is that Job serves as a type for someone who has a properly adjusted hermeneutical framework, who is able to 'read' the world more clearly and effectively than his materialistic counterpart. Though Job enjoyed temporal goods, he *recognized* that these goods were merely temporal, bearing in mind that only God could provide him with lasting happiness.[236] Job possessed a 'heart filled with God',[237] and took the Lord himself as his right hand.[238] Augustine also speaks to this 'hermeneutical hierarchy' when he exhorts his audience to let temporal things be temporal, and to situate them appropriately with respect to the rest of one's life.[239] For example, one's faith in Christ must take priority with respect to all temporal goods.[240] Speaking of one's *intentio*, Augustine describes it in terms of one's underlying reasons or motivations for action (*noli facere nisi propter uitam aeternam*).[241] When one performs a good action for the sake of some temporal good, one allows the left hand to know what the right hand is doing; one should only live from the desire for eternal life and for unchangeable goods.[242] Even when one does a good work for the sake of the kingdom, but is distracted by concerns about worldly gain, one mixes the left and the right, a situation which God forbids.[243] One divides or doubles one's heart, and becomes like those who 'with devotion's visage and pious action do sugar o'er the devil himself'.[244]

A similar opportunity Augustine provides for thinking about his theological programme in a hermeneutical modality is according to the notion of the soul and its loves. In *ep. Io. tr.*, he speaks of two loves, of God and of the world, respectively.[245] These two loves are mutually exclusive; those who possess the love of the world will prevent that of God from entering them.[246] As Augustine states shortly thereafter in the same tractate, 'If the love of the world is there, there will be no love of God there.'[247] When one rids oneself of earthly love, God's love may take its place.[248] As in *ciu.*, Augustine suggests in *ep. Io. tr.* that one's love determines one's habitation. So whilst everyone we meet dwells here on earth, some are citizens of the earthly city in virtue of the love of the world, whereas others inhabit heaven already here on earth, because their hearts are set on higher things.[249] (There is a great similarity here to C. S. Lewis' *The Great Divorce*.) The decision to love pulls one in a particular direction, influences what one sees as valuable and significant, and determines the system of relations in which one places those things.[250] In a sense, one becomes the things that one loves, and so if one loves temporal things, the kinds of things which are inherently limited and ultimately fade, one will suffer a similar fate.[251] When we use created things intemperately, we fail to love God, worshipping his creation rather than the Creator.[252]

In contrast, if one loves eternal things, one will become eternal.[253] Indeed, we shall become like gods.[254] The goodness of created things ought to lead us to love the Creator.[255] Augustine makes clear that we should not reject or condemn worldly, temporal things, as they are good in themselves. Rather, one must recognize that they have their source in God, their maker, who possesses all of their good qualities in himself beyond degree:[256] 'May the Spirit of God be in you, so that you may see that all these things are good. But woe to you if you love the things which have been made, and you abandon the Maker. They are beautiful to you; but how much more beautiful is the one who formed them?'[257] When we realize that God alone is to be loved and worshipped, we shall not be troubled by lower desires, and we shall be able truly to love God.[258] For Augustine, the life of sin and dissolution can be couched in epistemic and hermeneutical terms.[259] In other words, the soul makes an error in judgement concerning the worth of particular things. One erroneously treats temporal things like eternal ones, and attempts to enjoy them accordingly. This error for Augustine is simultaneously moral and epistemic.[260]

Conclusion

Our prejudices are most fruitfully challenged through an encounter with a particular content which somehow conflicts with or produces tension with our pre-understanding. And for Augustine, in my estimation, the ultimate answer to our prejudices, which frees us from the darkness of ignorance, is none other than Christ. Perhaps this is a way forward for thinking theologically and philosophically, that is, by applying hermeneutical methods to the text-analogue of nature. As I see it, Augustine's theory of knowledge is ultimately not about trying to reason to something, but rather about enabling oneself to see what is already present before one, in much the same way that concentrated study would allow one to make sense of a difficult text which one reads again and again.

The entire foregoing enquiry assumes the radical, incommensurable difference between God, the eternal and immutable Creator, and everything else, namely creation, things which came into existence out of nothing. *Sans* God's assistance, this ontological gulf is absolute and unbridgeable. In a paradoxical way, we are unable to realize the fullness of our own calling and identity, which as we have seen, is to rest in the eternal, immutable, incorporeal Creator. It is through him and him alone that we can hope to escape from the vicissitudes of our spatio-temporal 'vale of tears'.

CONCLUSION

In Augustine's thought, I believe we find powerful resources for thinking about the nature of knowledge and reality, and these insights arise as a direct result of his theological commitments and his attempt to account for creation in Wisdom. In particular I look to the principal and the gradual senses of being, which provide the basis for thinking about our knowledge. We are given to be in a timeless way and yet we realize ourselves insofar as we turn to God, our source and guide, within the extension of space and time. The principal and the gradual features of being are distinct but inseparable. Here I believe that Augustine provides us with a fundamental insight about the nature of being and of ourselves.

The presence of God is deep within each of us, in particular in virtue of our creation according to the divine image. The source of all being and truth, the summit of all knowledge, is more intimate to us than we are to ourselves. This observation suggests that knowledge is ultimately not only about the acquisition of facts, of 'scientific' knowledge, but is about a continuous, indefinite deepening, something which cannot be conducted according to the techniques of scientific method (a point which Gadamer and Buber appreciated). Augustine's questions are not even about *knowing* God per se. Augustine writes that he sought not to be more certain about God, but to rest more firmly in him. Augustine's thought also challenges us insofar as he grounds his theory of knowledge in a person, in particular the God-man Jesus Christ.

Just as the discarnate Logos is the agent of creation, so too is the incarnate Christ the agent of re-creation, restoring the fallen world. Augustine often couches sin in terms of a moral blindness, an obstruction which prevents one from seeing truth. Seeing the world as creation implies that evil is a negation of creation and a type of spiritual blindness. We come to see that the intellectual and the moral are closely linked, if not two aspects under which to view one and the same reality. Augustine speaks of a *sapientia superba*, a prideful wisdom of the world. Pride means seeing oneself as the source of one's own being and knowledge. When we fail to appreciate our finitude in knowing, whatever knowledge we do have can work against the further realization of truth.

The initial review of Augustine's discussion of creation revealed a further key aspect to his thought, namely that the creator is timeless and immaterial, in a word, incorporeal. Put differently, God is not a particular type of thing within the universe. Our status as creatures means that we are by nature material and temporal; how therefore can we have any knowledge of or relationship to a 'being' which escapes all categorization and admits of no material properties? We are challenged to think of knowledge in terms which go beyond the 'merely' empirical.

The broader context of Augustine's cosmology places us in a particular ontological position, that is, as beings who are situated within time and space and yet possess a faculty which puts us in touch with the transcendent. This observation has a relativizing effect on us, as we see the contingency of our place in the cosmos. This limitation suggests that we should seek to complement our own knowledge and experience with that of others. Moreover, we realize that not only are we *given* to be, but that our being given to be is simultaneously a being given *not* to be (an insight which Heidegger particularly appreciated). We can derive crucial insights from Augustine's attempt to negotiate this tension between being and non-being within himself. This further implies that in addition to our being, our knowing is simultaneously a not-knowing, as we struggle to collect and preserve the reports of our senses in the world. What Augustine attempts to understand, and what we are meant to come to see as remarkable, is how we can have *any* knowledge whatsoever, let alone knowledge of God, as beings in continuous flux. We follow Augustine in reflecting on and 're-describing' how we come to know in an ever-changing world. We also realize that the very fact that we think of the world in terms of flux and change also bespeaks a deeper awareness of an abiding truth beyond the vicissitudes of our spatio-temporal matrix.

The fact of creation in the divine Wisdom implies that the world is intelligible. Moreover, the particular way in which it is intelligible is of further significance. The world is imbued with vestiges of its creator. Augustine holds that these properties, though present in physical states of affairs, are nonetheless not reducible to them, and therefore not immediately obvious to the viewer. Rather, they require appropriate foreknowledge and interpretive discernment. We are led to see the world not as a realm evacuated of meaning and inertly awaiting our investigative efforts, but as the repository of truths to be uncovered and understood. It implies an interaction of a hermeneutical or interpretive nature. Augustine challenges us to think of the world as like a text. But what could this mean? In virtue of reflecting the divine Wisdom, the world can truly interrupt us and speak to us. What does the world say, and how do we respond? Augustine reverses the dynamic of knowledge. The truth is present to us, but we may not be present to it. The task is to remove the blockages within us so that we can see what is already there.

Once we begin to read the world, what do we learn? We become aware of our contingency, our dependency, in a contemporary idiom, our finitude. What seems like a trivial observation is replete with epistemic significance for Augustine. Creation implies both a reception of being and a response to its source to complete God's initial act of creation. We are not the source of our own being or our knowing.

The appreciation of our finitude does not stop there. Recall that in addition to Genesis, the Gospel of John is a key source of inspiration for Augustine's thought on creation. He held that these two biblical books both deal with creation, but from different perspectives. The discussion in previous chapters prepared us for a discussion of transcendence. In his exegesis of the prologue, Augustine remarks that John could not have come to a realization of the divine Word at the beginning of all things had he not transcended all of creation and arrived at the timeless Creator. Moreover, Augustine sees John as a model for all of us, encouraging us to transcend the created universe. But what does it mean, what could it mean, to go beyond oneself? Ultimately, the path to self-transcendence entails a recognition of the world and of oneself as created.

In the opening chapters, we discussed the inherent limitations of our being, due to our status as creatures. Due to these, we cannot maintain our ecstatic ascent, and we descend. Yet this descent is not in vain, as we are enabled to see the world in a new light. Creation implies that the spatial and the temporal are not the mark of the real. We realize that we have been led to think of the real in terms of what can be seen, touched, quantified and manipulated, often for our own (practical) ends. The dominant narrative sees value in terms of the practical, and the true in terms of the scientifically verifiable. The confrontation with Augustine's thought challenges us to critique our inherited epistemic assumptions and normative frameworks.

With all of this said, I should note one further aspect of a theology of creation: The search for knowledge is never complete. Creation's source is incomprehensible and inexhaustible, and so we can never settle in our search for truth. This bears directly on the content of this book. My interest in Augustine is not one of nostalgia; here we are reading not hagiographies but sources. I am not advocating a simple return to the past or a 're-enchantment' but rather a critical appraisal of the foregoing dispensation. We may pursue our enquiries with Augustine's help, but keeping in mind the finite nature of all of our efforts at arriving at knowledge. Nonetheless, Augustine also provides a helpful resource here, as he emphasizes the importance of raising questions, which he would understand as standing open to the address of God in and through the creation he has formed and fashioned. It is in the tension, the *metaxu*, that we are most open to a truth that we do not define but rather which defines and conditions us.

NOTES

General Introduction

1 Hans-Georg Gadamer, 'Was ist Wahrheit?', in *Idem*, *Gesammelte Werke*, Band 2: Hermeneutik II (Tübingen: Mohr Siebeck, 1986), 44–56, here 45: 'Ist die Wissenschaft wirklich, wie sie von sich beansprucht, die letzte Instanz und der alleinige Träger der Wahrheit?'
2 Gadamer, 'Was ist Wahrheit?', 47–8.
3 Gadamer, 'Was ist Wahrheit?', 48.
4 Cf. Gadamer, 'Was ist Wahrheit?', 48.
5 Gadamer, 'Was ist Wahrheit?', 49. Gadamer also suggests a distinction between truth and certainty. Ibid., 48.
6 Gadamer, 'Was ist Wahrheit?', 45.
7 Gadamer, 'Was ist Wahrheit?', 51.
8 Gadamer, 'Was ist Wahrheit?', 54.
9 Gadamer, 'Was ist Wahrheit?', 54.
10 Cf. Richard Bernstein, *Beyond Objectivism and Relativism: Science, Hermeneutics, and Praxis* (Oxford: Blackwell, 1983), 40.
11 Bernstein, *Beyond Objectivism and Relativism*, 34. Peter Winch, *The Idea of a Social Science and Its Relation to Philosophy* (London: Routledge & Kegan Paul, 1958).
12 Thomas S. Kuhn, *The Structure of Scientific Revolutions*, 2nd rev. ed. (Chicago: University Press, [1962] 2012).
13 Bernstein, *Beyond Objectivism and Relativism*, 41.
14 Bernstein, *Beyond Objectivism and Relativism*, 34.
15 Bernstein, *Beyond Objectivism and Relativism*, 36.
16 Bernstein, *Beyond Objectivism and Relativism*, 37.
17 Jean Grondin, *Der Sinn für Hermeneutik* (Darmstadt: Wissenschaftliche Buchgesellschaft, 1994), 25 (n. 2).

18 I have presented and explained this schema in Anthony Dupont and Matthew W. Knotts, 'In Dialogue with Augustine's *Soliloquia*: Interpreting and Recovering a Theory of Illumination', *International Journal of Philosophy and Theology* 74, no. 5 (2013): 432–65.
19 Cf. Stephen Menn, 'The Desire for God and the Aporetic Method in Augustine's *Confessions*', in *Augustine's* Confessions: *Philosophy in Autobiography*, ed. W. Mann (New York: Oxford University Press, 2014), 92.
20 E.g. *Io. eu. tr.* 1.19.
21 *ep. Io. tr.* 2.10.
22 *ep. Io. tr.* 7.10.
23 *ep. Io. tr.* 7.10.
24 Cf. Roland Teske, *To Know God and the Soul: Essays on the Thought of St. Augustine* (Washington, DC: Catholic University of America Press, 2008), 47.
25 Throughout this work, Milton's words will be used to express and reinforce certain points, especially ones made by Augustine with respect to creation. That being said, it is important to acknowledge that Milton's Arianism clearly separates him from Augustine.
26 *diu. qu.* 46.2, trans. Mosher, p. 80.
27 *diu. qu.* 51.3.
28 *diu. qu.* 51.2.
29 *diu. qu.* 51.3.
30 *diu. qu.* 46.2, CCSL 44A, pp. 71–2: 'Et ea quidem ipsa rationalis anima non omnis et quaelibet, sed quae sancta et pura fuerit, haec asseritur illi uisioni esse idonea, id est, quae illum ipsum oculum, quo uidentur ista, sanum et sincerum et serenum et similem his rebus, quas uidere intendit, habuerit.' Trans. Mosher, p. 80.
31 *s.* 117.8.11, PL 38, p. 667: 'Voluit enim Deus inseminare omni animae initia intellectus, initia sapientiae.'
32 *ord.* 2.19.50, in Vincent Giraud, 'Delectatio interior: plaisir et pensée selon Augustin', *Études Philosophiques* 109, no. 2 (2014): 209, n. 39.
33 Scholars such as A. MacIntyre, B. Gregory and R. Brague have suggested positions along these lines.
34 For a more detailed and diachronic treatment of *imago Dei* in Augustine, see John Edward Sullivan, *The Image of God: The Doctrine of St. Augustine and its Influences* (Dubuque, IA: Priory Press, 1963); and Gerald P. Boersma, *Augustine's Early Theology of Image: A Study in the Development of Pro-Nicene Theology*, Oxford Studies in Historical Theology (Oxford: University Press, 2016).

35 My treatment of Augustine on (original) includes little of his material from the 420s and the Pelagian controversy. From the 420s, Augustine's thought becomes increasingly pessimistic about our knowledge after the fall. Furthermore, illumination and related themes are not prominent throughout the Pelagian writings.

36 See, for example, *Io. eu. tr.* 38.8, CCSL 36, p. 342, in which Augustine describes Christ as, amongst other things, 'hominis formator et reformator, creator et recreator, factor et refactor'. See also *s*.52.2.2; *s*. 277.2; *s. Mai* 94.1; *en. Ps.* 66.2.

37 Ragnar Holte, *Béatitude et sagesse. Saint Augustin et le problème de la fin de l'homme dans la philosophie ancienne* (Paris: Études augustiniennes, 1962), 350.

38 Cf. Charles Taylor, *Sources of the Self: The Making of Modern Identity* (Cambridge, MA: Harvard University Press, 1989), 140–1.

Chapter 1

1 *Gn. litt.* 1.5.10.
2 *Gn. litt.* 1.2.6.
3 *Gn. litt.* 1.5.11.
4 *Gn. litt.* 3.19.29.
5 *Gn. litt.* 2.6.12.
6 *Gn. litt.* 2.6.13.
7 *Gn. litt.* 1.18.36.
8 *Gn. litt.* 2.6.14–8.19.
9 *Gn. litt.* 5.5.13. See also ibid., 5.4.10.
10 *Gn. litt.* 5.14.31. Ps. 104.24.
11 *Gn. litt.* 5.14.31; trans. Hill, p. 291. Col. 1.16.
12 *Gn. litt.* 5.15.33.
13 *Gn. litt.* 5.13.29; trans. Hill, p. 290.
14 *Gn. litt.* 1.2.4.
15 *Gn. litt.* 5.17.35.
16 *Gn. litt.* 5.17.35; ibid., 5.11.27.
17 *Gn. litt.* 5.11.27, CSEL 28,1, pp. 154–5: 'sine ullis temporalium morarum interuallis [. . .] per temporum moras.' Trans. Hill, p. 289.
18 *Gn. litt.* 5.11.27.

19 *Gn. litt.* 5.3.6.
20 *Gn. litt.* 5.3.6.
21 *Gn. litt.* 1.15.29.
22 *Gn. litt.* 5.3.6.
23 *Gn. litt.* 5.6.19.
24 *Gn. litt.* 5.12.28.
25 *Gn. litt.* 5.12.28.
26 *Gn. litt.* 5.12.28.
27 *Gn. litt.* 5.12.28.
28 *Gn. litt.* 5.15.33; trans. Hill, p. 292.
29 *Gn. litt.* 5.20.40. Jn 5.17.
30 *Gn. litt.* 5.21.42.
31 *Gn. litt.* 5.20.40.
32 *Gn. litt.* 5.20.40.
33 *Gn. litt.* 5.7.20.
34 *Gn. litt.* 5.4.11.
35 *Gn. litt.* 5.6.18.
36 *Gn. litt.* 2.8.19.
37 *Gn. litt.* 3.20.32.
38 *Gn. litt.* 1.10.20; cf. ibid., 1.4.9.
39 *Gn. litt.* 1.17.32; cf. ibid., 2.8.16.
40 Milton, *Paradise Lost* bk 5, lines 486–7.
41 *Gn. litt.* 1.5.10.
42 *Gn. litt.* 1.17.32.
43 *Gn. litt.* 3.24.37.
44 *Gn. litt.* 3.12.20.
45 *Gn. litt.* 3.24.37.
46 *Gn. litt.* 3.20.31.
47 *Gn. litt.* 3.20.32.
48 *Gn. litt.* 1.9.17; cf. 1.1.2–3.
49 *Gn. litt.* 1.4.9.
50 *Gn. litt.* 1.4.9.
51 *Gn. litt.* 1.4.9–5.10.
52 *Gn. litt.* 1.1.1; 1.9.15.

53 *Gn. litt.* 1.18.36.
54 *Gn. litt.* 1.15.29.
55 *Gn. litt.* 2.8.17.
56 *Gn. litt.* 1.8.14.
57 *s.* 1.2. This sermon was composed ca. 391–5.
58 *s.* 1.2.
59 Gerd Van Riel, 'Augustine's Exegesis of 'Heaven and Earth' in *Conf.* XII: Finding Truth amidst Philosophers, Heretics and Exegetes', *Quaestio* 7 (2007): 191–228.
60 Van Riel, 'Augustine's Exegesis', 226.
61 *Io. eu. tr.* 1.16.
62 Marie-François Berrouard, *Introduction aux Homélies de saint Augustin sur l'évangile de saint Jean*, Collection des études augustiniennes, Série Antiquité 170 (Paris: Études augustiniennes, 2004), 49.
63 *Io. eu. tr.* 1.16.
64 *Io. eu. tr.* 1.16; Ps. 103.24; F. Arsenault, *Augustin: Qui est Jésus-Christ?* (Paris: Desclée, 1974), 54.
65 *Io. eu. tr.* 2.2.
66 *Io. eu. tr.* 2.2.
67 *Io. eu. tr.* 2.2.
68 Lewis Ayres, 'Into the Poem of the Universe: *Exempla*, Conversion, and Church in Augustine's *Confessiones*', *Zeitschrift für Antikes Christentum* 13, no. 2 (2009): 276.
69 *Io. eu. tr.* 3.4.
70 *Io. eu. tr.* 3.4.
71 Milton, *Paradise Lost* bk 3, lines 60–1.
72 *Io. eu. tr.* 3.4.
73 *Io. eu. tr.* 3.4.
74 *Io. eu. tr.* 3.4.
75 *Io. eu. tr.* 3.4.
76 *Io. eu. tr.* 3.4.
77 Berrouard, *Introduction aux Homélies*, 46.
78 *Io. eu. tr.* 3.19.
79 *Io. eu. tr.* 3.19.
80 *Io. eu. tr.* 3.19. Augustine's reading of the Jewish tradition is debatable, considering what Michael Fishbane says about the

'Illimitable' character of God, derived from sources such as Deut. 4:12 and Exod. 3:14. See Michael Fishbane, *Sacred Attunement: A Jewish Theology* (Chicago and London: University of Chicago Press, 2008), 53.
81   *s.* 342.2.
82   *Io. eu. tr.* 1.18.
83   *Io. eu. tr.* 1.18. Cf. Arsenault, *Qui est Jésus-Christ?*, 16; *f. et symb.* 1.2. See also *s.* 88.6, RB 94 (1984), p. 80, in which Augustine aligns the motifs of light and wisdom, and goes on to link these with creation and the human person when he writes, 'lux illa est aeterna sapientia. Fecit autem te Deus, o homo, ad imaginem suam.'
84   *Io. eu. tr.* 3.4.
85   *Io. eu. tr.* 3.4. Cf. ibid., 3.5, 7.
86   *Io. eu. tr.* 3.4.
87   *Io. eu. tr.* 3.4.
88   *Io. eu. tr.* 3.4.
89   *Io. eu. tr.* 1.8.
90   E.g. *uera rel.* 31.58; *lib. arb.* 2.8.23.
91   *Io. eu. tr.* 3.18.
92   *Io. eu. tr.* 3.18, CCSL 36, p. 28: 'Sapientia Dei uideri oculis non potest. Fratres, si Christus Sapientia Dei, et Virtus Dei; si Christus Verbum Dei; uerbum hominis oculis non uidetur, Verbum Dei uideri sic potest?'
93   *Io. eu. tr.* 3.18.
94   *Io. eu. tr.* 3.18.
95   *Io. eu. tr.* 3.18; Mt. 5.8. Cf. *Io. eu. tr.* 1.17, CCSL 36, p. 10; 2.4, CCSL 36, pp. 13–14.
96   *Io. eu. tr.* 3.18.
97   *Io. eu. tr.* 3.18.
98   *Io. eu. tr.* 3.18.
99   *Io. eu. tr.* 3.18.
100 *Io. eu. tr.* 3.17.
101 Cf. *Io. eu. tr.* 3.17.
102 *Io. eu. tr.* 3.20.
103 *Io. eu. tr.* 3.5; cf. Lope Cilleruelo, '"Deum uidere" en San Augustín', *Salmanticensis* 12 (1965): 28.
104 *Io. eu. tr.* 1.15.
105 *Io. eu. tr.* 1.17.

NOTES

106 *Io. eu. tr.* 1.17.
107 *Io. eu. tr.* 2.10.
108 Arsenault, *Qui est Jésus-Christ?*, 18.
109 *Io. eu. tr.* 3.5.
110 *Io. eu. tr.* 3.5, CCSL 36, pp. 22–3: 'Et ubi erat ista? *In hoc mundo erat.* Et quomodo *in hoc mundo erat?* numquid sicut ista lux solis, lunae, lucernarum, sic et ista lux in mundo est? Non. Quia *mundus per eum factus est, et mundus eum non cognouit*: hoc est, *lux in tenebris lucet, et tenebrae eam non comprehenderunt.*'
111 *Io. eu. tr.* 3.4.
112 *Io. eu. tr.* 3.4, CCSL 36, pp. 21–2: 'Ipse est quidem, sed non totus illud quod uiderunt Iudaei; non hoc est totus Christus. Et quid est? *In principio erat Verbum.* In quo principio? *Et Verbum erat apud Deum.* Et quale Verbum? *Et Deus erat Verbum.*'
113 *Io. eu. tr.* 3.5.
114 *Io. eu. tr.* 3.5.
115 *Io. eu. tr.* 3.5.
116 *Io. eu. tr.* 3.5.
117 *Io. eu. tr.* 3.5.
118 *Io. eu. tr.* 3.6.
119 *Io. eu. tr.* 3.5, CCSL 36, p. 22: 'Lux non est absens sed uos absentes estis a luce. Caecus in sole praesentem habet solem, sed absens est ipse soli.'
120 Carol Harrison, *Beauty and Revelation in the Thought of St. Augustine*, Oxford Theological Monographs (Oxford: Clarendon, 1992), 59.
121 *Io. eu. tr.* 3.5.
122 *Io. eu. tr.* 3.5.
123 Berrouard, *Introduction aux Homélies*, 227.
124 Berrouard, *Introduction aux Homélies*, 228; *Io. eu. tr.* 37.1; 38.3; 40.11.
125 Berrouard, *Introduction aux Homélies*, 228.
126 Berrouard, *Introduction aux Homélies*, 228.
127 Berrouard, *Introduction aux Homélies*, 228.
128 Berrouard, *Introduction aux Homélies*, 228.
129 *Io. eu. tr.* 3.12, CCSL 36, p. 26: 'cum traduce peccati'.
130 *Io. eu. tr.* 3.7.

NOTES

131 *Io. eu. tr.* 3.7.
132 *Io. eu. tr.* 3.15.
133 *Io. eu. tr.* 2.8.
134 *Io. eu. tr.* 1.19.
135 *Io. eu. tr.* 1.19; 2.16.
136 *Io. eu. tr.* 1.19.
137 *Io. eu. tr.* 2.16.
138 *Io. eu. tr.* 2.8.
139 *Io. eu. tr.* 1.19; Mt. 5.8.
140 *Io. eu. tr.* 3.6.
141 *Io. eu. tr.* 1.12. See also ibid., 2.15.
142 Wolinski, *Chez Augustin*, 47.
143 Wolinski, *Chez Augustin*, 36.
144 *Io. eu. tr.* 1.11.
145 *Io. eu. tr.* 3.12.
146 *Io. eu. tr.* 3.12.
147 *Io. eu. tr.* 3.20; cf. Cilleruelo, '"Deum uidere" en San Augustín', 21.
148 Cf. A.W. Moore, *Points of View* (Oxford: Clarendon Press, 1997); Jerome's *Dialogi contra Pelagianos*.
149 Philippe Eberhard, 'Gadamer and Theology', *International Journal of Systematic Theology* 9, no. 3 (2007): 296.
150 Jens Zimmermann, *Recovering Theological Hermeneutics: An Incarnational-Trinitarian Theory of Interpretation* (Grand Rapids, MI: Baker, 2004), 163.
151 Jean Grondin, 'La thèse de l'herméneutique sur l'être', *Revue de Métaphysique et de Morale* 4 (2006): 470.
152 Eberhard, 'Gadamer and Theology', 297; Zimmerman, *Recovering Theological Hermeneutics*, 185.
153 Zimmermann, *Recovering Theological Hermeneutics*, 186.
154 Cf. Zimmermann, *Recovering Theological Hermeneutics*, 179–80.
155 Cf. Taylor, *Sources of the Self*, 140–1.
156 Cf. *en. Ps.* 146.13.
157 Zimmermann, *Recovering Theological Hermeneutics*, 179.
158 Eberhard, 'Gadamer and Theology', 294.
159 Beckmann-Lamb apud Gadamer. 'Heidegger war auch sein Leben lang auf der Gottsuche.' Cf. Catherine Vincie, RSHM, *Worship and*

the New Cosmology: Liturgical and Theological Challenges (Collegeville, MN: Liturgical Press, 2014), 12, 15, 40–1.
160 Vincie, *Worship and the New Cosmology*, 12, 15, 40–1.
161 Beckmann-Lamb apud Gadamer.
162 Sturm apud Gadamer, 'Rituale sind wichtig', 305.
163 Sturm apud Gadamer, 'Rituale sind wichtig', 305.

Chapter 2

1 Milton, *Paradise Lost* bk 5, lines 71–2. Satan tempts Eve with these words in her dream which presages the fall.
2 Credit is due to the Rev Dr George W. Rutler for this point, which he mentioned during the course of a private conversation. For more on the historical context, see e.g. Anna Schur Kaladiouk, 'On "Sticking to the Fact" and "Understanding Nothing": Dostoevsky and the Scientific Method', *The Russian Review* 65, no. 3 (2006): 417–38, esp. 420–1; David Oldroyd, *The Arch of Knowledge: An Introductory Study of the History of the Philosophy and Methodology of Science* (Methuen, NY: 1986), 142.
3 Cilleruelo, '"Deum uidere" en San Augustín', 28; cf. Pârvan, 'La relation', 87.
4 This approach is demonstrated by Justin Martyr. See Vladimir de Beer, 'The Patristic Reception of Hellenic Philosophy', *St. Vladimir's Theological Quarterly* 55, no. 4 (2014): 381. Of course, it is worth noting that Augustine assumes the rectitude of his Christian position. In other words, could Augustine have some correct intuition regarding this framework for knowledge, but be incorrect about his own situation within it? That being said, it is difficult to tell whether the two could be separated. Nonetheless, the fact remains that Augustine sees himself as in the possession of the truth, and he does not question this position.
5 *s.* 184.1.1.
6 *s.* 184.1.1.
7 *s.* 184.1.1.
8 Berrouard, *Introduction aux Homélies*, 49–50.
9 *s.* 184.1.1.
10 *s.* 184.1.1.

11 Cf. Alexandra Pârvan, 'La relation en tant qu'élément-clé de l'illumination augustinienne', *Chora: Journal of Ancient and Medieval Studies* 7–8 (2009–10): 87.
12 s. 184.1.1.
13 s. 190.1.1.
14 s. 188.3.3.
15 s. 188.3.3.
16 s. 117.10.17, PL 38, p. 671: 'Non praesumatis, et quasi anteponatis scientiam praecepto Dei; ne inferiores, non solidiores remaneatis.'
17 Harrison, *Beauty and Revelation*, 49.
18 Manfred Svensson, 'Scientia y sapientia en De Trinitate XII: San Agustín y las formas de la racionalidad', *Teología y Vida* 51 (2010): 101.
19 Svensson, 'Scientia y sapientia en *De Trinitate* XII', 101.
20 Meijer, *De* Sapientia, 100; Cilleruelo, '"Deum uidere" en San Agustín', 9; Gerd Van Riel, 'La sagesse chez Augustin: de la philosophie à l'Écriture', in *Augustin philosophe et prédicateur. Hommage à Goulven Madec*, ed. I. Bochet (Paris: Institut d'Études Augustiniennes, 2012), 393.
21 Harrison, *Beauty and Revelation*, 47.
22 s. 117.3.5, PL 38, p. 663: 'Magis pia est talis ignorantia, quam praesumpta scientia.' See also ibid.: 'Sit pia confessio ignorantiae magis, quam temeraria professio scientiae.'
23 s. 117.2.3; 3.5. Cf. Stefan Heßbrüggen-Walter, 'Augustine's Critique of Dialectic: Between Ambrose and the Arians', in *Augustine and the Disciplines*, ed. K. Pollmann and M. Vessey (Oxford and New York: Oxford University Press, 2005), 191.
24 s. 117.3.5.
25 s. 117.10.17.
26 s. 117.10.15.
27 s. 117.10.15.
28 s. 117.5.8.
29 Johannes Brachtendorf, 'Augustine on the Glory and the Limits of Philosophy', in *Augustine and Philosophy*, ed. P. Cary, J. Doody and K. Paffenroth, *Augustine in Conversation: Tradition and Innovation* (Totowa: Rowman and Littlefield, 2010), 7–8. According to Meijer, at least in his early works, Augustine considered himself amongst the foolish (*stulti*), and did not see himself as wise. See Meijer, *De* Sapientia, 118. See also Heßbrüggen-Walter, 'Augustine's Critique of Dialectic', 184–205.

30 *Io. eu. tr.* 2.3.
31 According to Berrouard, John described himself using this phrase, following a traditional formula for modestly referring to oneself. Berrouard, *Introduction aux Homélies*.
32 *Io. eu. tr.* 2.3.
33 *Io. eu. tr.* 2.3.
34 *Io. eu. tr.* 2.3.
35 Berrouard, *Introduction aux Homélies*, 230.
36 Berrouard, *Introduction aux Homélies*, 230.
37 Berrouard, *Introduction aux Homélies*, 230.
38 Berrouard, *Introduction aux Homélies*, 230.
39 Berrouard, *Introduction aux Homélies*, 231.
40 Gaëlle Jeanmart, *Herméneutique et subjectivité dans les* Confessions *d'Augustin*, Monothéismes et Philosophie 8 (Turnhout: Brepols, 2006), 65.
41 Cilleruelo, '"Deum uidere" en San Agustín', 24; Heßbrüggen-Walter, 'Augustine's Critique of Dialectic', 205.
42 *Io. eu. tr.* 2.4; trans. Hill, pp. 57–8; Rom. 1.20-2. The key phrase which concludes the sentence is *ut sint inexcusabiles*. Ultimately, Augustine viewed the conception of the world by the Greeks as an absurdity, as it lacked the foundation necessary to make it intelligible and meaningful. Cilleruelo, '"Deum uidere" en San Agustín', 12.
43 *Io. eu. tr.* 2.4. Cf. Cynthia Nielsen, 'St. Augustine on Text and Reality (and a little Gadamerian Spice)', *Heythrop Journal* 50, no. 1 (2009): 100.
44 *Io. eu. tr.* 2.4.
45 Mathijs Lamberigts, 'Peccatum', in *Augustinus-Lexikon* 4 3/4, ed. C. P. Mayer (Basel: Schwabe, 2004), 584.
46 Cf. Dominique Doucet, 'Recherche de Dieu, Incarnation et philosophie : *Sol.* I, 1, 2–6', *Revue des Études Augustiniennes et Patristiques* 36 (1990): 103–4; Charles Mathewes, 'Augustinian Anthropology: *Interior intimo meo*', *The Journal of Religious Ethics* 27, no. 2 (1999): 201, 207; Teske, *To Know God and the Soul*, 67. Though of course, Augustine did not thereby see all of the propositional positions of the philosophers as unproblematic. Consider, for example, 'magna magnorum deliramenta doctorum' (*s.* 241.6, PL 38, p. 1137), and 'omnes omnium philosophorum uanas opiniones' (*ciu.* 8.1).
47 Cilleruelo, '"Deum uidere" en San Agustín', 24.
48 Cilleruelo, '"Deum uidere" en San Agustín', 24.

49 Jeanmart, *Herméneutique et subjectivité*, 64–5.

50 Nielsen, 'St. Augustine on Text and Reality', 100.

51 Michael Foley, 'Cicero, Augustine, and the Philosophical Roots of the Cassiciacum Dialogues', *Revue des Études Augustiniennes* 45 (1999): 66, 68, 69.

52 Svensson, '*Scientia* y *sapientia* en *De Trinitate* XII', 98.

53 Meijer, *De* Sapientia, 109, 111.

54 Jean-Louis Chrétien, *L'espace intérieur* (Paris: Minuit, 2014), 62; cf. Jeanmart, *Herméneutique et subjectivité*, 64.

55 Chrétien, *L'espace intérieur*, 62.

56 Brachtendorf, 'Augustine on the Glory and the Limits of Philosophy', 7–8; Klingshirn, 'Divination and the Disciplines of Knowledge', 129; *doct.* 2.13.20; 38.57; 42.63.

57 Jeanmart, *Herméneutique et subjectivité*, 65.

58 *s.* 196.1.

59 *s.* 117.10.17; Mt. 11.29.

60 *s.* 117.10.17.

61 *s.* 117.4.5.

62 Marie Comeau, *Saint Augustin: Exégète du quatrième évangile*, 3rd ed., Études de théologie historique (Paris: Gabriel Beauchesne, 1930), 317.

63 *s.* 117.10.17.

64 *s.* 185.1, PL 38, p. 997: 'Natalis Domini dicitur, quando Dei Sapientia se demonstrauit infantem, et Dei Verbum sine uerbis uocem carnis emisit.'

65 Comeau, *Saint Augustin: Exégète du quatrième évangile*, 337.

66 *s.* 190.3.3.

67 *s.* 190.3.3.

68 *s.* 190.3.3.

69 *s.* 117.10.17.

70 *s.* 117.10.17.

71 *s.* 117.10.17.

72 Cf. *s.* 117.10.17.

73 *s.* 189.2.

74 *s.* 189.2.

75 *s. Dolbeau* 26.36–8. One should note that there is an ambiguity in Augustine's language. At certain points, Augustine suggests that it is

God's grace or mercy, and not our own works or virtue, which is responsible for our purgation. See *ciu.* 10.22.

76 *s. Dolbeau* 26.27–32.

77 Goulven Madec, *Chez Augustin* (Paris: Institut d'études augustiniennes, 1998), 14; cf. de Beer, 'The Patristic Reception of Hellenic Philosophy', 389–90.

78 Isabelle Bochet, 'Herméneutique, apologétique et philosophie: recherches sur Augustin', *Revue d'Études Augustiniennes et Patristiques* 48, no. 2 (2002): 325.

79 F.-J. Thonnard, 'Saint Augustin et les Grands Courants de la Philosophie Contemporaine', *Revue des Études Augustiniennes et Patristiques* 50 (2004): 203.

80 Georges Folliet, '"La spoliatio aegyptiorum" (Exode 3:21–3; 11:2–3; 12:35–6): les interpretations de cette image chez les pères et autres écrivains ecclésiastiques', *Traditio* 57 (2002): 12.

81 Bochet, 'Herméneutique, apologétique et philosophie', 323.

82 As Augustine writes in *doctr. chr.* 2.60, SIMONETTI, p. 162, 'ipsis Aegyptiis nescienter commodantibus ea quibus non bene utebantur.'

83 Folliet, '"La spoliatio aegyptiorum"', 12. Considering the various citations in *ciu.*, Bochet suggests that Augustine sees the study of pagan philosophy as propaedeutic to the study of the Bible. Bochet, 'Herméneutique, apologétique et philosophie', 325.

84 Cf. William Klingshirn, 'Divination and the Disciplines of Knowledge according to Augustine', in *Augustine and the Disciplines*, ed. K. Pollmann and M. Vessey (Oxford and New York: Oxford University Press, 2005), 135; *doct.* 2.38.57; 42.63.

85 *doctr. chr.* 2.60.

86 Klingshirn, 'Divination and the Disciplines of Knowledge', 138.

87 Carol Harrison, *Augustine: Christian Truth and Fractured Humanity*, Christian Theology in Context (Oxford University Press, 2000), 37.

88 But of course, 'knowledge' here is not the most useful term, since every aspect of one's encounter with Christ transcends the merely intellectual; rather, any knowledge or understanding regarding Christ implies a deeply spiritual and moral component. Indeed, as Mathewes ('Augustinian Anthropology', 201) writes, matters of knowledge and intellection are integrally connected with moral considerations, in particular concerning the soul's will (*uoluntas*) and that to which it gives its love (*amor*). Doucet also notes the close interplay of the intellectual and the moral life for Augustine. Doucet, 'Recherche de Dieu, incarnation et philosophie', 103–4.

89 Madec, *Chez Augustin*, 14.
90 Madec, *Chez Augustin*, 14–15. He goes on to add that this distinction 'ne correspond donc pas à discernement thomiste. Je laisse le soin à un théologien de calculer les conséquences de cette différence' (Madec, *Chez Augustin*, 15). Indeed, as Madec's disciple Bochet has noted at various points, one must avoid the danger of anachronistically applying the scholastic distinction to Augustine's oeuvre (Bochet, 'Herméneutique, apologétique et philosophie', 326). Indeed, this task to which Madec summons the theologian remains to be completed.
91 Cf. Isabelle Bochet, 'The Role of Scripture in Augustine's Controversy with Porphyry', *Augustinian Studies* 41, no. 1 (2010): 38.
92 Cf. Bochet, 'The Role of Scripture', 11.
93 Bochet, 'The Role of Scripture', 40; see *ep.* 102.3.19.
94 Bochet, 'The Role of Scripture', 48, 50.
95 Anna Schur Kaladiouk, 'On "Sticking to the Fact" and "Understanding Nothing": Dostoevsky and the Scientific Method', *The Russian Review* 65.3 (2006): 417–38.
96 Kaladiouk, 'On "Sticking to the Fact"', 419.
97 Kaladiouk, 'On "Sticking to the Fact"', 430.
98 Kaladiouk, 'On "Sticking to the Fact"', 426, 427.
99 Kaladiouk, 'On "Sticking to the Fact"', 429.
100 Kaladiouk, 'On "Sticking to the Fact"', 419.
101 Cf. Kuhn, *Structure*, 122–3; Hans-Georg Gadamer, 'The Universality of the Hermeneutical Problem', in *The Hermeneutic Tradition from Ast to Ricoeur*, ed. G. Ormiston and A. Schrift, trans. D. Linge (Albany, NY: State University of New York Press, 1990), 154.

Chapter 3

1 Here I borrow a phrase from C. Taylor.
2 Cf. Cyril O'Regan, 'Answering Back: Augustine's Critique of Heideger', in *Human Destinies: Philosophical Essays in Memory of Gerald Hanratty*, ed. F. O'Rourke (South Bend, IN: University of Notre Dame Press, 2012), 136.
3 *ep.* 18.2. See also Maurice Huftier, *Le tragique de la condition chrétienne chez saint Augustin* (Paris: Desclée, 1964), 201–2 and

Étienne Gilson, 'Notes sur l'être et le temps chez saint Augustin', *Recherches Augustiniennes* 2 (1962): 205–23, here 212, both of whom believe that Augustine speaks of time in a positive or at least a neutral sense, as it simply denotes an aspect of creation. Teske is less certain of this. See Teske, *To Know God and the Soul*, 247–8.

4   *en. Ps.* 146.11.
5   *Gn. adu. Man.* 1.2.3.
6   *Gn. adu. Man.* 1.2.3.
7   *Gn. adu. Man.* 1.2.3.
8   *conf.* 11.13.15. Cf. *conf.* 12.11.13. See also *conf.* 12.13.16, in which Augustine claims that God's knowledge consists in knowing eternally, with no passage of time. See also *conf.* 12.7.7, in which Augustine discusses the notion of creation *in principio* and *ex nihilo*, and *conf.* 12.12.15, in which he writes that *in principio* implies a state of being beyond or outside of time.
9   *conf.* 11.13.16, CCSL 27, p. 202.
10 Cf. Mirela Oliva, *Das innere Verbum in Gadamers Hermeneutik*, Hermeneutische Untersuchungen zur Theologie 53 (Tübingen: Mohr Siebeck, 2009), 31–2.
11 Cf. Cilleruelo, '"Deum uidere" en San Agustín', 11: 'En cambio, el ser creado es espacio, tiempo, composición, extensión, etc.'
12 Cf. Paul Helm, 'Thinking Eternally', in *Augustine's* Confessions: *Philosophy in Autobiography*, ed. W. Mann (New York: Oxford University Press, 2014), 136.
13 Christian Tornau, 'Intelligible Matter and the Genesis of Intellect', in *Augustine's* Confessions: *Philosophy in Autobiography*, ed. W. Mann (New York: Oxford University Press, 2014), 182.
14 Tornau, 'Intelligible Matter and the Genesis of Intellect', 194–5. Cf. *Gn. litt.* 4.30.47, CSEL 28,1, pp. 128–9.
15 Tornau, 'Intelligible Matter and the Genesis of Intellect', 197.
16 Tornau, 'Intelligible Matter and the Genesis of Intellect', 197.
17 *conf.* 12.13.16, CCSL 27, p. 224: 'simul sine ulla uicissitudine temporum.'
18 Cf. *Gn. litt.* 4.29.46, CSEL 28,1, p. 128: 'sed eorum mentem mirabili facilitate haec omnia simul posse.' In Book 5 of *Paradise Lost*, Milton depicts Raphael speaking to Adam, describing reason as either 'Discursive, or intuitive; discourse oftest is yours, the latter most is ours' (*Paradise Lost* bk 5, lines 488–9). This is another way of expressing Augustine's understanding of the difference between the

knowledge of angels and of men, respectively. However, it is doubtful that Augustine would endorse what follows immediately thereafter: 'Differing but in degree, of kind the same' (ibid., bk 5, line 490).

19 Cf. Teske, *To Know God and the Soul*, 211–12.

20 Cf. John Arthos, *The Inner Word in Gadamer's Hermeneutics* (Notre Dame, IN: University of Notre Dame Press, 2009), 114, 126–7.

21 For more on the structural elements of the *conf.*, see, e.g. E. Williger, 'Der Aufbau der Konfessionen Augustins', *Zeitschrift für Neutestamentliche Wissenschaft und die Kunde der Älteren Kirche* 28, no. 1 (1929): 81–106; and Goulven Madec, 'Une lecture de Confessions VII,IX,13–XXI,27. Notes critiques à propos d'une thèse de R.-J. O'Connell', *Revue des Études Augustiniennes* 16.1 (1970): 79–137.

22 *conf.* 7.1.1, CCSL 27, p. 92: 'non te cogitabam, Deus, in figura corporis humani: ex quo audire aliquid de sapientia coepi.'

23 James O'Donnell, *Augustine, Confessions: Commentary*, 3 Volumes (Oxford: Clarendon Press), 392.

24 Teske, *To Know God and the Soul*, 140–1.

25 Teske, *To Know God and the Soul*, 140–1.

26 *conf.* 7.1.1.

27 *conf.* 7.1.2.

28 *conf.* 7.1.2.

29 *ep. Io. tr.* 7.10.

30 Helm, 'Thinking Eternally', 120–1.

31 Helm, 'Thinking Eternally', 120–1.

32 *conf.* 7.10.16. Cf. C.P. Mayer, *Die Zeichen in der geistigen Entwicklung und in der Theologie des jungen Augustinus*, Cassiciacum 24/1-2 (Würzburg: Augustins-Verlag, 1969–74), 146; Graziano Ripanti, 'Il problema dell comprensione nell'ermeneutica agostiniana', *Revue des Études Augustiniennes* 20, no. 1–2 (1974): 92.

33 See *conf.* 7.17.23.

34 Menn, 'The Desire for God', 93.

35 Menn, 'The Desire for God', 99.

36 Menn, 'The Desire for God', 103.

37 *conf.* 7.11.17.

38 In *trin.* 8, Augustine speaks of a notion of the supreme Good as conditioning our knowledge of and our approach to individual good things in the world. God is the fullness of goodness, the Good itself, as

well as *esse* itself. See *trin.* 8.1.2; 2.3; 3.4; 3.5. For more on the theme of participation, see e.g. Gregory T. Doolan, *Aquinas on the Divine Ideas as Exemplar Causes* (Washington, DC: The Catholic University of America Press, 2008).
39 *conf.* 7.11.17.
40 *conf.* 7.10.16.
41 *conf.* 7.14.20.
42 *en. Ps.* 146.14.
43 *en. Ps.* 146.14.
44 *conf.* 7.15.21.
45 Helm, 'Thinking Eternally', 136. However, even if he separates time and space conceptually, it seems that de facto we cannot separate time and space, or rather that our experience of time and space are part and parcel of one another.
46 Cf. Craig Callender, 'Le temps, est-il une illusion?', *Pour la Science* 397 (November 2010). Available at www.pourlascience.fr/ewb_pages/a/article-le-temps-est-il-une-illusiona-26041.php (last accessed on 23 July 2016).
47 Though scholars such as Tornau emphasize the distinctively Christian character of this doctrine, G. May has nuanced this assertion. See Gerhard May, *Schöpfung aus dem Nichts: die Entstehung der Lehre von der* Creatio ex Nihilo, Arbeiten zur Kirchengeschichte 48 (Berlin: De Gruyter, 1973), 9–26.
48 O'Regan, 'Answering Back', 136.
49 Khaled Anatolios, 'Oppositional Pairs and Christological Synthesis: Rereading Augustine's *De Trinitate*', *Theological Studies* 68 (2007): 246.
50 *Gn. litt.* 5.18.36.
51 *Gn. litt.* 5.16.34.
52 *Gn. litt.* 5.16.34. See James Swetnam, 'A Note on *Idipsum* in St. Augustine', *The Modern Schoolman* 30 (1952–3): 328 and Teske, *To Know God and the Soul*, 120–3.
53 *Gn. litt.* 5.16.34. See also *doctr. Chr.* 1.32.35; *diu. qu.* 19.
54 *Gn. litt.* 5.11.27.
55 *Gn. litt.* 5.16.34; trans. Hill, p. 293.
56 *Gn. litt.* 5.19.38.
57 *Gn. litt.* 5.13.30.
58 *Gn. litt.* 5.5.16.

59 *Gn. litt.* 5.1.1.
60 *Gn. litt.* 5.17.35.
61 *Gn. litt.* 5.5.12.
62 *Gn. litt.* 5.5.12: 'Factae itaque creaturae motibus coeperunt currere tempora.' Trans. Hill, p. 182.
63 *Gn. litt.* 5.5.12.
64 *Gn. litt.* 5.5.12.
65 Teske, *To Know God and the Soul*, 227; see also 229–30.
66 *Gn. litt.* 5.5.12.
67 *Gn. litt.* 5.5.12.
68 Kurt Flasch, *Was ist Zeit? Augustinus von Hippo. Das XI. Buch der Confessiones. Historisch-Philosophische Studie* (Frankfurt am Main: Klostermann, 1993), 93.
69 Flasch, *Was ist Zeit?*, 93.
70 Flasch, *Was ist Zeit?*, 93.
71 Tornau, 'Intelligible Matter and the Genesis of Intellect', 192.
72 Flasch, *Was ist Zeit?*, 93. Tornau, 'Intelligible Matter and the Genesis of Intellect', 192.
73 *Gn. litt.* 1.15.29.
74 *Gn. litt.* 5.1.2; trans. Hill, p. 277.
75 *Gn. litt.* 5.23.44.
76 *Gn. litt.* 5.5.15–16.
77 *Gn. litt.* 5.5.16.
78 *Gn. litt.* 5.5.16.
79 *Gn. litt.* 5.5.12.
80 *Gn. litt.* 5.5.13.
81 *Gn. litt.* 5.19.37.
82 *Gn. litt.* 5.14.31.
83 *Gn. litt.* 5.19.39. Cf. *Gn. litt.* 5.16.34.
84 *Gn. litt.* 5.13.30.
85 *Gn. litt.* 5.4.10.
86 *Gn. litt.* 5.4.10.
87 *Gn. litt.* 5.4.10.
88 *Gn. litt.* 5.4.10.
89 *ciu.* 11.4.2.

90 *ciu.* 11.10.3.
91 *ciu.* 11.10.3.
92 *ciu.* 11.10.1.
93 *ciu.* 11.8.
94 Oliva, *Das innere Verbum in Gadamers Hermeneutik*, 30.
95 *ciu.* 11.4.2.
96 *ciu.* 11.5, 6. See also *ciu.* 15.20.
97 *ciu.* 11.6.
98 *ciu.* 11.6.
99 *ciu.* 11.6.
100 *ciu.* 11.9.
101 *ciu.* 11.9.
102 *ciu.* 11.9.
103 *ciu.* 11.4.1.
104 *ciu.* 11.3.
105 *ciu.* 11.3.
106 *ciu.* 11.2.
107 *ciu.* 11.2.
108 *ciu.* 11.2.
109 *ciu.* 11.2.
110 See Act I, Scene ii of the Scottish play.
111 *conf.* 11.14.17.
112 *conf.* 7.11.17.
113 Cilleruelo, '"Deum uidere" en San Augustín', 12.
114 *conf.* 11.23.30.
115 *conf.* 11.26.33.
116 *conf.* 9.4.10; trans. Boulding, p. 217. Ps. 4.8.
117 Cf. D.A. Napier, *En route to the* Confessions: *The Roots and Development of Augustine's Philosophical Anthropology*, Late Antique History and Religion 6 (Leuven: Peeters, 2013), 99–101; *conf.* 9.4.10.
118 Cf. Helm, 'Thinking Eternally', 154; Paige Hochschild, *Memory in Augustine's Theological Anthropology*, Oxford Early Christian Studies (Oxford: University Press, 2012), 168; Andrea Nightingale, *Once out of Nature: Augustine on Time and the Body* (Chicago: University of Chicago Press), 64; Napier, *En route*, 99–101.

119 Helm, 'Thinking Eternally', 154.
120 Hochschild, *Memory in Augustine's Theological Anthropology*, 168.
121 *conf.* 10.17.26, CCSL 27, pp. 168–9.
122 Nightingale, *Once out of Nature*, 64.
123 Nightingale, *Once out of Nature*, 86; *conf.* 11.28.37.
124 Hochschild, *Memory in Augustine's Theological Anthropology*, 152. In *conf.* 11.29.39, Augustine contrasts *distentio* with *intentio* and *extentus*. The latter terms concern the corrective to the distressing results of the human struggle with(in) temporality, as man is called to an eternal home. The term *intentio*, according to O'Daly, also implies a sense of contemplation. See Gerard O'Daly, 'Time as *Distentio* and St. Augustine's Exegesis of Philippians 3, 12–14', *Revue d'Études Augustiniennes et Patristiques* 23, no. 3 (1977): 265–71, here 269, 271. Augustine understands the terms *intentio* and *attentio* as denoting an aspect crucial to perception. Such uses, according to O'Daly, are discovered throughout many of Augustine's early works and even in *trin*. O'Daly, 'Time as *Distentio*', 271.
125 O'Daly, 'Time as *Distentio*', 269.
126 Hochschild, *Memory in Augustine's Theological Anthropology*, 157.
127 Nightingale, *Once out of Nature*, 58.
128 Nightingale, *Once out of Nature*, 90.
129 Jeanmart, *Herméneutique et subjectivité*, 36.
130 Jeanmart, *Herméneutique et subjectivité*, 36.
131 Jeanmart, *Herméneutique et subjectivité*, 36.
132 Jeanmart, *Herméneutique et subjectivité*, 36.
133 Jeanmart, *Herméneutique et subjectivité*, 36; *conf.* 3.4.7–8.
134 Jeanmart, *Herméneutique et subjectivité*, 36.
135 Jeanmart, *Herméneutique et subjectivité*, 36.
136 Jeanmart, *Herméneutique et subjectivité*, 37.
137 Cf. Gottlieb Söhngen, *Die Einheit in der Theologie* (München, 1952), 105.
138 Söhngen, *Die Einheit*, 101.
139 Jeanmart, *Herméneutique et subjectivité*, 64.
140 Boersma, *Augustine's Early Theology of Image*, 232, 235–6, 240–2, 252; *uera rel.* 11.21; 12.24; 20.38; 45.83.
141 Chrétien, *L'espace intérieur*, 63; *en. Ps.* 33.2.8.

142 Nightingale, *Once out of Nature*, 62; cf. 63; *conf.* 10.11.18.
143 Nightingale, *Once out of Nature*, 99.
144 Cf. Nick Trakakis, '*Deus Loci*: The Place of God and the God of Place in Philosophy and Theology', *Sophia* 52, no. 2 (2013): 319–20.
145 *conf.* 11.22.28.
146 *conf.* 11.22.28.
147 Sean Hannan, 'To See Coming: Augustine and Heidegger on the Arising and Passing Away of Things', *Medieval Mystical Theology* 21, no. 1 (2012): 90.
148 Hannan, 'To See Coming', 90.
149 Menn, 'The Desire for God', 93.
150 O'Regan, 'Answering Back', 165, cf. 154.

Chapter 4

1 *trin.* 12.15.25.
2 *ep.* 147.2.7.
3 *en. Ps.* 148.3.
4 *Gn. litt.* 3.4.6–5.7.
5 Cf. *Gn. litt.* 3.8.12.
6 Boersma, *Augustine's Early Theology of Image*, 250; cf. *uera rel.* 31.58, CCSL 32, p. 225.
7 *conf.* 10.6.10.
8 Ayres, 'Into the Poem', 271, n. 31; Gerard O'Daly, *Augustine's Philosophy of Mind* (Berkeley and Los Angeles: University of California Press, 1987), 11–15.
9 *lib. arb.* 2.3.8; *conf.* 10.10.17.
10 Even if this is the case, it does not explain why there would be differences or disagreements between two persons 'gazing' upon a form. Essentially, Augustine sees disagreement as a result of the darkness of the intellect due to finitude and sin.
11 *lib. arb.* 2.7.19.
12 Cf. *lib. arb.* 2.7.16.
13 *en. Ps.* 146.14. *lib. arb.* 2.8.21–2.
14 *Io. eu. tr.* 18.10.
15 *Io. eu. tr.* 18.10.

16 Jean-Louis Chrétien, *L'appel et la réponse* (Paris, 1992), 45. In this respect, Chrétien quotes Paul Claudel's curious formulation, 'l'œil écoute' (ibid.).
17 *trin.* 15.10.18, CCSL 50A, p. 485: 'non est aliud atque aliud uidere et audire.'
18 *ep. Io. tr.* 7.10.
19 *ep. Io. tr.* 8.1.
20 *ep. Io. tr.* 8.1.
21 *ep. Io. tr.* 8.2.
22 Cilleruelo, '"Deum uidere" en San Augustín', 5.
23 Cilleruelo, '"Deum uidere" en San Augustín', 5.
24 Cilleruelo, '"Deum uidere" en San Augustín', 5.
25 *Io. eu. tr.* 18.10.
26 *Io. eu. tr.* 18.10.
27 *Io. eu. tr.* 18.10.
28 *Io. eu. tr.* 18.10. For more on the theme of interiority in Augustine, see e.g. Charles T. Mathewes, 'Augustinian Anthropology: *Interior intimo meo*', *The Journal of Religious Ethics* 27.2 (Summer 1999): 195–221; Kim Sang Ong-Van-Cung, 'Le moi et l'interiorité chez Augustin et Descartes', *Chora: Journal of Ancient and Medieval Studies* 9/10 (2011–12): 321–38; David Peddle, 'Re-Sourcing Charles Taylor's Augustine', *Augustinian Studies* 32, no. 2 (2001): 207–17; Thomas Harmon, 'Reconsidering Charles Taylor's Augustine', *Pro Ecclesia* 20, no. 2 (2011): 185–209; Emmanuel Housset, 'L'invention de la personne par saint Augustin et la métaphysique contemporaine', *Quaestio* 6 (2006): 463–82; Jean-Louis Chrétien, *L'espace intérieur* (Paris: Minuit, 2014).
29 *lib. arb.* 2.8.22; trans. Russell, p. 131.
30 *conf.* 10.12.19.
31 Vincent Giraud, '*Signum* et *vestigium* dans la pensée de saint Augustin', *Revue des Sciences Philosophiques et Théologiques* 95, no. 2 (2011): 265, 266–7.
32 Giraud, '*Signum* et *vestigium*', 263.
33 *doct. chr.* 1.10.
34 *s. Dom. m.* 1.11.
35 *en. Ps.* 25.2.3.
36 *trin.* 1.4. Cf. *acad.* 3.27. See also *trin.* 1.3.
37 *s.* 143.3; see also *s.* 126.14.
38 *c. Adim.* 9.

39 *s. Dolbeau* 22.10.
40 *s. Dolbeau* 26.38.
41 *c. Faust.* 12.46. However, the idea that God is invisible is also present in the Greeks.
42 *s. Dom. m.* 1.11.
43 Cf. Cilleruelo, '"Deum uidere" en San Augustín', 4.
44 *ep. Io. tr.* 7.10. See also *s.* 4.4.
45 Cf. William Parsons, *Freud and Augustine in Dialogue: Psychoanalysis, Mysticism, and the Culture of Modern Spirituality*, Studies in Religion and Culture (Charlottesville, VA and London, England: University of Virginia Press, 2013), 63–4.
46 *s. Mai* 15.4.
47 However, certain Greek philosophers, mainly Platonists, also held that God was invisible. (Cilleruelo, '"Deum uidere" en San Augustín', 3).
48 Berrouard, *Introduction aux Homélies*, 52.
49 *s.* 6.1.
50 *s.* 4.5.
51 *s.* 4.6–7.
52 Cf. *s.* 4.4.
53 *s.* 4.4.
54 *s.* 6.1–2.
55 *s.* 6.1–2, 5.
56 *s.* 6.5.
57 *s.* 5.7.
58 *s.* 5.7.
59 *s.* 6.5.
60 *trin.* 1.13.30.
61 *trin.* 1.13.30.
62 *trin.* 1.13.30.
63 *trin.* 1.13.30.
64 Cf. Boersma, *Augustine's Early Theology of Image*, 250; *uera rel.* 31.58; *conf.* 10.6.10.
65 *conf.* 10.6.10.
66 Cf. *retr.* 1.6.
67 *trin.* 1.13.30. In another location, Augustine says that the Jews did in fact see the Son, but they did not know that he was God Incarnate,

revealing the Father (*Io. eu. tr.* 70.2; Evan Kuehn, 'The Johannine Logic of Augustine's Trinity: A Dogmatic Sketch', *Theological Studies* 68 (2007): 588). See also Arthos, *The Inner Word*, 105.

68 *doct. chr.* 2.11.
69 *Gn. litt.* 5.14.32.
70 *c. ep. Man.* 42.48.
71 Harrison, *Beauty and Revelation*, 66.
72 *Gn. litt.* 12.5.13.
73 *Gn. litt.* 12.4.12.
74 *Gn. litt.* 12.4.10; cf. Erich Naab, *Über Schau und Gegenwart des unsichtbaren Gottes*, Mystik in Geschichte und Gegenwart: Texte und Untersuchungen, Abteilung I, Christliche Mystik, Band 14 (Stuttgart-Bad Canstatt: Fromann-Holzboog, 1998), 28.
75 Cf. *Gn. litt.* 12.5.14.
76 Cf. Parsons, *Freud and Augustine in Dialogue*, 62–3.
77 *Gn. litt.* 12.19.41.
78 *Gn. litt.* 12.6.15. Augustine suggests a close link between thinking and seeing, as one's way of understanding images in the memory is by way of thinking (*cogitando*): 'intuere coelum et terram cogitando, sicut oculis corporeis cernendo consuesti' (*ep.* 147.17.43, CSEL 44, p. 317).
79 *Gn. litt.* 12.6.15.
80 *Gn. litt.* 12.4.10.
81 *Gn. litt.* 12.3.6; 6.15; 7.16.
82 *Gn. litt.* 12.27.55.
83 *Gn. litt.* 12.4.12.
84 *Gn. litt.* 12.4.12.
85 *Gn. litt.* 12.4.9. Augustine calls for sensitivity in interpreting corporeal language in scripture; it may not be intended in a literal sense, but rather to illustrate a point metaphorically (*Gn. litt.* 12.7.17.)
86 *Gn. litt.* 12.11.22.
87 *Gn. litt.* 12.24.51.
88 *Gn. litt.* 12.9.20.
89 Cf. Nightingale, *Once out of Nature*, 64.
90 Cf. Nightingale, *Once out of Nature*, 64.
91 *Gn. litt.* 12.24.51; cf. 8.19.
92 *Gn. litt.* 12.7.18.

93   *Gn. litt.* 12.11.22.
94   *Gn. litt.* 12.24.51.
95   *Gn. litt.* 12.9.20.
96   Cf. Naab, *Über Schau und Gegenwart Gottes*, 28.
97   *Gn. litt.* 12.3.6.
98   *Gn. litt.* 12.8.19.
99   *Gn. litt.* 12.24.50.
100 *Gn. litt.* 12.8.19.
101 *Gn. litt.* 12.26.54.
102 *Gn. litt.* 12.26.54.
103 *Gn. litt.* 12.5.13; cf. 11.22; 31.59.
104 *Gn. litt.* 12.24.50.
105 *Gn. litt.* 12.6.15.
106 *Gn. litt.* 12.24.51.
107 Cf. Giraud, '*Signum* et *vestigium*', 258.
108 Cf. *Gn. litt.* 12.11.23; *Gn. litt.* 12.14.29.
109 Cf. Arthos, *The Inner Word*, 110.
110 *Gn. litt.* 12.11.23.
111 *Gn. litt.* 12.14.29; cf. Naab, *Über Schau und Gegenwart Gottes*, 29.
112 *f. inuis.* 3.
113 *f. inuis.* 2.
114 *f. inuis.* 2.
115 *f. inuis.* 3.
116 Menn, 'Desire for God', 84.
117 Menn, 'Desire for God', 81.
118 Menn, 'Desire for God', 81.

Chapter 5

1 Willemien Otten, 'Nature and Scripture: Demise of a Medieval Analogy', *Harvard Theological Review* 88, no. 2 (1995): 261. For more on this theme, see Susannah Ticciati, *A New Apophaticism: Augustine and the Redemption of Signs*, Studies in Systematic Theology 14 (Leiden and Boston: Brill, 2013).
2 Otten, 'Nature and Scripture', 261.

3 Otten, 'Nature and Scripture', 261–2.
4 Otten, 'Nature and Scripture', 262.
5 Otten, 'Nature and Scripture', 262–3.
6 Otten, 'Nature and Scripture', 264ff.
7 Brad S. Gregory, *The Unintended Reformation: How a Religious Revolution Secularized Society* (Cambridge, MA and London, England: The Belknap Press of Harvard University Press, 2012), 45; cf. *conf.* 12.7.7.
8 Gregory, *The Unintended Reformation*, 67.
9 Gregory, *The Unintended Reformation*, 64.
10 Gregory, *The Unintended Reformation*, 43.
11 Victor Lee Austin, *Up with Authority: Why We Need Authority to Flourish as Human Beings* (Bloomsbury T&T Clark, 2010), 13; cf. ibid., 10–13.
12 Gregory, *The Unintended Reformation*, 42–3.
13 Gregory, *The Unintended Reformation*, 67.
14 Ticciati, *A New Apophaticism*, 25–6.
15 Gregory, *The Unintended Reformation*, 43.
16 Gregory, *The Unintended Reformation*, 67–8.
17 Gregory, *The Unintended Reformation*, 66 (cf. n. 128).
18 Gregory, *The Unintended Reformation*, 65.
19 Chrétien, *L'appel et la réponse*, *passim*. In this context, ethics may have a contribution to make as well, insofar as ethicists are always engaged in a hermeneutical enquiry which takes into account abstract principles and particular circumstances and situations.
20 Michael Fishbane, *Sacred Attunement: A Jewish Theology* (Chicago and London: University of Chicago Press, 2008). See also: Willemien Otten, 'On "Sacred Attunement," its Meaning and Consequences: A Meditation on Christian Theology', *The Journal of Religion* 93, no. 4 (October 2013): 478–94.
21 Mats Wahlberg, *Reshaping Natural Theology: Seeing Nature as Creation* (Palgrave Macmillan, 2012). See also James K. A. Smith, *The Fall of Interpretation: Philosophical Foundations for a Creational Hermeneutic* (Downers Grove, IL: InterVarsity Press, 2000).
22 Wahlberg, *Reshaping Natural Theology*, 1–2. Wahlberg is not a 'creationist' in the sense that he believes that an account of the development of human life, for instance, in evolutionary terms is false and incompatible with a theological account of creation. Indeed, one

of the main tasks of his monograph is to disabuse his audience of the false dichotomy between 'creation' on the one hand and 'evolution' on the other. He also rejects 'intelligent design' theory. See, for example, Wahlberg, *Reshaping Natural Theology*, 181: 'Today, however, we know that God did not build organisms by "hands-on-design".' See also ibid., 1–2, 12, 181, 188.

23 Chrétien, *L'appel et la réponse*, 12.
24 Chrétien, *L'appel et la réponse*, 11.
25 Chrétien, *L'appel et la réponse*, 12. Our interior voice would only be interior with respect to that of our body. Hence we ourselves represent a dialogue with our bodies.
26 Chrétien, *L'appel et la réponse*, 48–9; *ciu.* 11.27.2.
27 Chrétien, *L'appel et la réponse*, 46; *conf.* 10.6.9.
28 Chrétien, *L'appel et la réponse*, 9.
29 Chrétien, *L'appel et la réponse*, 9.
30 Chrétien, *L'appel et la réponse*, 11.
31 Chrétien, *L'appel et la réponse*, 11.
32 Chrétien, *L'appel et la réponse*, 47–8.
33 Chrétien, *L'appel et la réponse*, 47–8.
34 Chrétien, *L'appel et la réponse*, 47–8.
35 Chrétien, *L'appel et la réponse*, 49. See also Chrétien, *L'appel et la réponse*, 48: 'Augustin définit ici la beauté comme réponse.' Chrétien notes the interesting example of Roger Piles, an artist of the seventeenth century, who echoes this sentiment in a treatise on the principles of painting.
36 Chrétien, *L'appel et la réponse*, 50.
37 Giraud, '*Signum* et *vestigium*', 264–5.
38 Cf. Arthos, *The Inner Word*, 116–17.
39 Cf. Arthos, *The Inner Word*, 116–17.
40 Giraud, '*Signum* et *vestigium*', 265.
41 Harrison, *Beauty and Revelation*, 13.
42 Harrison, *Beauty and Revelation*, 37.
43 *trin.* 12.5.5; Giraud, '*Signum* et *vestigium*', 271, n. 80.
44 Harrison, *Beauty and Revelation*, 46–7.
45 Harrison, *Beauty and Revelation*, 46; cf. Jan Lemmens, 'Zo zie je God, volgens Augustinus', *Innerlijk Leven* 41 (1987): 24; Boersma, *Augustine's Early Theology of Image*, 235.

46 Harrison, *Beauty and Revelation*, 11.
47 Harrison, *Beauty and Revelation*, 42.
48 Cf. Ticciati, *A New Apophaticism*, 25–6.
49 Giraud, '*Signum* et *vestigium*', 267; *mus.* 6.14.44.
50 Giraud, '*Signum* et *vestigium*', 267; *lib. arb.* 2.16.43.
51 Harrison, *Beauty and Revelation*, 23.
52 Giraud, '*Signum* et *vestigium*', 267; *lib. arb.* 2.16.43.
53 Giraud, '*Signum* et *vestigium*', 267; *lib. arb.* 2.16.43.
54 Giraud, '*Signum* et *vestigium*', 266. Cf. Tornau, 'Intelligible Matter and the Genesis of Intellect', 199. Plotinus speaks of beauty perceived intellectually and how it fills one with a great desire to unite oneself with it. In a sense, beauty constitutes a summons to the soul. Peter King, 'Augustine's Anti-Platonist Ascents', in *Augustine's* Confessions: *Philosophy in Autobiography*, ed. W. Mann (New York: Oxford University Press, 2014), 15; *Enn.* 1.6.7.
55 *en. Ps.* 148.7, CCSL 40, p. 2169.
56 Giraud, '*Signum* et *vestigium*', 264; cf. *conf.* 10.6.9.
57 Giraud, '*Signum* et *vestigium*', 266–7; *trin.* 6.10.12.
58 Giraud, '*Signum* et *vestigium*', 264.
59 Giraud, '*Signum* et *vestigium*', 264.
60 Isabelle Bochet, 'Notes complementaires', in *Saint Augustin, La Doctrine chrétienne*, ed. M. Moreau, BA 11,2 (Paris: Institut d'études augustiniennes, 1997), 429–570, here 475.
61 *en. Ps.* 148.3, 9, 15. See also *en. Ps.* 148.12.
62 *en. Ps.* 148.15, CCSL 40, p. 2175. For more on Augustine's aesthetics, cf. *infra*. See also: Vincent Giraud, *Augustin, les signes et la manifestation*, Épiméthée (Paris: Presses Universitaires de France, 2013); Ayres, 'Into the Poem', 263–81; Karel Svoboda, *L'Esthétique de saint Augustin et ses sources*, Opera Facultatis philosophicae universitatis Masarykianae Brunensis 35 (Brno: Filosofická Fakulta, 1933); Anne-Isabelle Bouton-Toubholic, *L'ordre caché. La notion d'ordre chez saint Augustin*, Série Antiquité 174 (Paris: Coll. Études Augustiniennes, 2004).
63 *en. Ps.* 148.10.
64 *en. Ps.* 148.15.
65 *en. Ps.* 148.9.
66 *en. Ps.* 148.9, 15.
67 *en. Ps.* 148.15.

68 *en. Ps.* 18.1.1.
69 *en. Ps.* 18.2.2.
70 *en. Ps.* 18.2.3.
71 *en. Ps.* 18.2.3.
72 *en. Ps.* 18.1.2.
73 *en. Ps.* 18.2.2.
74 *en. Ps.* 18.2.2.
75 *en. Ps.* 18.2.3.
76 *en. Ps.* 18.1.3.
77 *en. Ps.* 18.1.3. This is interesting as in the second *enarratio* on this same psalm, Augustine interprets *nox nocti* in different, and indeed, negative terms. In the latter, he compares Christ to the day and Judas to the night. See *en. Ps.* 18.2.4.
78 *conf.* 10.6.9.
79 *conf.* 10.6.9.
80 *conf.* 10.6.8.
81 *conf.* 10.6.9; cf. *Io. eu. tr.* 2.4.
82 *conf.* 10.6.10.
83 *conf.* 10.6.10. See Boersma, *Augustine's Early Theology of Image*, 250.
84 *conf.* 10.6.9. See also *conf.* 10.6.9, CCSL 27, p. 160. See also *supra*; Plato, *Tht.*, 184c–e.
85 Nightingale, *Once out of Nature*, 64.
86 Napier, *En route*, 99–101; María Guadalupe Llanes, 'Gadamer y la igualdad sustancial de pensamiento y lenguaje en San Agustín', *Studia Gilsoniana* 2 (2013): 151; Nightingale, *Once out of Nature*, 99; cf. Arthos, *The Inner Word*, 126.
87 *conf.* 10.6.9.
88 *conf.* 10.6.9.
89 Giraud, '*Signum* et *vestigium*' 271.
90 Giraud, '*Signum* et *vestigium*', 273–4; cf. Ayres, 'Into the Poem', 269.
91 *conf.* 10.6.9.
92 *conf.* 10.6.9.
93 *conf.* 10.27.38.
94 Cf. Hannan, 'To See Coming', 84.
95 Ayres, 'Into the Poem', 277–8, 281.

96 Ayres, 'Into the Poem', 278.
97 Ayres, 'Into the Poem', 281. Cf. Ticciati, *A New Apophaticism*, *passim*.
98 *conf.* 10.27.38.
99 *conf.* 10.27.38.
100 *conf.* 10.6.10. Cf. Boersma, *Augustine's Early Theology of Image*, 250.
101 *conf.* 10.6.10.
102 Cf. Cilleruelo, '"Deum uidere" en San Augustín', 7; Nielsen, 'St. Augustine on Text and Reality', 99. Tertullian, *Carn. Chr.* 11.4, CCSL 2, p. 895; Carl W. Griffin and David L. Paulsen, 'Augustine and the Corporeality of God', *Harvard Theological Review* 95, no. 1 (2002): 106 n. 51; Teske, *To Know God and the Soul*, 202–3.
103 Cf. Desmond, *God and the Between*, 117.
104 *s.* 241.1.
105 *s.* 241.1.
106 See William Congreve's libretto for the operetta 'The Judgment of Paris'.
107 *s.* 241.1.
108 *s.* 241.2.
109 Chrétien, *L'appel et la réponse*, 48.
110 Giraud, '*Signum* et *vestigium*', 266.
111 Harrison, *Beauty and Revelation*, 96.
112 Giraud, '*Signum* et *vestigium*', 267; *lib. arb.* 2.16.43.
113 Cf. Giraud, '*Signum* et *vestigium*', 268; *lib. arb.* 2.16.41; *mus.* 6.7.17.
114 *ciu.* 11.27.2, CCSL 48, p. 347; Chrétien, *L'appel et la réponse*, 48–9.
115 Chrétien, *L'appel et la réponse*, 47–8.
116 Chrétien, *L'appel et la réponse*, 50.
117 *s.* 241.2, PL 38, p. 1134. Einstein too was apparently affected by beauty, even to the point of something like a transcendent or mystical experience of the divine. See Denis Brian, *Einstein: A Life* (Wiley, 1996), 193, cited in Max Jammer, *Einstein and Religion* (Princeton University Press, 1999), 19 (n. 6).
118 *s.* 241.2.
119 *s.* 241.2.
120 Cf. Cilleruelo, '"Deum uidere" en San Augustín', 8.

121 Charles Taylor, 'Interpretation and the Sciences of Man', *The Review of Metaphysics* 25, no. 1 (1971): 3.
122 Gadamer, 'The Universality of the Hermeneutical Problem', 154.
123 Philip Burton, 'The Vocabulary of the Liberal Arts in Augustine's *Confessions*', in *Augustine and the Disciplines*, ed. K. Pollmann and M. Vessey (Oxford and New York: Oxford University Press, 2005), 162; cf. Foley, 'Cicero, Augustine, and the Philosophical Roots', 62–3.
124 E.g. *ep. Io. tr.* 8.12, PL 35, p. 2043: 'Paulum interroga apostolum'; *s.* 380.6, PL 39, p. 1679: 'interroga ipsum Ioannem'; *Io. eu. tr.* 4.2, CCSL 36, p. 31: 'interroga Isaiam.'
125 Chrétien, *L'appel et la réponse*, 47–8.
126 For more on this theme, one may consider J. Searle's renowned Chinese room thought-experiment. The literature on this topic is vast, though this conversation begins from John Searle, 'Minds, Brains and Programs', *Behavioral and Brain Sciences* 3 (1980): 417–57.
127 Michael J. Buckley, *What Do You Seek? The Questions of Jesus as Challenge and Promise* (Grand Rapids, MI: Eerdmans, 2016), 10.
128 Rabbi Abraham Joshua Heschel, quoted in Paul G. Crowley and Stephen J. Pope, 'Foreword', in Buckley, *What Do You Seek?*, xi.
129 Buckley, *What Do You Seek?*, 10.
130 Buckley, *What Do You Seek?*, 7.
131 Buckley, *What Do You Seek?*, 10.
132 Buckley, *What Do You Seek?*, 10.
133 Buckley, *What Do You Seek?*, 6.
134 Buckley, *What Do You Seek?*, 8.
135 Buckley, *What Do You Seek?*, 10.
136 Buckley, *What Do You Seek?*, 10.
137 Buckley, *What Do You Seek?*, 5, 6, 7.
138 Buckley, *What Do You Seek?*, 7.
139 Buckley, *What Do You Seek?*, 7.
140 Buckley, *What Do You Seek?*, 7.
141 Chrétien, *L'appel et la réponse*, 49.
142 Cf. *Gn. litt.* 4.30.47; Tornau, 'Intelligible Matter and the Genesis of Intellect', 194–5.
143 Kuhn, *Structure*, 126.

144 This is how the point was explained to me in a conversation with R. Bernstein. This point is discussed more elaborately in his *Beyond Objectivism and Relativism*.
145 Kuhn, *Structure*, 96.
146 Kuhn, *Structure*, 96.
147 Kuhn, *Structure*, 38.
148 Lawrence, '*Ontology* of *and* as *Horizon*: Gadamer's Rehabilitation of the Metaphysics of Light', *Revista Portuguesa di Filosofia* 56, no. 3/4 (2000): 402.
149 Jean-Claude Petit, 'Herméneutique philosophique et théologie', *Laval théologique et philosophique* 41, no. 2 (1985): 166.

Chapter 6

1 Chrétien, *L'espace intérieur*, 66.
2 Chrétien, *L'espace intérieur*, 66, 72.
3 Cilleruelo, '"Deum uidere" en San Agustín', 18.
4 Cilleruelo, '"Deum uidere" en San Agustín', 18.
5 Cilleruelo, '"Deum uidere" en San Agustín', 18; cf. Lemmens, 'Zo zie je God', 31.
6 Chrétien, *L'espace intérieur*, 61.
7 Chrétien, *L'espace intérieur*, 61–2.
8 Chrétien, *L'espace intérieur*, 61–2.
9 Chrétien, *L'espace intérieur*, 62.
10 *en. Ps.* 148.4.
11 *en. Ps.* 148.4.
12 Ripanti, 'Ermeneutica Agostiniana', 91.
13 *en. Ps.* 148.4.
14 *en. Ps.* 146.2.
15 Here I am invoking the presentation of Protagoras' position in Plato's *Theatetus*.
16 Cf. *Io. eu. tr.* 96.2.
17 Cf. *Io. eu. tr.* 20.12.
18 Ayres, 'Into the Poem', 272.
19 *conf.* 10.29.40.

20 *conf.* 10.29.40. Interestingly, the form he uses is the passive, suggesting the outside activity of God on the soul.
21 *conf.* 11.29.39.
22 Ayres, 'Into the Poem', 276.
23 Nightingale, *Once out of Nature*, 69.
24 Chrétien, *L'espace intérieur*, 53–4; *conf.* 10.29.40.
25 Chrétien, *L'espace intérieur*, 53–4; *conf.* 10.29.40.
26 Nightingale, *Once out of Nature*, 70.
27 Nightingale, *Once out of Nature*, 70.
28 *s. Dom. m.* 2.9, CCSL 35, p. 100.
29 Hochschild, *Memory in Augustine's Theological Anthropology*, 151. Perhaps Augustine was inspired by the Platonic image of time as the moving image of eternity in *Timaeus* 37c–e.
30 Nightingale, *Once out of Nature*, 74.
31 *conf.* 11.28.38, CCSL 27, p. 214.
32 Augustine makes the same point in *uera rel.* 22.42–3.
33 *conf.* 11.28.38. Augustine puts forward a similar example in *mus.* Cf. Harrison, *Beauty and Revelation*, 56.
34 *conf.* 11.28.38.
35 *conf.* 11.28.38.
36 *conf.* 11.28.38.
37 *conf.* 11.28.38.
38 Menn, 'The Desire for God', 93.
39 *trin.* 8.1.2.
40 *trin.* 8.2.3.
41 Josef Lössl, '"The One": A Guiding Concept in Augustine's *De vera religione*', *Revue des Études Augustiniennes* 40 (1994): 101.
42 Lössl, 'The One', 87.
43 Lössl, 'The One', 100.
44 Lössl, 'The One', 101.
45 Lössl, 'The One', 93; *uera rel.* 18.35.94. Augustine also speaks of the beauty of creation (*pulchritudine uniuersae creaturae*). Lössl, 'The One', 94; *uera rel.* 23.44.121.
46 Lössl, 'The One', 93; *uera rel.* 18.35.94, CCSL 32, pp. 203ff.
47 Lössl, 'The One', 97.

48 Cf. Lössl, 'The One', 101; Paul Van Geest. *The Incomprehensibility of God: Augustine as a Negative Theologian*, Late Antique History and Religion, The Mystagogy of the Church Fathers 1 (Leuven, Paris and Walpale, MA: Peeters, 2011), 117–18.
49 Lössl, 'The One', 101.
50 Lössl, 'The One', 101.
51 Lössl, 'The One', 101.
52 *uera rel.* 39.72, CCSL 32, p. 234. See Boersma, *Augustine's Early Theology of Image*, 224–53.
53 *uera rel.* 39.72.
54 *uera rel.* 39.72.
55 *uera rel.* 39.72.
56 Chrétien, *L'espace intérieur*, 59; cf. *uera rel.* 39.72.
57 James Wetzel, *Augustine and the Limits of Virtue* (Cambridge: University Press, 1992), 160, quoted in Ayres, 'Into the Poem', 273, n. 40.
58 Chrétien, *L'espace intérieur*, 60.
59 *Io. eu. tr.* 20.11.
60 *Io. eu. tr.* 20.12.
61 *Io. eu. tr.* 20.12.
62 *Io. eu. tr.* 20.12.
63 *Io. eu. tr.* 20.12.
64 *Io. eu. tr.* 20.12.
65 *Io. eu. tr.* 20.12.
66 *Io. eu. tr.* 20.12.
67 *Io. eu. tr.* 20.12.
68 *Io. eu. tr.* 23.9.
69 *Io. eu. tr.* 20.12.
70 *Io. eu. tr.* 20.12.
71 *Io. eu. tr.* 20.12.
72 *Io. eu. tr.* 20.12.
73 *Io. eu. tr.* 20.12.
74 *Io. eu. tr.* 20.12.
75 *Io. eu. tr.* 20.11.
76 *Io. eu. tr.* 20.11.
77 *Io. eu. tr.* 20.11.

78 *Io. eu. tr.* 20.11, CCSL 36, p. 209: 'Adtolle te a corpore, transi etiam te.'
79 *Io. eu. tr.* 20.11, CCSL 36, p. 209; cf. Lemmens, 'Zo zie je God', 31.
80 *Io. eu. tr.* 20.11.
81 Cf. *Io. eu. tr.* 20.13.
82 *Io. eu. tr.* 20.13.
83 *Io. eu. tr.* 20.13, CCSL 36, pp. 210–11: 'transcendit omnes spiritus qui non uidentur, transcendit mentem suam ipsa ratione animi sui.'
84 *Io. eu. tr.* 20.13.
85 *Io. eu. tr.* 20.13.
86 *Io. eu. tr.* 1.4.
87 Cf. *Gn. litt.* 4.29.46, CSEL 28,1, p. 128: 'sed eorum mentem mirabili facilitate haec omnia simul posse.'
88 *Io. eu. tr.* 1.4.
89 *Io. eu. tr.* 1.4.
90 *Io. eu. tr.* 1.4.
91 *Io. eu. tr.* 1.4.
92 *Io. eu. tr.* 1.4.
93 *Io. eu. tr.* 1.4.
94 *Io. eu. tr.* 20.12.
95 Arthos, *The Inner Word*, 112.
96 *Io. eu. tr.* 96.4.
97 *Io. eu. tr.* 38.4; cf. Svensson, '*Scientia* y *sapientia* en *De Trinitate* XII', 95.
98 *Io. eu. tr.* 20.13.
99 *Io. eu. tr.* 20.13.
100 As Parsons writes, 'mystical truth is always there, but that ordinary experience stands in the way and must be put aside just as one removes a veil to reveal a treasure that existed all along.' Parsons, *Freud and Augustine in Dialogue*, 64.
101 Here I am informed by Drever's aforementioned term 'soteriological reversal'. Matthew Drever, 'The Self Before God? Rethinking Augustine's Trinitarian Thought', *Harvard Theological Review* 100, no. 2 (2007): 235.
102 Cf. Menn, 'The Desire for God', 92.
103 See William Blake's 'The Marriage of Heaven and Hell'.
104 Menn, 'The Desire for God', 93.

105 Drever, 'The Self before God?', 237.
106 Drever, 'The Self before God?', 237.
107 *Io. eu. tr.* 20.13.
108 *Io. eu. tr.* 20.13.
109 *Io. eu. tr.* 1.7.
110 *Io. eu. tr.* 1.7.
111 *Io. eu. tr.* 1.7.
112 *Io. eu. tr.* 96.2.
113 *Io. eu. tr.* 96.2.
114 *Io. eu. tr.* 96.2.
115 I am grateful to C. Harrison for this insight.
116 Boersma, *Augustine's Early Theology of Image*, 236.
117 Boersma, *Augustine's Early Theology of Image*, 250 n. 107; *uera rel.* 31.58.
118 Boersma, *Augustine's Early Theology of Image*, 250 n. 107; *uera rel.* 31.58.
119 Boersma, *Augustine's Early Theology of Image*, 225.
120 Boersma, *Augustine's Early Theology of Image*, 237.
121 Boersma, *Augustine's Early Theology of Image*, 238; cf. Lemmens, 'Zo zie je God', 24.
122 Boersma, *Augustine's Early Theology of Image*, 238.
123 Boersma, *Augustine's Early Theology of Image*, 248; *uera rel.* 29.52.
124 *conf.* 9.10.24.
125 *conf.* 7.10.16; cf. Svensson, '*Scientia* y *sapientia* en De Trinitate XII', 100.
126 *conf.* 7.20.26; 17.23.
127 Naab, *Über Schau und Gegenwart Gottes*, 30.
128 King, 'Augustine's Anti-Platonist Ascents', 8–9.
129 Boersma, *Augustine's Early Theology of Image*, 248.
130 *uera rel.* 21.41, CCSL 32, pp. 212–13, quoted in Boersma, *Augustine's Early Theology of Image*, 248 n. 98.
131 Boersma, *Augustine's Early Theology of Image*, 238 n. 52; *uera rel.* 35.65.
132 Boersma, *Augustine's Early Theology of Image*, 232, 235–6, 240–2, 252; *uera rel.* 11.21; 12.24; 20.38; 45.83.
133 Boersma, *Augustine's Early Theology of Image*, 235; *uera rel.* 3.3; 37.68–38.69.

134 Boersma, *Augustine's Early Theology of Image*, 235; *uera rel.* 3.3; 37.68–38.69.
135 Boersma, *Augustine's Early Theology of Image*, 235.
136 Boersma, *Augustine's Early Theology of Image*, 235–6.
137 Boersma, *Augustine's Early Theology of Image*, 236, 237; *uera rel.* 34.63.
138 Boersma, *Augustine's Early Theology of Image*, 238, 240.
139 Boersma, *Augustine's Early Theology of Image*, 240.
140 Boersma, *Augustine's Early Theology of Image*, 253.
141 Hannan, 'To See Coming', 84.
142 Hannan, 'To See Coming', 84. What is less clear is how this hermeneutical element might be applied in particular situations, and how it may look at the local level when social and political circumstances are radically different.
143 Menn, 'The Desire for God', 93.
144 Meijer, *De* Sapientia, 114.
145 Cf. Meijer, *De* Sapientia, 112.
146 I am grateful to M. Lamberigts for this insight.
147 Ayres, 'Into the Poem', 268.
148 Ayres, 'Into the Poem', 268; cf. A. Kotze, *Augustine's* Confessions*: Communicative Purpose and Audience*, Supplements to Vigiliae Christianae 71 (Leiden: Brill 2004), 65.
149 Giraud, '*Signum* et *vestigium*', 272–3.
150 *trin.* 15.16.26.
151 *trin.* 15.16.26.
152 Cf. Ryan Coyne, 'A Difficult Proximity: The Figure of Augustine in Heidegger's Path', *Journal of Religion* 91, no. 3 (2011): 372.
153 Rowan Williams, 'Sapientia and Trinity: Reflections on *De Trinitate*', in *Collectanea Augustiniana: Mélanges T. J. van Bavel*, ed. B. Bruning, M. Lamberigts and J. van Houtem, Bibliotheca Ephemeridum Theologicarum Lovaniensium XCII-A (Louvain: Leuven University Press), 320; Boersma, *Augustine's Early Theology of Image*, 255.
154 Philippe Eberhard, 'Gadamer and Theology', *International Journal of Systematic Theology* 9, no. 3 (2007): 283–300, here 291.
155 Eberhard, 'Gadamer and Theology', 291.
156 Chrétien, *L'espace intérieur*, 57.

157 Williams, 'Sapientia and Trinity', 320, quoted in Boersma, *Augustine's Early Theology of Image*, 255.
158 Charles Taylor, *A Secular Age* (Cambridge, MA: Belknap Press of Harvard University Press, 2007).
159 Cf. Coyne, 'A Difficult Proximity', 372.
160 Cf. *s. Dom. m.* 2.9.32. God speaks within every soul, good and evil, in particular in the conscience through the approval or disapproval of one's actions. *s.* 12.4.
161 Chrétien, *L'espace intérieur*, 72.
162 *Gn. litt.* 1.1.2.
163 *Gn. litt.* 5.16.34.
164 Milton, *Paradise Lost* bk 5, line 80.
165 Milton, *Paradise Lost* bk 5, line 763.
166 Chrétien, *L'appel et la réponse*, 10.
167 Alberto Romele, 'The Ineffectiveness of Hermeneutics: Another Augustine's Legacy in Gadamer [sic]', *International Journal of Philosophy and Theology* 75, no. 5 (2014): 431.
168 Zimmermann, *Recovering Theological Hermeneutics*, 173.
169 *ep.* 147.9.21; Eberhard, 'Gadamer and Theology', 294.
170 Fishbane, *Sacred Attunement*, 203.
171 Fishbane, *Sacred Attunement*, 203.
172 Fishbane, *Sacred Attunement*, 65.
173 Fishbane, *Sacred Attunement*, 203.
174 Jean Grondin, *The Philosophy of Gadamer*, trans. K. Plant, Continental European Philosophy (Chesham, UK: Acumen, 2003), 148.
175 Brice R. Wachterhauser, 'Prejudice, Reason and Force', *Philosophy* 63 (1988): 253.
176 Fishbane, *Sacred Attunement*, 204. See also Desmond, *God and the Between*, 78–82 on God and evil. Quoting Blake's 'The Tiger', Desmond describes God as master of both life and death.
177 For more on Augustine as an interpreter and exegete of scripture, see e.g. Thomas William, 'Biblical Interpretation', in E. Stump and N. Kretzman (eds.), *The Cambridge Companion to Augustine* (Cambridge: University Press, 2001), 59–70; G. Bonner, 'Augustine as a Biblical Scholar', in P. R. Ackroyd and C. F. Evans (eds.), *The Cambridge History of the Bible*, vol. 1 (Cambridge: University Press, 1970), 541–62.

178 Gareth Matthews, 'Augustine on Reading Scripture as Doing Philosophy', *Augustinian Studies* 39 (2008): 145–62, here 158. See also Gerd van Riel, 'Augustine's Exegesis of "Heaven and Earth" in *Conf.* XII: Finding Truth amidst Philosophers, Heretics, and Exegetes', *Quaestio* 7 (2007): 191–228.

179 Matthews, 'Augustine on Reading Scripture as Doing Philosophy', 147.

180 Blake D. Dutton, 'The Privacy of the Mind and the Fully Approvable Reading of Scripture: Augustine on Genesis 1:1', in *Augustine's Confessions: Philosophy in Autobiography*, ed. W. Mann (New York: Oxford University Press, 2014), 176.

181 Dutton, 'The Privacy of the Mind', 177.

182 Matthews, 'Augustine on Reading Scripture as Doing Philosophy', 159.

183 Matthews, 'Augustine on Reading Scripture as Doing Philosophy', 159, 161; Van Riel, 'Augustine's Exegesis', 211.

184 Matthews, 'Augustine on Reading Scripture as Doing Philosophy', 160.

185 Matthews, 'Augustine on Reading Scripture as Doing Philosophy', 160–161.

186 Dutton, 'The Privacy of the Mind', 174.

187 Cf. Otten, 'Nature and Scripture', 262–3.

188 *en. Ps.* 146.11.

189 *en. Ps.* 146.11.

190 *en. Ps.* 146.11.

191 *en. Ps.* 146.11.

192 *en. Ps.* 146.11.

193 *en. Ps.* 146.11.

194 *en. Ps.* 146.11.

195 *en. Ps.* 146.11.

196 *en. Ps.* 146.11.

197 *en. Ps.* 146.11.

198 *en. Ps.* 146.11.

199 *en. Ps.* 146.11.

200 *en. Ps.* 146.11.

201 Edmund Hill, 'Unless You Believe, You Shall Not Understand: Augustine's Perception of Faith', *Augustinian Studies* 25 (1994): 60.

202 Hill, 'Unless You Believe', 60.
203 Hill, 'Unless You Believe', 61.
204 Hill, 'Unless You Believe', 62.
205 *en. Ps.* 120.5.
206 *en. Ps.* 120.5.
207 *en. Ps.* 120.14.
208 *en. Ps.* 120.14.
209 *en. Ps.* 120.14.
210 *en. Ps.* 120.14.
211 *en. Ps.* 120.5.
212 *ep. Io. tr.* 8.7.
213 *en. Ps.* 120.5.
214 *en. Ps.* 120.5.
215 *en. Ps.* 120.5.
216 *ep. Io. tr.* 8.2.
217 *en. Ps.* 120.8.
218 Giraud, '*Signum* et *vestigium*', 269–70; *ciu.* 11.28.
219 *en. Ps.* 120.8.
220 Glenn McCullough, 'Heidegger, Augustine, and *Poiêsis*: Renewing the Technological Mind', *Theology Today* 59, no. 1 (2002): 30–1.
221 *en. Ps.* 120.8.
222 *en. Ps.* 120.8.
223 *en. Ps.* 120.8.
224 *en. Ps.* 120.8.
225 Cf. *en. Ps.* 120.8.
226 Cf. *en. Ps.* 120.8.
227 Ayres, 'Into the Poem', 270. This is also apropos of Desmond's understanding of the reconfigured *ethos* and how it may obscure certain parts of the primal *ethos*.
228 *conf.* 4.7.12.
229 Ayres, 'Into the Poem', 270–1; *conf.* 4.7.12.
230 Napier, *En route*, 99–100; Menn, 'The Desire for God', 93.
231 *conf.* 11.29.39.
232 *en. Ps.* 96.10.
233 *s. Dom. m.* 2.14. Cf. *ep.* 242.4.

234 *s. Dom. m.* 2.9.
235 *en. Ps.* 120.8.
236 *en. Ps.* 120.8. The French Carmelite Sœur Elisabeth de la Trinité captures this point well when she writes, 'Oh! Que la terre et les choses d'ici-bas sont néant au regard de l'éternité!' and 'Tout ce qui finit ne peut nous satisfaire, il nous faut l'Eternel.' Sœur Elisabeth de la Trinité, *Vers le double abîme*, 47.
237 *en. Ps.* 120.8.
238 *en. Ps.* 120.8.
239 *en. Ps.* 120.9.
240 *en. Ps.* 120.9.
241 *en. Ps.* 120.10.
242 *en. Ps.* 120.10.
243 *en. Ps.* 120.10.
244 Shakespeare, *Hamlet*.
245 *ep. Io. tr.* 2.8.
246 *ep. Io. tr.* 2.8.
247 *ep. Io. tr.* 2.14.
248 *ep. Io. tr.* 2.8.
249 *ep. Io. tr.* 2.12.
250 *ep. Io. tr.* 2.8.
251 *ep. Io. tr.* 2.10.
252 *ep. Io. tr.* 2.11.
253 *ep. Io. tr.* 2.10, 14.
254 *ep. Io. tr.* 2.14.
255 *ep. Io. tr.* 2.11.
256 *ep. Io. tr.* 2.11.
257 *ep. Io. tr.* 2.11.
258 *ep. Io. tr.* 2.14.
259 Menn, 'The Desire for God', 93.
260 Menn, 'The Desire for God', 93.

REFERENCES

Primary Sources/Critical Editions

De Civitate Dei Libri I–X, edited by B. Dombart and A. Kalb, Corpus Christianorum Series Latina, 47. Turnholti: Brepols, 1955.

De Civitate Dei Libri XI–XXII, edited by B. Dombart and A. Kalb, Corpus Christianorum Series Latina, 48. Turnholti: Brepols, 1955.

Confessionum libri XIII, edited by L. Verheijen, O.S.A., Corpus Christianorum Series Latina, 27. Turnholti: Brepols, 1981.

De consensu evangelistarum libri qvattor, edited by F. Weihrich, Corpus Scriptorum Eccliasticorum Latinorum, 43. Vindobonae: Tempsky, 1904.

Contra Academicos, De beata uita, De ordine, De magistro, De libero arbitrio, edited by W. Green, et al., Corpus Christianorum Series Latina, 29. Turnholti: Brepols, 1970.

Corpus Augustinianum Gissense, edited by C. Mayer. Basel: Schwabe, 2005.

De diuersis quaestionibus octoginta tribus, edited by A. Mutzenbecher, Corpus Christianorum Series Latina 44A. Turnhout: Brepols, 1975.

De doctrina christiana, edited by M. Simonetti. Roma: Fondzione Lorenzo Valla, 1994.

Enarrationes in Psalmos I–L, edited by D. E. Dekkers, O.S.B. and I. Fraipont, Corpus Christianorum Series Latina, 38. Turnholti: Brepols, 1956.

Enarrationes in Psalmos LI–C, edited by D. E. Dekkers, O.S.B. and I. Fraipont, Corpus Christianorum Series Latina, 39. Turnholti: Brepols, 1956.

Enarrationes in Psalmos CI–CL, edited by D. E. Dekkers, O.S.B. and I. Fraipont, Corpus Christianorum Series Latina, 40. Turnholti: Brepols, 1956.

Epistulae I–XXX, edited by Al. Goldbacher, Corpus Christianorum Series Latina, 34/1. Vindobonae: Tempsky, 1895.

Epistulae XXXI–CXXIII, edited by Al. Goldbacher, Corpus Scriptorum Eccliasticorum Latinorum, 34/2. Vindobonae: Tempsky, 1898.

Epistulae CXXIV–CLXXXIV A., edited by Al. Goldbacher, Corpus Scriptorum Eccliasticorum Latinorum, 44. Vindobonae: Tempsky, 1904.
Epistulae CLXXXV–CCLXX, edited by Al. Goldbacher, Corpus Scriptorum Eccliasticorum Latinorum, 57. Vindobonae: Tempsky, 1911.
De fide et symbolo, De fide et operibus, De agone christiano, De continentia, De bono coniugali, De sancta virginitate, De bono viduitatis, De adulterinis coniugiis, De mendacio, Contra mendacium, De opere monachorum, De divinatione daemonum, De cura pro mortuis gerenda, De patientia, edited by I. Zycha, Corpus Scriptorum Ecclesiasticorum Latinorum, 41. 1900.
De fide rerum inuisibilium, edited by M. P. J. van den Hout, Corpus Christianorum Series Latina, 46, 1–19. Turnholti: Brepols, 1955.
De Genesi ad Litteram Libri Duodecim, edited by I. Zycha, Corpus Scriptorum Ecclesiasticorum Latinorum 28, 1–456. Vindobonae: Tempsky, 1894.
De Genesi aduersus Manichaeos, edited by D. Weber, Corpus Scriptorum Eccliasticorum Latinorum, 91. Wien: Verlag der Österreichischen Akademie der Wissenschaften, 1998.
In Iohannis euangelium tractatus CXXIV, edited by D. Willems, O.S.B. Corpus Christianorum Series Latina, 36. Turnhout: Brepols, 1954.
De libero arbitrio libri tres, edited by W. M. Green, Corpus Scriptorum Ecclesiasticorum Latinorum, 74. 1956.
De musica: liber VI, edited by M. Jacobsson, Acta Universitatis Stockholdmiensis: Studia Latina Stockholmiensa, 47. Stockholm: Almqvist and Wiksell, 2002.
Opera Omnia, edited by J.-P. Migne, Patrologia Latina, 35, 38, 39, 44. Paris, 1841–6.
Retractationum libri II, edited by A. Mutzenbecher, Corpus Christianorum Series Latina, 57. Turnholti: Brepols, 1984.
'Le sermon CXXVI de saint Augustin sur le thème foi et intelligence et sur la vision du verbe', edited by C. Lambot, *Revue Bénédictine* 69 (1959), 177–90.
'Le sermon CCXIV de saint Augustin pour la tradition du symbole', edited by P. Verbraken, *Revue Bénédictine* 72.1–2 (1962), 7–21.
'Le sermon LXXXVIII de saint Augustin sur la guérison des deux aveugles de Jéricho', edited by P.-P. Verbraken, *Revue Bénédictine* 94.1–2 (1984), 71–101.
'Le sermon 53 de saint Augustin sur les Béatitudes selon saint Matthieu', edited by P.-P. Verbraken, *Revue Bénédictine* 104.1–2 (1994), 19–33.
De sermone Domini in monte libros duos, edited by A. Mutzenbecher, Corpus Christianorum Series Latina, 35. Turnhout: Brepols, 1967.

Sermones de Vetere Testamento, id est Sermones I–L, edited by
C. Lambot, O.S.B., Corpus Christianorum Series Latina, 41. Turnholti:
Brepols, 1961.
Sermones post Maurinos Reperti, Miscellanea Agostiniana, 1. Roma:
Tipografia Poliglotta Vaticana, 1930.
Sermones selecti duodeviginti, edited by D. C. Lambot, O.S.B., Stromata
Patristica et Mediaevalia, 1. Brussels: Spectrum, 1950.
Sermons pour la Pâque, edited by S. Poque, Sources chrétiennes, 116.
Paris: Cerf, 1966.
Soliloquiorum libri duo, De inmortalitate animae, De quantitate animae,
edited by W. Hörmann, Corpus Scriptorum Ecclesiasticorum
Latinorum, 89. 1986.
De spiritu et littera, edited by C. Urba and I. Zycha, Corpus Scriptorum
Eccliasticorum Latinorum, 60, 155–230. Vindobonae: Tempsky,
1913.
De Trinitate libri XV, edited by W. Mountain, Corpus Christianorum
Series Latina, 50–50A. Turnholti: Brepols, 1968.
De uera religione, edited by Kl. Daur, et al., Corpus Christianorum Series
Latina, 32. Turnhout: Brepols, 1962.
*De utilitate credendi, De duabus animabus, Contra Fortunatum
Manichaeum, Contra Adimantum, Contra epistulam fundamenti,
Contra Faustum Manichaeum,* edited by I. Zycha, Corpus Scriptorum
Eccliasticorum Latinorum, 25/1. Vindobonae: Tempsky, 1891.
Vingt-six sermons au peuple d'Afrique, edited by F. Dolbeau, Série
Antiquité, 147A. Paris: Institut d'études augustiniennes, 2001.

Translations

The Confessions, translated by M. Boulding, edited by J. Rotelle, The
Works of Saint Augustine: A Translation for the 21st Century, I/1.
Hyde Park, New York: New City Press, 1996.
Eighty-Three Different Questions, translated by D. L. Mosher, The
Fathers of the Church: A New Translation, 70. Washington, DC: The
Catholic University of America Press, 1982.
The Literal Meaning of Genesis, translated by E. Hill, The Works of Saint
Augustine: A Translation for the 21st Century, I/13. New York: New
City Press, 2008.
On the Free Choice of the Will, translated by R. Russell, The Fathers of
the Church. Washington, D.C.: Catholic University of America Press,
1968.
Origen. *On First Principles*, translated by G. W. Butterworth. London:
Society for Promoting Christian Knowledge, 1936.

Secondary

Anatolios, Khaled. 'Oppositional Pairs and Christological Synthesis: Rereading Augustine's *De Trinitate*'. *Theological Studies* 68 (2007): 231–53.

Arsenault, F. *Augustin: Qui est Jésus-Christ?* Paris: Desclée, 1974.

Arthos, John. *The Inner Word in Gadamer's Hermeneutics*. Notre Dame, IN: University of Notre Dame Press, 2009.

Austin, Victor Lee. *Up with Authority: Why We Need Authority to Flourish as Human Beings*. Bloomsbury T&T Clark, 2010.

Ayres, Lewis. 'Into the Poem of the Universe: *Exempla*, Conversion, and Church in Augustine's *Confessiones*'. *Zeitschrift für Antikes Christentum* 13, no. 2 (2009): 263–81.

Beckmann-Lamb, Sigrid. "Sigrid Beckmann-Lamb sprach am 02.08 2001 mit dem Philosophen Hans-Georg Gadamer." http://www.seifenermodell.de/gruenderin/interviews/108-interview-mit-hans-georg-gadamer.html (last accessed on 1 November 2016).

Beer, Vladimir de. 'The Patristic Reception of Hellenic Philosophy'. *St. Vladimir's Theological Quarterly* 55, no. 4 (2014): 373–98.

Bernstein, Richard. *Beyond Objectivism and Relativism: Science, Praxis, and Hermeneutics*. Oxford: Blackwell, 1983.

Berrouard, Marie-François. *Introduction aux Homélies de saint Augustin sur l'évangile de saint Jean*. Collection des études augustiniennes, Série Antiquité 170. Paris: Études augustiniennes, 2004.

Blake, William. (1982), D. Erdman (ed), *The Complete Poetry and Prose of William Blake*. New York: Anchor Books.

Bochet, Isabelle. 'Notes complementaires'. In *Saint Augustin, La Doctrine chrétienne*, edited by M. Moreau, Bibliothèque Augustinienne 11,2, 429–570. Paris: Institut d'études augustiniennes.

Bochet, Isabelle. 'Herméneutique, apologétique et philosophie: recherches sur Augustin'. *Revue d'Études Augustiniennes et Patristiques* 48, no. 2 (2002): 321–9.

Bochet, Isabelle. 'The Role of Scripture in Augustine's Controversy with Porphyry'. *Augustinian Studies* 41, no. 1 (2010): 7–52.

Boersma, Gerald. *Augustine's Early Theology of Image: A Study in the Development of Pro-Nicene Theology*. Oxford Studies in Historical Theology. New York: Oxford University Press, 2016.

Bonner, G. 'Augustine as a Biblical Scholar'. In *The Cambridge History of the Bible*, edited by P. R. Ackroyd and C. F. Evans, Volume 1, 541–62. Cambridge: University Press.

Bouton-Toubholic, Anne-Isabelle. *L'ordre caché. La notion d'ordre chez saint Augustin*. Série Antiquité 174. Paris: Coll. Études Augustiniennes, 2004.

Brachtendorf, Johannes. 'Augustine on the Glory and the Limits of Philosophy'. In *Augustine and Philosophy*, edited by P. Cary, J. Doody and K. Paffenroth, Augustine in Conversation: Tradition and Innovation, 3–22. Totowa: Rowman and Littlefield.

Brian, Denis. *Einstein: A Life*. Wiley, 1996.

Buckley, Michael J. *What Do You Seek? The Questions of Jesus as Challenge and Promise*. Foreword by P. Crowley, SJ, and S. Pope. Grand Rapids, MI: Eerdmans, 2016.

Burton, Philip. 'The Vocabulary of the Liberal Arts in Augustine's *Confessions*'. In *Augustine and the Disciplines*, edited by K. Pollmann and M. Vessey, 141–64. Oxford and New York: Oxford University Press.

Byers, Sarah. 'Augustine and the Philosophers'. In *A Companion to Augustine*, edited by M. Vessey, Blackwell Companions to the Ancient World, 175–87. Chichester: Wiley Blackwell.

Callender, Craig. 'Le temps, est-il une illusion?' *Pour la Science* 397, November 2010. Available at pourlascience.fr/ewb_pages/a/article-le-temps-est-il-une-illusiona-26041.php (last accessed on 23 July 2016).

Chrétien, Jean-Louis. *L'appel et la réponse*. Paris, 1992.

Chrétien, Jean-Louis. *L'espace intérieur*. Paris: Minuit, 2014.

Cilleruelo, Lope. '"Deum uidere" en San Agustín'. *Salmanticensis* 12 (1965): 3–31.

Comeau, Marie. *Saint Augustin : Exégète du quatrième évangile*. 3rd ed. Études de théologie historique. Paris: Gabriel Beauchesne, 1930.

Congreve, William. 'The Judgement of Paris: A Masque'. Eighteenth-Century Collections Online. University of Michigan.

Coyne, Ryan. 'A Difficult Proximity: The Figure of Augustine in Heidegger's Path'. *Journal of Religion* 91, no. 3 (2011): 365–96.

Desmond, William. *God and the Between*. Illuminations: Theory and Religion. Malden, MA: Blackwell, 2008.

Doolan, Gregory T. *Aquinas on the Divine Ideas as Exemplar Causes*. Washington, DC: The Catholic University of America Press, 2008.

Doucet, Dominique. 'Recherche de Dieu, Incarnation et philosophie : Sol. I, 1, 2v6'. *Revue des Études Augustiniennes et Patristiques* 36 (1990): 91–119.

Drever, Matthew. 'The Self before God? Rethinking Augustine's Trinitarian Thought'. *Harvard Theological Review* 100, no. 2 (2007): 233–42.

Dupont, Anthony and Matthew W. Knotts. 'In Dialogue with Augustine's *Soliloquia*: Interpreting and Recovering a Theory of Illumination'. *International Journal of Philosophy and Theology* 74, no. 5 (2013): 432–465.

Dutton, Blake D. 'The Privacy of the Mind and the Fully Approvable Reading of Scripture: Augustine on Genesis 1:1'. In *Augustine's*

Confessions: *Philosophy in Autobiography*, edited by W. Mann, 155–80, New York: Oxford University Press.

Eberhard, Philippe. 'Gadamer and Theology'. *International Journal of Systematic Theology* 9, no. 3 (2007): 283–300.

Elisabeth de la Trinité, Sœur. *Vers le double abîme: Ses pensées profondes à méditer et à vivre*. Recueillies et présentées par A. Lybaert, OCD. Montsurs: Editions Résiac, 1977.

Fishbane, Michael. *Sacred Attunement: A Jewish Theology*. Chicago and London: University of Chicago Press, 2008.

Flasch, Kurt. *Was ist Zeit? Augustinus von Hippo. Das XI. Buch der Confessiones. Historisch-Philosophische Studie*. Frankfurt am Main: Klostermann, 1993.

Foley, Michael. 'Cicero, Augustine, and the Philosophical Roots of the Cassiciacum Dialogues'. *Revue des Études Augustiniennes* 45 (1999): 51–77.

Folliet, Georges. '"La spoliatio aegyptiorum" (Exode 3:21–23; 11:2–3; 12:35–36): les interprétations de cette image chez les pères et autres écrivains ecclésiastiques'. *Traditio* 57 (2002): 1–48.

Gadamer, Hans-Georg. *Gesammelte Werke*. 10 Volumes. Tübingen: Mohr Siebeck, 1986–95.

Gadamer, Hans-Georg. 'The Universality of the Hermeneutical Problem'. In *The Hermeneutic Tradition from Ast to Ricoeur*, edited by Gayle L. Ormiston and Alan D. Schrift, translated by D. Linge, 147–58. Albany, NY: State University of New York Press.

Gadamer, Hans-Georg. *Truth and Method*, translated by J. Weinsheimer and D. Marshall. 2nd rev. ed. London, New Delhi, New York, and Sydney: Bloomsbury, 2013.

Gilson, Étienne. 'Notes sur l'être et le temps chez saint Augustin'. *Recherches Augustiniennes* 2 (1962): 205–223.

Giraud, Vincent. '*Signum* et *vestigium* dans la pensée de saint Augustin'. *Revue des Sciences Philosophiques et Théologiques* 95, no. 2 (2011): 251–74.

Giraud, Vincent. *Augustin, les signes et la manifestation*. Épiméthée. Paris: Presses Universitaires de France, 2013.

Giraud, Vincent. 'Delectatio interior: plaisir et pensée selon Augustin'. *Études Philosophiques* 109, no. 2 (2014): 201–17.

Gregory, Brad S. *The Unintended Reformation: How a Religious Revolution Secularized Society*. Cambridge, MA and London, England: The Belknap Press of Harvard University Press, 2012.

Griffin, Carl W. and David L. Paulsen. 'Augustine and the Corporeality of God'. *Harvard Theological Review* 95, no. 1 (2002): 97–118.

Grondin, Jean. *Der Sinn für Hermeneutik*. Darmstadt: Wissenschaftliche Buchgesellschaft, 1994.

Grondin, Jean. *The Philosophy of Gadamer*, translated by Kathryn Plant. Continental European Philosophy. Chesham, UK: Acumen, 2003.
Grondin, Jean. 'La thèse de l'herméneutique sur l'être'. *Revue de Métaphysique et de Morale* 4 (1 October 2006): 469–81.
Hannan, Sean. 'To See Coming: Augustine and Heidegger on the Arising and Passing Away of Things'. *Medieval Mystical Theology* 21, no. 1 (2012): 75–91.
Harmon, Thomas. 'Reconsidering Charles Taylor's Augustine'. *Pro Ecclesia* 20, no. 2 (2011): 185–209.
Harrison, Carol. *Beauty and Revelation in the Thought of St. Augustine*. Oxford Theological Monographs. Oxford: Clarendon, 1992.
Harrison, Carol. *Augustine: Christian Truth and Fractured Humanity*. Christian Theology in Context. Oxford University Press, 2000.
Helm, Paul. 'Thinking Eternally'. In *Augustine's Confessions: Philosophy in Autobiography*, edited by W. Mann, 135–54, New York: Oxford University Press.
Heßbrüggen-Walter, Stefan. 'Augustine's Critique of Dialectic: Between Ambrose and the Arians'. In *Augustine and the Disciplines*, edited by K. Pollmann and M. Vessey, 184–205. Oxford and New York: Oxford University Press.
Hill, Edmund. 'Unless You Believe, You Shall Not Understand: Augustine's Perception of Faith'. *Augustinian Studies* 25 (1994): 51–64.
Hochschild, Paige. *Memory in Augustine's Theological Anthropology*. Oxford Early Christian Studies. Oxford: University Press, 2012.
Holte, Ragnar. *Béatitude et sagesse. Saint Augustin et le problème de la fin de l'homme dans la philosophie ancienne*. Paris: Études augustiniennes, 1962.
Housset, Emmanuel. 'L'invention de la personne par saint Augustin et la métaphysique contemporaine'. *Quaestio* 6 (2006): 463–82.
Huftier, Maurice. *Le tragique de la condition chrétienne chez saint Augustin*. Paris: Desclée, 1964.
Jammer, Max. *Einstein and Theology*, Princeton: University Press, 1999.
Jeanmart, Gaëlle. *Herméneutique et subjectivité dans les* Confessions *d'Augustin*. Monothéismes et Philosophie 8. Turnhout: Brepols, 2006.
Kaladiouk, Anna Schur. 'On "Sticking to the Fact" and 'Understanding Nothing': Dostoevsky and the Scientific Method'. *The Russian Review* 65, no. 3 (2006): 417–38.
King, Peter. 'Augustine's Anti-Platonist Ascents'. In *Augustine's* Confessions: *Philosophy in Autobiography*, edited by W. Mann, 6–27. New York: Oxford University Press.
Klingshirn, William. 'Divination and the Disciplines of Knowledge according to Augustine'. In *Augustine and the Disciplines*, edited by

K. Pollmann and M. Vessey, 113–40. Oxford and New York: Oxford University Press.

Kotze, A. *Augustine's Confessions: Communicative purpose and audience*. Supplements to Vigiliae Christianae 71. Leiden: Brill, 2004.

Kuehn, Evan. 'The Johannine Logic of Augustine's Trinity: A Dogmatic Sketch'. *Theological Studies* 68 (2007): 572–94.

Kuhn, Thomas. *The Structure of Scientific Revolutions*. 2nd rev. edn. Chicago: University of Chicago Press, [1962] 2012.

Lamberigts, Mathijs. 'Peccatum'. In *Augustinus-Lexikon*, 4 ¾, 581–99. Basel: Schwabe.

Lawrence, Fred. '*Ontology* of *and* as *Horizon*: Gadamer's Rehabilitation of the Metaphysics of Light'. *Revista Portuguesa di Filosofia* 56, no. 3/4 (2000): 389–420.

Lemmens, Jan. 'Zo zie je God, volgens Augustinus'. *Innerlijk Leven* 41 (1987): 23–32.

Llanes, María Guadalupe. 'Gadamer y la igualdad sustancial de pensamiento y lenguaje en San Agustín'. *Studia Gilsoniana* 2 (2013): 145–59.

Lössl, Josef. '"The One": A Guiding Concept in Augustine's *De vera religione*'. *Revue des Études Augustiniennes* 40 (1994): 79–103.

Madec, Goulven. 'Une lecture de Confessions VII,IX,13-XXI,27. Notes critiques à propos d'une thèse de R.-J. O'Connell'. *Revue des Études Augustiniennes* 16, no. 1 (1970): 79–137.

Madec, Goulven, et al. *Chez Augustin*. Collection des Études Augustiniennes, Série Antiquité 160. Paris: Institut d'études augustiniennes, 1998.

Mathewes, Charles. (1999), 'Augustinian Anthropology: *Interior intimo meo*'. *The Journal of Religious Ethics* 27, no. 2 (1999): 195–221.

Matthews, Gareth B. 'Knowledge and Illumination'. In *The Cambridge Companion to Augustine*, edited by E. Stump, 171–85. Cambridge: University Press.

Matthews, Gareth. 'Augustine on Reading Scripture as Doing Philosophy'. *Augustinian Studies* 39 (2008): 145–162.

May, Gerhard. *Schöpfung aus dem Nichts: die Entstehung der Lehre von der Creatio ex Nihilo*, Arbeiten zur Kirchengeschichte 48. Berlin: De Gruyter, 1978.

Mayer, Cornelius Petrus. *Die Zeichen in der geistigen Entwicklung und in der Theologie des jungen Augustinus*. Cassiciacum 24/1–2. Würzburg: Augustinus-Verlag, 1969–74.

McCullough, Glenn. 'Heidegger, Augustine and *Poiêsis*: Renewing the Technological Mind'. *Theology Today* 59, no. 1 (2002): 21–38.

Meconi, David. 'Becoming Gods by Becoming God's: Augustine's Mystagogy of Identification'. *Augustinian Studies* 39 (2008): 61–74.

Meijer, M. *De Sapientia in de eerste geschriften van s. Augustinus*. Brakkenstein-Nijmegen: Eucharistische Boekhandel, 1937.
Menn, Stephen. 'The Desire for God and the Aporetic Method in Augustine's *Confessions*'. In *Augustine's Confessions: Philosophy in Autobiography*, edited by W. Mann, 71–107. New York: Oxford University Press.
Milton, John. *Paradise Lost*, edited by C. Ricks, Signet Classic Poetry. New York: Penguin, 2001.
Moore, A.W. *Points of View*. Oxford: Clarendon Press, 1997.
Naab, Erich. *Über Schau und Gegenwart des unsichtbaren Gottes*. Mystik in Geschichte und Gegenwart: Texte und Untersuchungen, Abteilung I, Christliche Mystik, Band 14. Stuttgart-Bad Canstatt: Frommann-Holzboog, 1998.
Napier, D.A. *En route to the* Confessions: *The Roots and Development of Augustine's Philosophical Anthropology*. Late Antique History and Religion 6. Leuven: Peeters, 2013.
Nielsen, Cynthia. 'St. Augustine on Text and Reality (and a Little Gadamerian Spice)'. *Heythrop Journal* 50, no. 1 (2009): 98–108.
Nightingale, Andrea. *Once out of Nature: Augustine on Time and the Body*. Chicago: University of Chicago Press, 2011.
O'Daly, Gerard. 'Time as *Distentio* and St. Augustine's Exegesis of Philippians 3,12–14'. *Revue d'Études Augustiniennes et Patristiques* 23, no. 3 (1977): 265–71.
O'Daly, Gerard. *Augustine's Philosophy of Mind*. Berkeley and Los Angeles: University of California Press, 1987.
O'Donnell, James. *Augustine, Confessions: Commentary*. 3 Volumes. Oxford: Clarendon Press, 1992.
Oldroyd, David. *The Arch of Knowledge: An Introductory Study of the History of the Philosophy and Methodology of Science*. Methuen, NY: 1986.
Oliva, Mirela. *Das innere Verbum in Gadamers Hermeneutik*. Hermeneutische Untersuchungen zur Theologie 53. Tübingen: Mohr Siebeck, 2009.
Ong-Van-Cung, K.S. 'Le moi et l'interiorité chez Augustin et Descartes'. *Chora: Journal of Ancient and Medieval Studies* 9/10 (2011–12): 321–38.
O'Regan, Cyril. 'Answering Back: Augustine's Critique of Heidegger'. In *Human Destinies: Philosophical Essays in Memory of Gerald Hanratty*, edited by F. O'Rourke, 134–84. South Bend, IN: University of Notre Dame Press.
Otten, Willemien. 'Nature and Scripture: Demise of a Medieval Analogy'. *Harvard Theological Review* 88, no. 2 (1995): 257–84.
Otten, Willemien. 'On "Sacred Attunement", its Meaning and Consequences: A Meditation on Christian Theology'. *The Journal of Religion* 93, no. 4 (2013): 478–94.

Parsons, William. *Freud and Augustine in Dialogue: Psychoanalysis, Mysticism, and the Culture of Modern Spirituality*. Studies in Religion and Culture. Charlottesville, VA and London, England: University of Virginia Press, 2013.

Pârvan, Alexandra. '*La relation* en tant qu'élément-clé de l'illumination augustinienne'. *Chora: Journal of Ancient and Medieval Studies* 7–8 (2009–10): 87–103.

Peddle, David. 'Re-Sourcing Charles Taylor's Augustine'. *Augustinian Studies* 32, no. 2 (2001): 207–17.

Petit, Jean-Claude. 'Herméneutique philosophique et théologie'. *Laval théologique et philosophique* 41, no. 2 (1985): 159–70.

Plato, and Francis Macdonald Cornford. *Plato's Cosmology; the Timaeus of Plato*. International Library of Psychology, Philosophy and Scientific Method. K. Paul, Trench, Trubner & Co. ltd., 1937. https://search.ebscohost.com/login.aspx?direct=true&AuthType=sso&db=cat05408a&AN=gan.6532&site=eds-live.

Ripanti, Graziano. 'Il problema della comprensione nell'ermeneutica agostiniana'. *Revue des Études Augustiniennes* 20, no. 1–2 (1974): 88–99.

Romele, Alberto. 'The Ineffectiveness of Hermeneutics: Another Augustine's [sic] Legacy in Gadamer'. *International Journal of Philosophy and Theology* 75, no. 5 (2014): 422–39.

Searle, John. 'Minds, Brains and Programs'. *Behavioral and Brain Sciences* 3 (1980): 417–57.

Shakespeare, William. The Complete Works.

Smith, J.K.A. *The Fall of Interpretation: Philosophical Foundations for a Creational Hermeneutic*. Downers Grove, IL: InterVarsity Press, 2000.

Söhngen, Gottlieb. *Die Einheit in der Theologie*. München, 1952.

Sturm, Thomas. "Rituale sind wichtig." Der Spiegel (21 February 2000). http://www.spiegel.de/spiegel/print/d-15737880.html (last accessed on 1 November 2016).

Sullivan, John Edward. *The Image of God: The Doctrine of St. Augustine and its Influences*. Dubuque, IA: Priory Press, 1963.

Svensson, Manfred. '*Scientia* y *sapientia* en *De Trinitate* XII: San Agustín y las formas de la racionalidad'. *Teolgía y Vida* 51 (2010): 79–103.

Svoboda, Karel. *L'Esthétique de saint Augustin et ses sources*. Opera Facultatis philosophicae universitatis Masarykianae Brunensis 35. Brno: Filosofická Fakulta, 1933.

Swetnam, James. 'A Note on *Idipsum* in St. Augustine'. *The Modern Schoolman* 30 (1952–3): 328–31.

Tavola cronológica dei discorsi. http://www.augustinus.it/latino/discorsi/tavola_discorsi.htm (last accessed on 1 March 2017).

Tavola cronológica delle lettere. http://www.augustinus.it/latino/lettere/tavola_lettere.htm (last accessed on 1 March 2017).

Tavola cronológica: Nella tavola, vengono riportate le indicazioni cronologiche dello Zarb (Z.), del Rondet (H.) e di La Bonnardière (La B.). http://www.augustinus.it/latino/esposizioni_salmi/tavola_cronologica.htm (last accessed on 1 March 2017).

Taylor, Charles. 'Interpretation and the Sciences of Man'. *The Review of Metaphysics* 25, no. 1 (1971): 3–51.

Taylor, Charles. *Sources of the Self: The Making of Modern Identity.* Cambridge: University Press, 1989.

Taylor, Charles. *A Secular Age.* Cambridge, MA: Belknap Press of Harvard University Press, 2007.

Teske, Roland. *To Know God and the Soul: Essays on the Thought of St. Augustine.* Washington, DC: The Catholic University of America Press, 2008.

Thonnard, F.-J. 'Saint Augustin et les Grands Courants de la Philosophie Contemporaine'. *Revue des Études Augustiniennes et Patristiques* 50 (2004): 195–206.

Ticciati, Susannah. *A New Apophaticism: Augustine and the Redemption of Signs.* Studies in Systematic Theology 14. Leiden and Boston: Brill, 2013.

Tornau, Christian. 'Intelligible Matter and the Genesis of Intellect: The Metamorphosis of a Plotinian Theme in *Confessions* 12–13'. In *Augustine's* Confessions: *Philosophy in Autobiography*, edited by W. Mann, 181–214. New York: Oxford University Press.

Trakakis, Nick. '*Deus Loci*: The Place of God and the God of Place in Philosophy and Theology'. *Sophia* 52, no. 2 (2013): 315–33.

Van Geest, Paul. *The Incomprehensibility of God: Augustine as a Negative Theologian.* Late Antique History and Religion, The Mystagogy of the Church Fathers 1. Leuven, Paris and Walpole, MA: Peeters, 2011.

Van Riel, Gerd. 'Augustine's Exegesis of "Heaven and Earth" in *Conf.* XII: Finding Truth amidst Philosophers, Heretics and Exegetes'. *Quaestio* 7 (2007): 191–228.

Van Riel, Gerd. 'La sagesse chez Augustin: de la philosophie à l'Écriture'. In *Augustin philosophe et prédicateur. Hommage à Goulven Madec*, edited by Isabelle Bochet, 389–405. Paris: Institut d'Études Augustiniennes.

Vincie, Catherine, RSHM. *Worship and the New Cosmology: Liturgical and Theological Challenges.* Collegeville, MN: Liturgical Press, 2014.

Wachterhauser, Brice R. 'Prejudice, Reason and Force'. *Philosophy* 63 (1988): 231–53.

Wahlberg, Mats. *Reshaping Natural Theology: Seeing Nature as Creation.* Palgrave Macmillan, 2012.

Wetzel, James. *Augustine and the Limits of Virtue.* Cambridge: University Press, 1992.

William, Thomas. 'Biblical Interpretation'. In *The Cambridge Companion to Augustine*, edited by E. Stump and N. Kretzman, 59–70. Cambridge: University Press.

Williams, Rowan. 'Sapientia and Trinity: Reflections on *De Trinitate*'. In *Collectanea Augustiniana: Mélanges T. J. van Bavel*, edited by B. Bruning, M. Lamberigts and J. van Houtem, Bibliotheca Ephemeridum Theologicarum Lovaniensium XCII-A, 317–332. Louvain: Leuven University Press.

Williger, E. 'Der Aufbau der Konfessionen Augustins', *Zeitschrift für Neutestamentliche Wissenschaft und die Kunde der Älteren Kirche* 28, no. 1 (1929): 81–106.

Winch, Peter. *The Idea of a Social Science and Its Relation to Philosophy*. London: Routledge & Kegan Paul, 1958.

Zimmermann, Jens. *Recovering Theological Hermeneutics: An Incarnational-Trinitarian Theory of Interpretation*. Grand Rapids, MI: Baker, 2004.

INDEX OF NAMES

Bernstein, Richard xiv, 79

Chrétien, Jean-Louis
   beauty 65, 65–6, 75
   interiority 45, 84–5, 90
   interrogation 76–9
   response xxi–xxii, 100
   senses 49

Descartes, René xiii–xiv, xviii, 99, 100
Desmond, William xxi, 75, 150 n.176, 152 n.227

Einstein, Albert 32, 36, 142 n.117

Fishbane, Michael xxi, xxii, 65, 101

Gadamer, Hans-Georg
   hermeneutics xxi, 58, 65, 101
   interrogation 76–7
   prejudice 83, 85, 102
   religion 15–17, 100
   science xiii–xv, 28, 109

Heidegger, Martin
   Augustine's influence on xv
   finitude 15, 17, 97
   limits of knowledge 16–17, 105
   Nihility 98–9, 103, 110
   time 46

John
   Evangelist 22, 84, 94
   prologue xix, 7, 21, 37, 52, 69–70
   Verbum 7–14

Kant, Immanuel 16, 27, 66, 75, 78–9
Kuhn, Thomas S. xiv, 28, 79

Paul 4, 12, 14, 21, 22, 54–5, 74, 86
Plato *see* Platonism
Plotinus *see* Platonism

Taylor, Charles 76, 99

INDEX OF SUBJECTS

apophatic 64, 66, 68, 72, 81

beauty xxii, 11, 35, 39, 50–1, 59, 65–81 (*see also pulchritudo*)

Cartesian *see* Descartes, René
Christ
    creator 7–8, 10, 41, 69
    faith in 22, 106
    incarnate 12, 14, 19, 24–5, 51–3, 103
    re-creator 6, 13, 27, 73, 108, 109, 115 n.36
    revelation 20, 23
    truth 26, 90
    words of in Gospels 5, 77, 94, 105
conscience 66, 99, 150 n.160
corporeal
    creation 4, 36, 40, 71, 73–4, 85, 91–2
    images in OT 9, 10, 13
    obstruction by 11, 67, 87, 106
    our situation 18, 31, 86, 89
    senses 7, 41–2, 48–53, 55–9, 97–8
creatio ex nihilo 36, 64, 68, 74, 76, 94, 127 n.8, 129 n.47

disenchantment 63–4 (*see also* Descartes, René)
distentio 36, 43–4, 83, 86–8, 96, 132 n.124

empirical 27–8, 48, 50, 53, 64, 76, 79, 80, 110
eternity *see also* time
    divine 5, 91, 103
    ideas 4, 67, 100
    Verbum 6, 8–10, 14, 17, 26, 53, 70
extension
    lack of 7, 18, 33, 34–7, 98, 127–8 n.18
    in time and space 31, 42–3, 81, 88, 93

Father (God) (*see also* Trinity)
    creation 4, 5
    knowledge of 14
    and the Son 11, 18, 24, 37, 41, 51, 53
finitude
    creation 31, 36, 42, 66, 70, 80
    critical discussion of 99–102
    and human knowledge 15–16, 18, 22, 35, 45, 47, 78
    prejudice 81, 84, 85–90
    transcendence of and renewed return 91–4, 94–9

Genesis
    creation 4, 5, 33 63, 64, 76
    and John 7
    and the Manichees 32
    two accounts 14, 39, 85
Geisteswissenschaften see science(s)

gradual
  creation 4, 85
  growth in knowledge 25, 67, 87, 95
  sense of reason 42, 51, 58, 102

hermeneutics (*see also* Gadamer, Hans-Georg)
  Augustine's
    Christian 19, 25
    scriptural 102
  contemporary philosophy xxiii, 14–16, 58, 72, 97, 99–100, 101
  model for interpretation of reality 65, 68, 86, 98, 103, 105, 106–8
  response to summons 67, 76–7, 79
Holy Spirit 4, 13, 94 (*see also* Father (God), Trinity)
horizon xiv, 85, 89 (*see also* finitude)

illumination
  basis for further growth 17, 22, 76
  gift from God 13, 25, 94, 102, 104
  incorporeality 10, 73–4
  reason 6, 9, 26–7, 41, 52
images
  in the mind 41, 44–5, 55–8, 67, 71, 136 n.78
  misleading nature of 9, 35, 92, 96–8, 104
imago (Dei)
  constitutive of human reason and identity 6, 9, 10, 17, 42, 49, 50
  completion of relationship 72, 94–5, 99
incorporeality
  in *conf.* 7 34–7

light 9, 41
  not extended in space or time 15, 18, 52, 86, 105, 108
  perception of 49, 53, 55, 93, 94, 100
  and scripture 8, 11
intentio
  dialogue with nature in *conf.* 68–71
  and *memoria* 44–5
  way of looking 53–4, 58, 59, 79, 80, 105
interiority
  divine presence 12, 49, 84, 90, 99
  inner senses 10, 41, 45, 66, 71, 72–3
  transcendence 91, 92
interrogatio 17, 48, 59, 70–2, 74–6, 75–80, 100

Jesus *see* Christ
Judaism
  Jewish people 9, 12, 117–18 n.80
  Jewish theological tradition 65, 101, 135–6 n.67

light *see* illumination
Logos *see* Verbum

Manichees 20, 32, 40, 101
matter
  Augustine's concept of 34–7
  categories of with respect to knowledge 34, 43, 88–9, 64, 96
  connection to time 37–42
  creation 17, 33, 36–7, 75, 87
  immaterial 18, 49, 55, 93
  judging in light of eternity 50, 95, 106
  medium 47, 59, 68, 86, 93

INDEX OF SUBJECTS

memoria
   capacity 45, 48, 73, 98
   individual images within 55–6, 88
   necessary for attaining *sapientia* 43, 44, 87

Neoplatonism *see* Platonism

participation 9, 35, 41, 67, 87, 95, 103, 128–9 n.38
peccatum see sin
Platonism
   Augustine's polemic against 22, 23, 25, 26
   beauty as a call 66
   incorporeality 33, 34, 135 n.47
   Plotinus' *Enneads* 67, 140 n.54
   purification 45
   Theaetetus 71, 86, 141 n.84, 144 n.15
   Timaeus 87, 145 n.29
prejudice
   Gadamer xvi, xxii, xxiii, 17, 78, 83
   ontological 13, 65, 73, 74, 80–1, 84–6, 88, 97–8, 105
   pride as 20, 102
pride *see superbia*
principium 6–7, 17, 32, 94, 101, 127 n.8
principal xix–xx, 4, 27, 42, 51, 58, 73
pulchritudo 7, 39, 66–70, 75–6, 145 n.45 (*see also* beauty)
purgatio
   asceticism 45, 76
   one's own efforts versus God's grace 23, 25, 106, 124–5 n.75
   time and space 45, 87, 96
   vision xvi–xvii, 10, 51–2, 54

purification *see purgatio*

questioning *see interrogatio*

sapientia
   advancing in 43, 44, 45, 87, 97
   Christ 4, 6, 7, 8, 17, 31, 37, 52, 89
   creation in 3–7, 11, 14, 40, 69, 70
   form of 10, 13, 48, 49, 52, 55, 57, 89, 95
   incorporeal 9, 18, 35, 95
   and knowledge (*scientia*) 26, 41, 76, 114 n.31
   reflected in the world 11, 47, 68, 75
   superba 19, 20–1, 23, 25, 104, 110
science(s) xiii–xv, xxii, 17, 27–8, 64, 79–80, 109, 112
senses
   bodily 7, 10, 18, 55, 73, 96
   interior 41, 45, 48–52, 66, 71
   levels of vision in *Gn. litt.* 12 52–9
simple 39, 43, 71, 87, 106
sin
   blindness and darkness 12, 13, 18, 88, 109
   damage to human reason 16, 20, 21, 45, 46, 67, 73
   healing of 14, 23, 27
   opposed to being 6, 89
   prejudice 102–7
space
   creation 31, 42, 37–40
   extension 33, 35, 36, 90, 93, 98
   God 7, 18, 34, 41, 64, 89
   prejudice 45, 74, 84, 88, 96, 102, 105
   and time 6, 43, 48, 83, 85, 86, 97

subjectivity *see* interiority
superbia 20–3, 68, 99–100, 102–5

text-analogue 63, 76
time
    attachment to temporal goods 96, 106–8
    creation and 4–6, 20, 36
    distentio 83, 87–8, 93, 97, 98
    eternity 23, 34, 44, 67, 95
    perception in 7, 33, 48–9, 84–5, 89
    reality 15, 43, 45, 74, 86
    re-descriptive account of 31–2, 46
    and space 18, 37–42, 81, 92, 98, 105
Trinity 4, 8, 31, 94 (*see also* Christ, Father (God), Holy Spirit)

uestigium
    in creation xxii, 31, 47, 51, 63, 110

and the human soul xxi, 17, 44, 67, 75
source thereof 67–8

Verbum
    discarnate 7, 14, 17, 21–2, 41, 69, 70, 109
    and human knowledge 9, 10, 26, 46, 103
    incarnate 18, 23, 24, 25, 51
vision
    beyond empirical 10, 76
    comprehension 100
    of God 11, 21
    objects of 48–50
    purification of 43, 51–2, 67, 73, 87, 94, 98, 106
    senses of 52–9
Vorurteil see Gadamer, Hans-Georg

Wissenschaft(en) see science(s)
Word *see Verbum*

INDEX LOCORUM

acad.
   3.27 51

c. Adim
   9 51
c. ep. Man.
   42.48 54
c. Faust.
   12.46 51
ciu.
   8.1 123 n.46
   10.22 25, 124–5 n.75
   11 37, 40–2, 130–1 n.89–109
   15.20 131 n.96
   22 54
conf.
   3 44, 132 n.133
   4 105–6, 152 n.228–9
   7 34–7, 43
   9 33, 95–6, 131 n.117
   10 xxii, 44, 45, 48, 50, 53, 66, 68, 70–4, 86–8,
   11 32, 43–6, 87, 88, 106, 132 n.123–4
   12 32, 33, 127 n.8, 138 n.7

diu. qu.
   19 37, 129 n.53
   46 xvii, 114 n.26, n.30
   51 xvii, 114, n.27–9
doctr. chr.
   1 51, 129 n.53
   2 26, 125 n.82

en. Ps.
   18 69–70, 141 n.77
   25 51
   33 45
   66 xx, 115 n.36
   96 106
   120 104–5, 106–7
   146 15–16, 32, 35, 48, 49, 86, 102–3
   148 48, 68, 69, 86
ep.
   18 32
   102 126 n.93
   147 11, 48, 54, 100, 136 n.78
   242 152 n.233
ep. Io. tr.
   2 xvi, 107
   7 xvi, 34, 49, 51–2
   8 49, 76, 104

f. inuis.
   2 59
   3 59

Gn. adu. Man.
   1.2.3 32
Gn. litt.
   2 4, 6, 7
   3 4, 6, 48
   4 33, 79, 93
   5 4–5, 37–40, 54, 99
   12 41, 54–9, 77

Io. eu. tr.
  1 xv–xvi, 7–8, 9, 10, 11, 93, 94, 96–7, 114 n.20, 118 n.95
  2 8, 11, 13, 21–2, 141 n.81
  3 8–9, 9–11, 11–12, 13, 14
  4 143 n.124
  18 49, 50
  20 86, 91–4
  23 91 (146 n.68)
  37 12–13, 119 n.124
  38 xx, 12–13, 93, 115 n.36
  40 12–13, 119 n.124
  70 135–6 n.67
  96 86, 93–4

lib. arb.
  2 10, 48–9, 50, 52, 75

mus.
  6 68, 75, 140 n.49, 142 n.113

ord.
  2.19.50 xviii

retr.
  1.6 53

s.
  1 7, 117 n.57
  4 52
  5 53
  6 52–3
  12 150 n.160
  52 xx
  88 118 n.83
  117 xviii, 20–1, 24–5
  126 134 n.37
  143 51
  184 20
  185 24
  188 20
  189 25
  190 20, 24–5
  196 23–4
  241 xxii, 39, 74–6
  277 xx
  342 9, 118 n.81
  380 76

s. Dolbeau
  22.10 51
  26.27–32 25
  26.36–8 25
  26.38 51

s. Dom. m.
  1.11 51
  2.9 87, 106
  2.9.32 99
  2.14 106

s. Mai
  15.4 52
  94.1 xx

sol.
  1 xv, 114 n.18, 123 n.46

trin.
  1 51, 53, 54
  6 68
  8 35, 59, 89, 128–9 n.38
  12 47, 67
  15 49, 98

uera rel.
  3.3 96
  11.21 96
  12.24 96
  18.35.94 89
  20.38 96
  21.41 96
  22.42–3 88
  29.52 95
  31.58 48, 53, 95
  34.63 96
  35.65 96
  37.68–38.69 96
  39.72 89–90
  45.83 96

INDEX OF REFERENCES

Genesis *see* Genesis in Index of Subjects

Exodus
   3.14 8
   3.21–3; 11.2–3; 12.35–6 26

Psalm
   18 69–70
   41 92
   103 4, 8

Wisdom
   11.21 8

Daniel
   5.5–28 58, 77

Matthew
   5 51–2
   5.8 10

John *see* John in Index of Names

Romans
   1.19–21 74
   1.20 65
   1.20–2 123 n.42

1 Corinthians
   2.14 12
   14.15 56

2 Corinthians
   5.6 86
   12.2–4 54–5

Colossians
   1.16 4, 115 n.11

Hebrews
   11.6 59

1 John
   3.2 21